An Ideological Death

CULTURAL EXPRESSIONS OF WORLD WAR II
INTERWAR PRELUDES, RESPONSES, MEMORY

PHYLLIS LASSNER, SERIES EDITOR

AN IDEOLOGICAL DEATH

SUICIDE IN ISRAELI LITERATURE

RACHEL S. HARRIS

NORTHWESTERN UNIVERSITY PRESS | EVANSTON, ILLINOIS

Northwestern University Press
www.nupress.northwestern.edu

Printed in the United States of America

10 9 8 7 6 5 4 3 2 1

ISBN 978-0-8101-4379-1

The Library of Congress has cataloged the original, hardcover edition of this
book as follows:

Harris, Rachel S. (Rachel Sylvia), 1977– author.
    An ideological death : suicide in Israeli literature / Rachel S. Harris.
       pages cm. — (Cultural expressions of World War II)
      ISBN 978-0-8101-2978-8 (cloth : alk. paper) — ISBN 978-0-8101-6765-0 (ebook)
    1. Israeli literature—History and criticism. 2. Hebrew literature, Modern—History
and criticism. 3. Suicide in literature. 4. Zionism in literature. I. Title. II. Series:
Cultural expressions of World War II.
    PJ5021.H37 2014
    892.4'093548—dc23
                                          2014017284

For my parents, Valerie and Jeffrey Harris

"You are the bows from which your children, as living arrows, are sent forth."

—GIBRAN KAHLIL GIBRAN (1883–1931)

CONTENTS

ACKNOWLEDGMENTS

This book has taken a long time to come into being from its earliest origins as my doctoral dissertation. In the process it has benefited from the wisdom of a great number of people to whom I am extremely grateful. My doctoral supervisor at the University of Oxford, Glenda Abramson, helped shepherd the first version as a thesis — forcing me to admit that all the renditions of death in Hebrew literature might be too large a topic to tackle, but that suicide somehow seemed manageable. Daphna Clifford was a wise advisor and important friend through my graduate work. I thank her for introducing me to Hebrew literature and for teaching me to think.

My colleagues at the University at Albany (SUNY) helped me begin the process of transformation from student to scholar. I thank Hilde Hoogenboom, Martha Rozett, Jacinto Fombona, Alethia Jones, Jennifer Burrell, and Jeffrey Berman for their generosity in reading early drafts and the guidance which followed.

Matti Bunzl and Dara Goldman read late drafts of parts of the manuscript and helped me find my focus. They have been generous colleagues since I arrived at the University of Illinois, Urbana-Champaign. My thanks to them extend far beyond this book, to everything they have done to make this position warm, welcoming, and a supportive intellectual environment.

To the many people who have lived with me during this project as roommates and friends, and who listened to endless recountings of the chapters as I worked through them, I extend my warmest affection, particularly Sonya Levin, Meytal Ozeri, Evelina Kuchuk, Marni Rosen, and Alex Buckley, who taught me how to use a comma. Randy Deshazo read through the final version and his helpful comments carried me to the finish line.

Phyllis Lassner steered this book through Northwestern Press and her assistance has been invaluable. I thank the press for all its support, and the anonymous reviewers whose kindness and words of wisdom delivered the text's final shape. Anne Gendler and her assistant Amanda Allan have been patient and diligent editors; I thank them for caring as much for this text as I have.

In the final account, it is my parents, Valerie and Jeffrey Harris, who have accompanied this project for the longest time. They have cheered from the sidelines and supported each incarnation of this work, from its first life as an essay during my master's at the School for Oriental and African Studies, during the years as a doctoral thesis at the University of Oxford, and later its turbulent development as a book manuscript, to its completion as a monograph. Through their support and their belief in the possibility that this book would one day become a reality, they have made it so. I am deeply grateful for their love and generous warmth and I dedicate this book to them.

ABBREVIATIONS

HR   Hilu, Alon. *The House of Rajani*. Translated by Evan Fallenberg. London: Harvill-Secker Random House, 2010.

CS   Katzir, Yehudit. *Closing the Sea*. San Diego: Harcourt, 1992.

I   Kenaz, Yehoshua. *Infiltration*. Translated by Dalya Bilu. New York: Random House, 2003.

KSK   Keret, Etgar. *Ha-Kaitanah shel Kneller*. Tel Aviv: Zemorah Keter, 1998.

JH   Oz, Amos. *Where the Jackals Howl, and Other Stories*. London: Chatto and Windus, 1981.

PC   Shabtai, Yaakov. *Past Continuous*. Philadelphia: Jewish Publication Society of America, 1985.

RN   Tammuz, Benjamin. *Requiem for Na'aman*. New York: New American Library, 1982.

MM   Yehoshua, A. B. *Mr. Mani*. New York: Doubleday, 1992.

An Ideological Death

Danny (A Note in Memory)
Amos Kenan

Even as a child, Danny was convivial, sociable, and took part in the collective. When he studied at Tova's kindergarten, he liked to sit in a group with all the other children and sing: *Hurrah, hurrah, what can we do without labor?*

When he went to primary school, he always liked to join in. Every break-time he would sit with the others and sing: *Neighbor, neighbor, what can we do without labor?*

At secondary school, he joined a youth movement, which he served in for ten years. There he received a collective secular education and learned to do everything with everybody else: to sing, to dance, to travel, to think, to talk, to write, and so forth. He even excelled at writing songs for the collective. He emphasized the petty egotism of the individual and in opposition pointed to the magnificent developments achieved by social groups.

When everyone went to protest, he went to protest. When everyone went on the illegal aliyah, he went on the illegal aliyah. When everyone was detained on Bari or Cyprus, he was detained on Bari or Cyprus. When everyone left, he left. When everyone went to war, he went too.

With thanks to Kenan's widow Nurit Gertz for permission to reprint this story. The short piece "Dani (Tziun lezikro)" originally appeared in the collection *Sefer ha-Satirot 1948–1984 and Vice Versa*. The translation is my own. Note that "Tziun" in the Hebrew title can also be read as "Tzion," a reference to Zion and Israeli nationalism.

When everyone obtained a discharge, he got discharged too. And when everyone went to search for the great tomorrow, he searched for it as well.

When he left the kibbutz (after a social crisis), every evening he would go to meet the gang and ask: *Hey gang, what are we doing today? Hey gang, what are we doing tomorrow? Hey gang, are we going to the cinema? Hey gang, how's the gang?* In fact, anywhere the gang was to be found, he would not be missing.

One day a terrible tragedy occurred; the whole gang left the city to attend the wedding of one of the comrades and Danny remained alone. The whole evening he wandered alone in the streets and didn't meet a soul. It sent him into a deep depression. For that reason, he killed himself. And even today no one understands how he did it on his own.

Introduction

An Ideological Death: Suicide in Israeli Literature explores the depiction of suicide within the Israeli literary canon. In literature this image serves to represent, in metaphorical terms, the rupture at the heart of Israeli society between its ideological narratives of creation, which in every sense may be considered to construct in Benedict Anderson's sense an imagined community, and the reality of life within the Israeli state.

During the nineteenth century, key European Jewish thinkers, writers, and political figures developed Jewish nationalism, building on Diasporic Jewish identity. This modern political movement known as Zionism called for a physical piece of land that would allow this nation to become a self-governing state. By its establishment in 1948 as the State of Israel, a clearly recognizable set of Zionist national narratives existed that were consciously constructed, reinforced, and maintained through national institutions, public rhetoric, and the fabric of daily life. The construction of the hegemonic discourse was the result of a consciously imagined community sharing ideas about a unifying past, beliefs about territorial claims, and commitment to the revitalization of the Hebrew language. Within Zionism there was a powerful cultural force with a deep desire to create an authentic local culture. A tension existed in this very notion that rejected many of the tenets of European Diasporic Jewish life (Yiddish, folk culture, traditional family structures) while attempting to re-create the values and institutions of the European world that had birthed precisely these manifestations of Jewish national identity.

Simultaneously, the encounter with the Levantine world with its Arab architecture, heat, and alien foods forced the hybridization of European values and aesthetic tastes with the local environment to create a new set of expectations appropriate to the circumstances.

At the heart of this enterprise to create a national collective was the expectation that the Jew himself would be remade. The new Jew would reject the yoke of European oppression and the insular and supposedly unhealthy life of the Diaspora in exchange for physical vigor, social equality, bravery, courage, independence, and liberty. The paradigmatic sabra generation born to the land or arriving as children in the 1920s were raised within the — by then — established expectations and institutions of Jewish life in Mandate Palestine. They represented the iconic understanding of the new Jew. By day the sabra would work the field, redeeming the land from its barren state — while in turn being redeemed by it for the investment of his (and her) labor. By night the sabra would be armed in order to defend the landscape from attack, keeping his brethren safe and protecting the borders of Israel. Once independence was declared in 1948, and the nation found itself at war with the surrounding countries, the rhetoric was already deeply rooted. The various forms of militia and defense groups that had existed in Mandate Palestine during the decades leading up to the war were unified under the guise of the IDF (the Israel Defense Forces) and centralized the already prominent role of military service (and success) in the national narratives.

Connecting the land to both a biblical right and the culture of physical labor meant that the landscape served prominently in the discourse of the movement to create a national homeland in Palestine (Zionism). In addition to protecting the borders and those who dwelled within them, working the land was constructed as an act of redemption, and agricultural activities were preeminent in the political discourse. Despite internal political divisions about ways in which this might manifest — the differences between the socialist labor movements in the creation of kibbutzim, the more individualist moshavim, the relatively independent pioneer farmers and their cooperatives, and the urban pioneers building new cities, the narrative remained fundamentally the same: the land was fallow, the new Jew would make it fruitful, and both he and the country would flourish.

Tel Aviv, the greatest of all urban development narratives, epitomized this ideology. Built both literally and figuratively as a city reclaimed from the very sands on which it stood, Tel Aviv was established in 1909 as a suburb of Jaffa, flourishing over the succeeding twenty years to become the dominant economic, cultural, and social center of the *Yishuv* (the Jewish settlement in Palestine). By the time the state was established, Tel Aviv and not Jerusalem, the historic and notional capital, was the most important civil and social representation of the transformation of a modern Jewish society.

While female pioneers, particularly in the early years, were expected to perform the same redemptive tasks as men, this notion evolved, and by the 1950s it had become clear that though women served in the military and in agricultural development, they were increasingly expected to fill the more traditionally domestic aspects of those roles. On kibbutzim women could be found in the laundry, the children's houses, or the kitchens, while in the army they were placed in auxiliary roles as secretaries, nurses, and assistants. Over time, their greatest contribution to the social experiment was seen as the birthing of the nation. As Ben Gurion declared, the nation needs "fertile women's bodies to bear and raise the next generation of citizens."[1] This ideology, articulated by Israel's first prime minister, in 1952, "equated men who evade military service with women who do not bear at least four healthy children."[2] Thus, just as males had expectations within Israeli society that increasingly informed and shaped hegemonic narratives, females also had national narratives with which they were expected to comply.

At every level, culture was deeply embedded in all of these political and social developments. As Benedict Anderson demonstrates, access to the means of printing and publishing is a key factor in the ways groups form nationalism and a national identity. Through the transmission of texts, Jews had maintained a sense of nationhood even in the Diaspora. Scriptures and rabbinical commentaries, as well as a substantial body of secular literature, had always been at the core of Jewish formulations of identity. Though we tend to refer to this process as religious observance it was a far more complex construction that included attention to culture, ethnicity, recent place of origin, and contact with the world at large as new ideas, words, and concepts found their way into Hebrew texts. The wider availability of text, which caused a fundamental shift in national identities following the advent of mass printing in general, was less markedly obvious within Jewish circles. But the dissemination of political nationalism through text was as radical in this milieu as the very presence of text was for others. Given the highly literate nature of European Jewish communities, Zionist ideas for a national homeland were articulated in pamphlets, lectures, and books. But it was fiction written by many of the great political activists of the day that truly captured the hearts and imagination of the young Zionists.

Modern Hebrew literature developed in earnest from the late nineteenth century alongside the ideas for a Jewish homeland, and these political aspects were often expressed in ideologically framed fiction in terms of the plot, the characters, and even the language chosen. By writing in Hebrew, authors were making a commitment in a cultural frame to a country that did not yet exist. The interconnections of Israeli literature and Zionist ideology and their mutual impact on the formation of Israeli identity lie at the heart of this book. Literature created Zionism as a fictional and fantastical dream, establishing values, beliefs, and ideals, even before reality had manifested—thus writing was an ideological project about the creation of the nation-state. Simultaneously, its producers were physically engaged in the transformation of the landscape and the national ideology. Poets worked on kibbutzim (Rahel Bluwstein, Hannah Senesh); novelists fought against the Arab population in local uprisings (Yosef Haim Brenner, Ze'ev [Vladimir] Jabotinsky); and journalists established national committees to bring about the establishment of Israel in Palestine (Theodor Herzl, Max Nordau). In turn, the populace, recognizing the importance of literature in creating the hegemonic Zionist narrative, named settlements, schools, and cafés after authors, book titles, and fictional landscapes, which had espoused in the imagination the world that was created as a reality.

Such a clearly developed and paradigmatic cultural, social, and symbolic capital existed within the early years of the State of Israel, with roots in the late nineteenth-century pioneering ideals, that despite differing political factions and voices internally, the dominance of this discourse was incontestable. Hence, from its very beginning, modern Hebrew literature possessed a high order of cultural capital capable of motivating individuals. The burden literature had borne in creating political enlightenment also imbued authors with the power to critique the manner in which Zionist ideology was realized. Since the 1970s, the authority of the foundational Zionist narratives has begun to teeter. Just as the establishment of these narratives can be traced in literature, we now find significant representations of a nation at odds with the dominant discourse in mainstream fiction and poetry. In Israel, the construction of a hegemonic master narrative, as Yael Zerubavel has argued extensively, came about through the filtering of the past and the creation of national memory, which involved the selection of experiences that could be formulated in the service of the national present, and the erasure of competing and alternative voices, at times in conflict with the dominant ideology and those agents who represented it.

The Yom Kippur War (1973) caught the citizens somewhat unprepared. Massive casualties and scenes of captured Israeli soldiers being led across television sets that were only newly prevalent in Israel presented the shocking possibility that Israel was not invincible, and the imagined community might lose its physical manifestation. Four years later, the Labor Party that had dominated the political landscape for the thirty years since the beginning of the state was overthrown in a landmark election, as a result of which the Likkud Party came to power. Then in 1978, Israel entered Lebanon. Though its earliest incursions into this neighboring state served to defend Israel's northern settlements from PLO artillery fire and terrorist activities, by 1982 the PLO had returned. Israel's aggressive attempts to clear Southern Lebanon of Palestinian paramilitary forces undermined Israel's long-standing diplomatic posture that its military served to defend the nation. Instead, by actively interfering in internal Lebanese politics and being seen as complicit in the massacres at Sabra and Shatila, the country and its army suddenly faced significant public censure within Israel and abroad. For the first time the IDF saw a significant decline in its public standing. The cultural hegemony of Labor-Socialist and military elites was shattered. Using the influence that Israeli writers traditionally possessed, fiction from the 1970s onward criticized the state in powerful and public ways, undertaking an unsympathetic examination of institutions that had been previously sacrosanct. The image of suicide became a way to suggest that many of the mythic symbols, stories, and institutions that the public took for granted and accepted as the only model of reality, had excluded all the other competing narratives that had existed simultaneously, but had been suppressed during the state-building years. For example, though 50 percent of Jews in Israel descend from migrants of Arab lands (*mizrachim*), many of whom continue to live in poverty due to disastrous settlement policies, it was only the narrative of the male cultural elite — socialists from Europe — that figured in the national image. By shattering the inviolability of the nation's sacred cows, writers opened up the possibility for new, differing histories to be heard.

With these changes, alternative narratives — often in conflict with the traditional European, Ashkenazi, male, militarized, kibbutz, Labor-Socialist position — began to emerge, including that of other pioneers, Jews who migrated from Arab lands, Jews who were settled in Palestine as part of the old *Yishuv* before the pioneers arrived, and in the most recent years, an increasing acceptance of the Palestinian counter-narrative. Though the Arab-Israeli conflict has underpinned almost every facet of Israeli life in one way or another, it has in many ways been absent from Israelis' identification of self. Seen as "them" in opposition to a pioneering and virtuous "us," the Palestinian was in turn romanticized and reviled. It was to escape what was perceived as the Arab backwardness of Jaffa that led to the building of Tel Aviv; the intense cultivation of the land was a response to an apparent underdevelopment by primitive native farmers with antiquated farming methods; and the narrative of the guard, the soldier, and finally the Israeli military machine emerged out of a need for self-protection (imagined and real) that was part of a Jewish legacy from Europe, filtered through the local lens of an Arab threat. Yet despite this constant and humming undercurrent, the Arab remained absent in most of mainstream Israeli literature. It was more than a hundred years after the beginning of Modern Hebrew literature in the nineteenth century that the Arab would get to speak in his own voice and represent his own experience in Hebrew fiction. Today, changes in Israeli-Jewish, Israeli-Arab, and Palestinian society have led to changes in the depiction of the Arab in Hebrew literature. This change in the Israeli psyche, which allowed the once heroic and resilient sabra to admit the presence of difference, has led to previously unimaginable narratives and new constructions of Israeli identity. This book explores the ways in which Israeli literature sets out to subvert, criticize, and even denounce the ideological conventions of Israel.

Israeli fiction continues to explore the imagined origins of its nation, ultimately reflecting on the failure of its ideals even while expressing support for Zionism and the State of Israel. Through a study of texts which have chosen to convey this crisis by representing the suicide of protagonists within its literature, this book examines critical responses to the Israeli narrative. Poetry by the generation of the War of Independence (1948), novels by A. B. Yehoshua, Benjamin Tammuz, Yaakov Shabtai, Yehoshua Kenaz, and Alon Hilu, novellas by Etgar Keret and Yehudit Katzir, and a short story by Amos Oz demonstrate a profound challenge to the foundational myths. In reconsidering and even criticizing Israel these novels imagine society's extremes and, paradoxically, by doing so they at times also reinforce the nation's narratives by framing social and political norms. This seeming inconsistency can be seen as a result of the overlapping threads that are often in conflict with one another and which are both hard to unravel and at times built on shifting sands. This book serves as a snapshot of mainstream Israeli fiction and its ability to engage in a critical and rhetorical process that examines its own formation. Though these texts demonstrate a nation questioning its own values and ideals, they cannot be seen as post-Zionist. Written by authors at the very center of Israeli society, mostly holding moderate political views, these texts instead reveal the inexorable struggle for identity that lies at the heart of a nation.

Taking an approach that focuses on the importance of reading Israeli literature within its cultural context, each chapter explores a different major narrative of Israeli national identity. Traced through the image of Samson and his development from a biblical archetype to a modern celebrity, chapter 1 explores the construction of the sabra hero in his military context and the creation of a myth of self-sacrifice for the national collective. The act of suicide signifies a rejection of the founding fathers by the "State Generation" of writers who succeeded them, and the inherent conflict between the expectations of heroism and of death. Chapter 2 presents the collapse of the incontestability of the IDF in Israeli society, raising questions about the construction of violence and camaraderie as rites of passage for Israeli males. Chapter 3 traces the development of the formal Zionist narrative from pioneer to modern nation-state with its exclusion of other contesting and competing histories that occurred concurrently, but have been relegated to the margins: the rise of counternarratives, including that of members of the first aliyah, of Mizrachis and Sephardis, of Palestinians and of women has led to a decline in the domination of the hegemonic elite, who were traditionally Ashkenazi, Labor-Socialist, and male. Through this chapter personal and family accounts are used to question the monolithic and linear representation of Zionist history. Chapter 4 is concerned with Tel Aviv, from its kernel as a Jewish garden suburb of Jaffa to its role as an international and metropolitan city, constantly pulled between the desire to be a manifestation of the local Zionist ideals that led to its construction and its desire to be a "city like any other." Chapter 5 reveals that despite the impending end of cultural hegemony for many of the nation's most central narratives, represented through the act of suicide, the expectation of women's fertility remains — so much so that the act of suicide in fact serves to reinforce this obligation! In chapter 6, the final chapter of this book, I examine the study of suicide in literature in a broader comparative context. Traditionally, the study of suicide in literature is examined in relation to theories which relate to suicide in life; whether that of the author exploring suicidal feelings (Hemingway, Plath, Woolf, Alvarez, Parker, and others); in relation to social-science studies such as Durkheim's sociological categories and Shneidman's psychological categorization systems; or as Jeffrey Berman seeks to do, presenting studies of suicide in literature in relation to students' psychological experiences of reading about suicide in literature, responding to such experiences as the "Werther effect."[3] This concluding chapter explores the impact of reading suicide through a culturally dependent lens and considers the micro context of Israeli literature within the broader discussions of suicide in fiction.

Not all Hebrew literature is concerned with Zionism, or even written for or about Israel. But in works that do engage with this cultural and political tradition, the image of suicide becomes a way of engaging with ideological constructions of Israel. In this book I explore Hebrew literature written primarily since the establishment of the State of Israel (1948) that uses the image of suicide to comment on society. Despite the many divisions in Israel — religious/secular, Ashkenazi/Sephardi, Left/Right, male/female, rich/poor — Israeli society in many ways can be seen as a cohesive unit. Writers who confront the national norms are engaged in a dialectical relationship with formative Zionist narratives.

What Are National Narratives in General and Why Are They at Times Ideological?

For suicide to be a compelling image, offering a dystopian view of a particular civilization, there must be a single unifying view for that society. Thus the imagined community, in order to articulate a concept of self, constructs its identity by filtering stories, language, cultural artifacts, and history about that society.[4] In essence a "cultural community" arises when a fictive kinship is created through "one language, myths of origin and common history, rituals consecrating the piece of territory which is the 'homeland' and a shared knowledge of the past."[5] These narratives about the society are used to explain the current identity of the group, and because this is often achieved with ideological intentions in mind, they are designed to reinforce that national identity. As Alan Confino shows, "the past is constructed not as fact but as myth to serve the interest of a particular community."[6] Although individuals in this society differ, these ideological narratives offer cultural, political, or moral values that transcend differences. Individual experiences within a culture are subsumed into the commonly constituted practices and representations. "National memory, for example, is constituted by different, often opposing, memories that, in spite of their rivalries, construct common denominators that overcome on the symbolic level real social and political differences to create an imagined community."[7] These features of culture, history, and so on about a given group or society, when collected and shared are often known as the collective memory of the group. National (or collective) memory is the result of the constructed common denominators that have overcome, on the symbolic level, real social and political differences in order to create an imagined, idealized community.

In discussing the attitudes of Israeli society, using Anderson's model of collective identity, it is possible to consider uniformity in belief, attitude, and values in relation to mainstream Zionist tropes and institutions. Though divisions of class, religion, and politics remain, there are aspects of Zionist identity that transcend the personal realm. Therefore some generalization may be made in referring to society as a body with a single mind. Collective memory feeds the collective identity of the group—shaping its conceptions and behavior. As Yael Zerubavel has explained: "collective memory creates a particular periodization and evaluation of the past, and turns certain events into political myths."[8] In turn these myths are uniformly accepted, and the image of suicide is then employed by Israeli authors to confront these myths. The term "myth" becomes confusing because of its multiple meanings: "myth as distortion or lie; myth as mythology, legend, or oral tradition; myth as literature per se; myth as shibboleth,"[9] but as Timothy Brennan has argued, "all of these meanings are present at different times in the writing of modern political culture." Accepting this multiplicity of meanings in no way challenges a hypothesis of collective memory, because whether myth is mythology or is literature, it has been constructed and interpreted for the political purposes of national memory. Importantly, it is the influence these narratives have by becoming motivating forces for the society that accepts and adopts them that makes them relevant, not whether they are constructed from provable truths. This collective memory expresses the shared identity that unites a social group even though its members may have different interests and motivations.

> The crucial issue in the history of memory is not how a part is represented but why it was received or rejected. For every society sets up images of the past. Yet to make a difference in a society, it is not enough for a certain past to be selected. It must steer emotions, motivate people to act, be received; in short, it must become a socio-cultural mode of action.[10]

A society will then model the beliefs about the past to shape goals for the future. Within a national narrative, the cultural, social, historical, political, and religious identities of a group converge to create a meta-narrative. The group is then described as a nation when these early elements of group identity (culture, history, religion) are combined with other symbols such as homeland, anthem, language, and flag. In a national narrative, there is the shared belief among the participants that a common past and a common future link the people, and that the group must work together toward this common future. Modern political movements combined these ingredients to construct nationalisms as motivating forces.

What Is the Zionist National Narrative?

Suicide in Hebrew literature creates tension by being in disharmony with the national narrative, which places central importance on the individual's responsibility to contribute to the nation. The particular Zionist narrative (the Jewish longing for a national homeland) has been defined concisely by Michael Feige as one that relates to the greatness of the Israelite nation in ancient times; the two thousand years of exile during which the people suffered and forfeited its national greatness until the glorious return to the ancient land; in sum, it is a process characterized by sacrifice and heroism.[11]

Nurit Gertz and Yael Zerubavel separately have explored many of the nation-building myths of Israeli society arguing that the process of constructing these myths includes rejecting the Diaspora and the Jewish past as a religious past.[12] Instead, they argue, the past has been historicized and made secular, which in turn has transformed this history into cultural commodity. The components of this commodification include a symbolic or physical bond with the Land of Israel, using the Hebrew language, identifying with biblical characters as real rather than symbolic ancestors, emphasizing the human qualities of their depiction rather than those elements that have been portrayed as superhuman, and embracing these archetypes, thereby making them part of a communal past.

Following the nineteenth-century tradition of the grand historical narrative, Zionism constructed a sweeping interpretation of Jewish history from Antiquity to the present, marked by its teleological orientation. Advocating continuity and identification with Antiquity and a dissociation from the period of exile, the Zionist narrative constructed historical dichotomies that highlighted the introduction of a radical shift in Jewish history: Its decline narrative from the "golden age" of Antiquity to Jewish life in exile was to be replaced by a progress narrative beginning with the Zionist return to the land of Israel and leading toward national redemption.[13]

Redeeming and rebuilding the land became central images of this new ideology. These images included drawing in Jews from the Diaspora, reclaiming land from swamps or the desert and even constructing cities and agricultural settlements. Even though this ideology "was challenged by anti-Zionists, certain Jewish communities, and even within the Zionist camp itself, the narrative of progress leading to redemption enjoyed a long period of uncontested dominance in Israeli society."[14] At its zenith, the Zionist narrative was accepted as self-evident, "but this hegemony had to be constructed, preserved, and reproduced."[15] This identity prevailed and, in the main, was uniformly accepted. The challenge to this historical construction only began to become evident from the late 1970s and 1980s, which is a period characterized by a "manifestation of the decline of the classical Zionist ethos and the renewed contest over Israeli identity."[16] Following these movements the Zionist narrative was then challenged by the public recognition of groups articulating alternative experiences that had been ignored and excluded from the earlier accepted constructions. The lines of identity in Israel then began to be redrawn. However, the earlier construction and codification of the Zionist ethos created tropes. These cultural codes became signifiers for the Israeli reality and created a language representing the hegemony of the Zionist narrative. Despite ideological changes, these earlier images of Zionism continue to possess meaning.

> The meaning of hegemony in this context is that the national narrative was understood as "objective history," and was taken at face value as irrefutable truth by most Israeli Jews. In this way it offered national meaning to private individuals on subjects close to their own experience — hardship, immigration, sacrifice and death.[17]

With the decline of a hegemonic discourse, alternative voices began to become more evident (though some had existed before, they did not gain prominence or public visibility until after the decline of "progress-to-redemption" Zionism). Henceforth the Israeli narrative became increasingly polyphonic, capturing and articulating the greater diversity in ethnicity, religious practice, gender, and place of origin.

Why Literature in General, and Hebrew Literature Specifically?

The image of suicide can disrupt the narrative, making the reader uneasy. The appearance of suicide in literature raises questions about existing social patterns, as part of a text's engagement with the society in which it appears, and which it may describe. As Gershon Shaked has argued, good literature can "overturn accepted forms" and also "attempts to reverse the meanings by the model it creates." It is the very essence of literature to create this attitude of opposition. This responsibility and this objective were even more evident "in the regimen of Israeli life in the 1970s and 1980s, where everything cries out for its opposite, and every truth for its contrary."[18] As Simon During has shown, "it is becoming a commonplace that the institution of literature works to nationalist ends."[19] Literature is a way to communicate nationalistic ideas, or to criticize those that currently exist. Through this medium "nationalism is . . . quite specifically, the battery of discursive and representational practices which define, legitimate, or valorize a specific nation-state or individuals as members of a nation-state."[20]

By using imagery, ideology is reframed in the modes of modern popular culture, where the patterns of analogies or archetypes are then available for further manipulation. In turn this provides a society with "a body of language, tropes and cultural signifiers."[21] These images are recognized and accepted by the audience for whom the text is intended. Since culture is the set of operating procedures governing social interactions, it becomes a relatively closed unit, serving a specific and invested audience, who both shape and are shaped by the group's culture. "Every individual in that cultural configuration carries the characteristic of that culture and behaves according to that pattern."[22] Culture has, by extension, created tropes that are familiar and therefore significant within the society.

The meaning of the suicide image will only be clear to someone who is able to interpret the image in the context of the work in which it is produced. As Pierre Bourdieu has argued, the meaning of a work of art is a code that can only be deciphered with the key. Meaning transpires only at a time during which the codes of the culture are known and understood. Bourdieu's method suggests that

> the full explanation of artistic works is to be found neither in the text itself, nor in some sort of determinant social structure. Rather, it is found in the history and structure of the field itself, with its multiple components, and in the relationship between that field and the field of power.[23]

Any analysis of a text must combine a study of the product, in this case a literary text, with knowledge about the cultural codes of the society that produced it, especially since the texts considered here are engaging with the cultural codes of that society. Given that the significance of a text will be based on the "position, cultural needs and capacities for analysis or symbolic appropriation"[24] of a group or individual — the reception of these cultural works requires a discussion about literary reception in general and further implies a consideration of "the values and systems of classification brought to bear on them at different moments." As symbols become reappropriated, so their meanings change. Thus, an analysis of cultural capital must be based on an evolving code that needs to be continually interpreted and understood according to changing social norms.

Literature represents a culture, but it also shapes it. The image of suicide can fracture traditional representations, thereby offering new readings. Yerach Gover, working within the framework of cultural discourse, derives a sociological explanation about cultural capital that is specific to Israel. Literature can produce and reinforce national ideology while also conserving the cultural signifiers; those images, icons, and values that have come to represent so much to so many as recognizable symbols with clearly identifiable meanings for the national narrative. Gover argues that literature in general and Hebrew literature specifically provides a measurable cultural medium in which to witness the effect of nationalism because a text contains examples of culturally conventional patterns. "It is through the literary heightening of the symbolic and allegorical aspects of this myth that Israeli Jewish culture presents itself as a historical force and can be presented as object for the critique of ideology."[25] What Gover calls Jewish Hebrew literature not only provides a vehicle for exploring these narratives and criticizing them on an elite level, but, according to Gover, it represents much wider beliefs and trends in Israel's culture.

In his discussion of the representation of suicide in art, Ron Brown demonstrates the applicability of Bourdieu's theory: that there is a separation between high and low culture, with high culture being the exclusive province of the elite, while in turn this elite rejects low culture.[26] "On the whole, high art paints a picture of heroic suicide to which popular culture illustrates an opposition."[27] This suggests that images are created for, and received by, different social groups. However, Gover explains that Israeli society does not have the social separation of high and low culture. Though both high culture and low culture are produced in Israel, they are also consumed across social strata, with different social groups often consuming both products. Divisions in (Jewish) Israeli society are not confined to economics and education as Bourdieu assumed for his cultural theories, but may be along ethnic (Ashkenazi/Sephardi), gender (male/female, gay/straight) or religious (orthodox/secular) lines. The divisions in society will influence the way in which suicide is represented and the role it has to play in the texts. According to Gover, class systems are weak structures in Israel and economic inequality has not led the privileged classes to "exhibit distinctive cultures and lifestyles."[28] Hence the relationship between Hebrew literature and Israeli culture is different from the general theory of culture described by Bourdieu and others. In fact, the circulation of literary texts in Israel is so widespread, and the texts and their authors so much a part of public life, that what in another society would be high and elite is in Israel popular and public.

Since the beginning, modern Hebrew literature has engaged with the public discourse and as a result it is not latent in Israeli society, passively absorbed only by the elite, but is instead material that becomes part of the cultural discourse which it is attempting to explore.[29] As a result, it can also be considered to lack the degree of autonomy that is usually attributed to literature. Until recently Hebrew literature created and re-created the national narrative. The writers did not function in a purely creative cultural sphere, isolated from their readers, but placed their work in the public, political, and social spheres. Generally, Israeli writing set in a political or national framework remained loyal to the Zionist image until the dawn of the late twentieth century. Hence, Hebrew literature is almost always connected to Zionism either as a nationalist entity, or as a way of criticizing this dominant ideological framework. Until recently Israeli writers continued to be deeply involved in current political events, and their books were judged in terms of politically charged standards.[30]

Following this argument it is possible to generalize that literature, culture, and politics are extensively interrelated in Israel and therefore the use of an image for literary effect will have a political effect, which will in turn become part of the dominant culture. This cyclical dynamic ensures that an image's meaning will then be available again to be reused or changed. In turn this will make a new political statement, which will influence the dominant culture subsequently becoming available again to be reused or changed. Even when this traditional vision abandons the hegemonic narrative that had existed, the literature is expected to, and does, shape other conflicting narratives in a way that still provides some meaning to a Zionist vision.

Gover has shown that Zionism conforms to the model of ideology as a counter-generative, repetitive, thematically discursive unit in the discourse it informs; a repetition that is frequently fragmented or challenged by the depiction of suicide. Zionism is pervasive and unavoidable within Israeli culture. As Nancy Ezer has argued, "at the foundation of every cultural creation lies a socio-political infrastructure."[31] Accordingly, any analysis that attempts to evaluate a text's semiotic codes without recourse to history remains more or less incomplete. This is all the more true when judging a literature in a culture where ideology is inextricably linked with text. Thus, Jewish Israeli society is grounded in its culture, and that culture is mediated by Zionist ideology; therefore political decisions, attitudes toward other groups, patterns of authority and obligation, and the limits of political and moral discourse should be examined in relation to that ideology. And literature, as a vehicle of that cultural system, provides a framework for viewing the state. The literary works are both part of the state, as they do not exist in a vacuum and must be written, produced, and published, and contrarily, are also in a position to observe the state by providing a critique. Therefore, texts form a dialogue with the national narrative, writing and rewriting the past. In doing so, they form an intertextual relationship with previous writers and future writers of this national narrative.

While Hebrew and later Israeli literature has been a vehicle for both the establishment and subsequent contestation of national narratives, the image of suicide draws on an older history of textual depiction. The use of suicide as an image is built upon a foundation of Jewish religious and historical attitudes — even though authors may draw on this cultural past unintentionally, merely because of its latent presence in Israeli society. Depictions of suicide exist in the Bible and early religious commentaries in the Mishnah and Talmud which considered the subject in detail. The subject was again taken up among religious scholars during the medieval period, with much written about suicide in rabbinical texts such as the *Shulchan Aruch* which codifies religious law. During this period rabbis were called on to engage with the needs of persecuted Jewish populations who often committed suicide rather than be killed at the hands of violent rabble. Simultaneously, a secular tradition of martyrological literature emerged that recognized these deaths and represented them using the language and imagery of the Bible. In turn this created an evolving tradition of images and tropes. Even in the modern nation-state of Israel today, religious commentary on suicide continues to be a prevalent aspect of the cultural discourse.

What Meaning Has the Image of Suicide Evoked in the Jewish Past?

The Jewish attitude to suicide broadly is one of prohibition. This is based on the verse in Genesis 9:5; "And surely your blood, of your lives I will require" which was understood to mean that a person's lifeblood belongs to God and may not be taken away by man. Jewish attitudes to suicide describe the soul as being literally cut off from God (*karet*) and, during the Talmudic period, the rules pertaining to the treatment of a suicide evolved. Medieval commentary stated that "anyone that knowingly kills themselves will descend to Gehenom."[32] This is the Jewish equivalent of hell, a place from which the soul cannot be redeemed.

However, this was not always the situation. The Hebrew Bible contains the stories of six men who commit suicide. Avimelech (Judges 9:54), Samson (Judges 16:25–31), Saul (I Samuel 31:3–4), Saul's arms bearer (I Samuel 31:5), Ahitophel (II Samuel 17:23), and Zimi (Kings 16:18–19). There are other early historical sources that report suicides, such as Josephus reporting on the death of the Zealots at Masada, and the stories that appear in the Deuterocanonical Apocrypha, including the story of Hannah and her sons, in I Maccabees.[33] These early sources became the foundational texts for a religious acceptance of suicide on occasions on which the sacrifice was deemed to be for political or religious reasons and is therefore considered martyrdom.

The *Shulchan Aruch*[34] takes Saul as an example of permitted suicide, and Samson's suicide is extolled. The rabbis defined a set of criteria based on these cases that permitted suicide in three instances. The first type of permissible suicide occurs in cases where a person would otherwise desecrate God's name (*hillul hashem*) and includes occasions of forced conversion or idol worship that would be a denial of the oneness of God. The second type would be an occasion on which one is forced to commit an act of sexual depravity, including adultery, incest, and bestiality. The third occasion occurs when a person is forced to commit an act of murder. From late antiquity and during the Middle Ages at times of persecution many Jews committed suicide because they believed that they would be forced into one of these situations. These suicides became known as acts for the sanctification of God's name, or *kiddush hashem*, and those who performed these acts were known as martyrs. During the Middle Ages, a culture developed that ostensibly valorized suicide-martyrdom, emerging more pragmatically, according to Susan Einbinder, from rabbis' fears about Jewish conversions to Christianity by Jews who were threatened with violence or death. Despite a large body of poetry acclaiming martyrs, "there is equally evidence that advocating suicide or slaughter was a policy that troubled the rabbis, as well it might. For the rabbis (and hence the literature) to have endorsed martyrdom as the solution to conversionary pressure would have been inconsistent with the ongoing, deliberative steps both advocated for the survival of the living."[35] Though rabbis were certainly hesitant to encourage suicide, they were concerned about the possibility of defection from within. Commemoration of martyrs was as much symbolic, aimed at emphasizing the devotion that led to such an act and demonstrating a commitment to the Jewish people, as it was an account of actual deaths.

Along with a large body of poetry and some religious liturgy, statues or memorials were often erected to commemorate martyrs. A variety of images was used to connect contemporary sacrifice in the Middle Ages, with the historical traditions of the Jewish people thereby elevating the immediate crisis and sanctifying it. The suffering of the present was equated with that of the past, stressing the ideological (and religious) lessons the rabbis hoped to focus upon. Samson frequently became a reference source for this act, thereby equating the recent sacrifice made by Jews with that of their ancestors.

> A fourth century sculpture of Samson can be found on the pavement of the Church of the Martyrs at Misis in Turkey, and from the ninth century Samson's death appears regularly in illuminated manuscripts. This may give recognition to the argument that a good death as a "martyr" was more readily represented and

that there was a blanket of silence over the deaths of Abimelech, Ahitophel, Zimi and Saul, which were less popular.[36]

As early as the second crusade (1144–47), conventions about the depiction of suicide in literature had arisen and medieval Jews preferred to record the loss of their brethren in verse. In France and Germany, there was "an established set of martyrological conventions, some new and some adapted from religious sources," and martyrs were described in "the language of cultic sacrifice drawing on images of pollution and purity"and were considered to be unblemished and therefore suitable as ritual offerings to God.[37] Their purity was contrasted with the corruption of the Christian who was depicted as idolatrous and abhorrent. The false salvation offered by Christians is repudiated with symmetrical images or counterimages of darkness and light, or the fires of damnation and divine truth.

Increasingly victims of "judicial violence" also became part of the martyrology canon. From 1171 the earlier emphasis on demographic diversity, numbering women and children among the dead, is replaced with a "focus on an elite corps of scholar-martyrs."[38] This meant the introduction of new motifs in the representation of martyrdom. Yael Shemesh has said that "suicide is a universal phenomenon found in all periods and in all societies. Nevertheless, the attitude of society toward suicide depends on the time and on the culture."[39] In *Beautiful Death*, Einbinder shows that the poetry depicting martyrs and suicide was not static but evolved, representing different artistic trends, audiences, and historical situations such as the changing popularity of conversion or the impact of particular pogroms.

The response of the religious establishment in the medieval period can, according to Einbinder, be seen in the Tosafists' responses:

> Allusions to prophetic or divine revelation [are compressed] into the idealised figure of a scholar-martyr. Over time, and coinciding with diminishing Tosafist hegemony, these images retreat to representations of the martyr's death as a moment of personal redemption and transfiguration. In contrast, a set of cruder images, drawing on deep-rooted taboos and often framed as a dialogue

between the martyr and his foe, denigrates the sacred symbols of Christianity.[40]

Despite much of this poetry having a startling combination of polemic and vulgarity, the general stress remains on the importance of Jewish solidarity and cohesion. This is represented through images of individuals and communities that would die rather than be willing to forfeit their fate. The language in the poems evokes images of togetherness and of taking part with "one heart."[41] Bravery was conveyed as the ideal. The martyrs were depicted like Rabbi Akiva, dying with the *shema* on their lips in order to convey religious piety.

> In dignified, formal cadences, [the poets] ushered into the glory of eternal sainthood the innocent victims of mob and judicial violence. Most of these men and women had suffered degradation, torture and mutilation while living, and incineration or exposure after death. Some had defied their oppressors, while others had fled, confessed under torture or implicated their neighbours, families and friends. Yet rarely does the poetry permit us a glimpse of frailty or doubt. Whatever their human flaws, the martyrs were memorialised as models of purity unsullied in their devotion to God. The poetry honoured their resistance to defilement in images of ritual purity, while it anchored the scene of their death in the language of covenantal renewal.[42]

The rabbinical tension between preparing Jews for martyrdom, and horror at the idea of accepting a policy that promoted suicide or slaughter, reflects larger rabbinical issues with suicide toward which Judaism has an ambivalent attitude. Nowhere in the Talmud is it expressly forbidden. However, post-Talmudic sources, often developed during the Middle Ages and including the *Shulchan Aruch*, considered it a heinous sin, a crime worse than murder. It abnegates the doctrines of reward and punishment, and denies the sovereignty of God who gives life and takes it away. It was only in the late post-Talmudic tractate *Semahot* that the laws regarding suicide were formulated.[43] It is laid down that no rites are to be performed in honor of the dead such as *keriah* (tearing clothes as a sign of mourning) or *hesed* (eulogizing the dead), though these rules do not exclude burial or shrouds.[44] However, everything which appertains to respect for the mourners is permitted such as sitting *shiva* (the weeklong period of mourning).[45]

The Talmud contains a debate about whether a proclamation should be made to inform mourners that the death was by suicide. R. Ishamel affirms that an announcement should be made concerning the suicide — "woe, he has taken his life" — but R. Akiva disagrees, saying "leave him in silence, neither honor him nor curse him."[46] This reflects the ambivalence surrounding much of the law on suicide in Judaism.

For a verdict of suicide to be pronounced there are specific and rigorous criteria in Jewish law. In fact, the law is constructed to discourage a ruling of suicide. Persons taking their own lives must be considered of sound mind, or the death will not be ruled a suicide. The *Shulchan Aruch* even contains some debate about whether anyone who commits suicide can be of sound mind. Moreover, to be ruled a suicide, a person must have clearly signaled that in performing the act the intention was to take his (or her) own life. If even half an hour has elapsed between the declaration and the act, it may not be considered a suicide. If the body is discovered after the act has taken place, the method of death may also prevent ruling the fatality a suicide. For example, if a man is found slumped over a sword, there may be other explanations for his cause of death, including accidental death or murder. Furthermore, the numbers of Jews who do commit suicide (or at least are judged to have committed suicide) rather than die as an act of *kiddush hashem* (martyrdom), is relatively small, a fact noted by Émile Durkheim in his nineteenth-century sociological study.[47]

Nor are these religious rulings on those aspects of suicide that relate to martyrdom relegated to the distant past. Examples exist in more recent Jewish history. On the eve of their execution, two soldiers fighting against the British in Palestine, Meir Feinstein and Moshe Barazani, blew themselves up in prison in Jerusalem 1947 in order to avoid the hangman. Their deaths were compared to the suicide of Saul, though their original plan to kill themselves on the way to the scaffold and thereby take down the executioner as well was justified using the model of Samson. Rabbi Shlomo Goren, the chief rabbi of the Israel Defense Forces, expressed the view that a soldier taken prisoner was entitled and even obliged to commit suicide if he feared that he might not be able to withstand torture, or that under it he might reveal military secrets.[48] In using biblical archetypes for their religious rulings, these contemporary texts about a secular situation demonstrate a similarity of approach to the Middle Ages, which combines religious ideas with modern life.

Suicide as an act of *kiddush hashem* became more prevalent as a way to die during periods of Jewish suffering in the Middle Ages. But while martyrdom gained currency and was seen as a noble sacrifice, committing suicide outside the framework of *kiddush hashem* was considered to be an abandonment or a rejection of God, and therefore a serious crime. Though returning to Zion had long been part of Jewish belief, the political movement of Zionism calling for the settlement of dispersed Jews of the Diaspora to create a Jewish state in Palestine was a secular movement. A suicidal death as a symbol of dedication to God and the Jewish people (martyrdom) which was contrasted with the rejection of God (suicide for personal reasons) no longer provides an adequate explanation for the use of the image in modern Hebrew literature. Without God (and the threat of conversion or massacres) being a significant factor in the literary descriptions of suicide, the image must be read for other reasons and not just in the framework of the Jewish past. The modern political present has come to replace this religious power in literary terms.

Although the Jewish population of Palestine, particularly that of the second aliyah, contained individuals who would commit suicide, nevertheless it was only the heroic, martyr-suicide that was depicted in nationalist literature about Palestine and the early years of the state.[49] Suicide as a result of depression, decay, emotional crisis, or weakness, as evident in literary depictions of Jews in modern Europe (and corresponding with European literary movements including Hebrew modernism), was not evident in Zionist nationalist literature.[50] This is unsurprising as the image of weakness was considered a failure of the Zionist cause. Nevertheless, during the same period there was a great deal of literature written in Hebrew that may be considered un-Zionist.

This writing was not literature that attacked national ideals; in the main it simply ignored them. The texts represented the life of simple folk in Israel, Europe, or America and though the literature was written in Hebrew, it did not construct national imagery. Often the works portrayed characters living in shtetls in Europe or a Palestine reminiscent of Eastern Europe, or within the ghetto walls as far afield as London.

Similar to the plot of Yiddish stories, these narratives presented protagonists who killed themselves because they had been betrayed in love, or because they had rejected God and assimilated, only to be betrayed by society. These suicides were prolific and reflected the influence of European writing of the period; much of this material has been written on extensively.[51]

The treatment of suicide in Hebrew literature is ubiquitous during the nineteenth and early twentieth century. Not only does it feature in poetry and prose fiction, but there were also a number of significant Hebrew writers that committed suicide. Nissan Turov explored in detail this phenomenon in Hebrew literature, investigating psychological and social factors among Hebrew writers.[52] His influential writing in the 1950s, in Israel, shaped later generations such as Amos Oz, who in his novel *Sippur 'al 'ahavah vehoshekh* (*A Tale of Love and Darkness*) returns to many of the themes and literary styles used to narrate suicide in this early period.[53] These themes of betrayal, lost love, as well as nihilistic existentialism were pervasive within the melodrama of early Hebrew fiction, while poetry often reflected the authors' personal preoccupation with suicide as a subtle undercurrent within the work, such as Bialik's *Megillat Ha'Esh*.

Sexual Dishonor and the Female Suicide

By contrast with the heroic narratives, or the representation of love and betrayal that characterized the suicide of men in Hebrew literature, the treatment of female suicides has been concerned with a response to humiliation and sexual degradation. One example of such a narrative is by Yehudah Leib Gordon (1831–92). He presents the suicide of a daughter and her mother in "Bi-mezulot Yam" ("In the Depths of the Sea," 1865) an epic narrative poem that appears in his collection *Songs of Judah*. Cast out to sea as refugees following the expulsion from Spain, the two women are the widow and daughter of the martyred Rabbi 'Abu Sha'am of Tortona. Penina, the beautiful daughter, agrees to submit to the captain's advances once they have reached the shore in order to prevent him drowning the other refugees — but she confesses to her mother that she will kill herself before she will submit to him. "I would prefer to die than to profane my virtue, / And like Jephthah's daughter, in my death I shall save my nation."[54] Penina's actions are framed within the importance of preserving her chastity and honor. Like Jephthah's daughter who died a maiden, and for whom the daughters of Israel mourned for four days each year, Penina's actions preserve her as both a heroine for saving her people and for maintaining her virginity in the face of coercion.

The comparison of Penina's sacrifice is nevertheless ironic since Jephthah's daughter is sacrificed by her father after he vows to dedicate to God whatever first comes out of his house if he conquers the Ammonites. Punished for his injudiciousness, Jephthah is dismembered limb by limb.[55] Gordon often worked with Jewish historical themes as a vehicle for commenting on Russian Jewish life. Believing that: "a gradual, liberal, sanguine transformation of the life and the culture of the Jews of Eastern Europe"[56] with its attendant spiritual deliverance was the key to liberating the Jewish people, he supported emigration to the West and particularly America, rather than specifically advocating for a Jewish national homeland.[57] "Bi-mezulot Yam" was part of a series of works in *Songs of Judah* that indicated Gordon's move toward a redemption for Jews that could be brought about through their own "economic religious and cultural reforms."[58] Neither the theme nor the locations used in this epic poem related to a political-nationalistic call to action. It was not until a generation later that Gordon's cries were adopted by a newer generation that saw Palestine, and hence Zionism, as the true path to personal salvation.

In Gordon's poem, the women's suicide reflects their desire to maintain their chastity in the face of dishonor. A variant of this theme can be seen in the work of Dvorah Baron. In *Ke-Aleh Nidaf* (*Like a Blown Leaf*), published in 1910, Baron explores a woman's humiliation and degradation. The heroine, having been abandoned by her intended fiancé, commits suicide. Though set against the background of immigration to Israel, the locale described could as easily be Russia, from where the author originally came. Though the heroine is living in Tel Aviv, she is disconnected from the experiences of the city. Instead, this story presents a jilted woman who, left without recourse, abandoned and alone, kills herself. This motif is seen in nationalistic literature, where it takes on a political significance—a theme that will be discussed further in chapter 5. But there is a second chain of tradition that can be traced from this pre-state Hebrew literature to Hebrew literature written during the state that does not engage with the national narrative or political ideology. Two examples of subsequent literary depictions of female suicide can be found in the works of Yehuda Burla and Yuval Shimoni. Yehuda Burla's "Maseh Norah" ("A Terrible Action," 1962), which appeared in *Nashim*, portrays the suicide of an emotionally abandoned woman, and Yuval Shimoni's *Me-Of Hayonah* (1990) portrays the suicide of a French girl jumping out of a Paris hotel window after being jilted. Even though these texts appear during the latter parts of the twentieth century, the universal nature of the suicide echoes an older tradition. The image of the exposed woman, whose suicide results from her sexual corruption (whether intentional as with Shimoni, or as a result of rape) and the image of the jilted woman have long been part of the European literary tradition. Representations of women's suicide in nineteenth-century Hebrew literature correspond in both style and theme with depictions in European literature during the eighteenth and nineteenth centuries. These conventions are later drawn on in Israeli fiction of the state period. Yet, as I shall show, in the modern Hebrew examples experiences are filtered through an ideological lens that engages with institutions in Israeli society, and reflects on national narratives that associate the sanctity of women's sexuality with a national project of procreation.

Suicide from Unrequited Love

David Patterson notes the considerable use of suicide in early Hebrew novels such as S. J. Abramowitz's *Ha-'Abhoth ve-ha-Banim* (*Fathers and Sons,* 1868), R. A. Braudes's *Ha-Dath ve-ha-Haim* (*Religion and Life,* 1885), a number of novels by Abraham Mapu including *'Ahavat Zion* (*Love of Zion,* 1853), P. Smolenskin's *Ha-To'eh be-Darkhei ha-Haim* (*The Wanderer in the Paths of Life,* 1905), and *Gaon ve-Shever* (*Pride and Fall,* 1905). The use of suicide is part of the "melodramatic flavor" of the novels, with Smolenskin's novels containing five cases of suicide, as well as many further examples of "threatened or attempted suicide."[59]

> Love plays an important if, perhaps, satirical role. A lovesick friend . . . declares that he is prepared to wait for one more year, but that if his love still remains unrequited he will then commit suicide as thousands do in London . . . Similarly, *The Joy of*

the Godless closes with a letter for the delinquent hero, David, protesting his love for the heroine and threatening to commit suicide.[60]

Certainly these melodramatic uses of suicide as a recourse following disappointment in love reflect the influences of European novels such as Goethe's *The Sorrows of Young Werther*. Another frequent trope in these novels is the use of letters to communicate the suicide, such as in Avraham Mapu's *The Hypocrite* when the young Zerah's clothes are found on the riverbank containing a letter "explaining that the cause of his suicide is unrequited love."[61] This pattern continues with the later Hebrew writers, such as in Haim Nahman Bialik's "Ayekh" where the protagonist dies for love, as well as in Uri Nissan Gnessin's 1910 story, "Etzel," where a woman doctor commits suicide perhaps as an expression of unrequited love, though the act contains elements of ambiguity. As these examples show, love, or more particularly, its failure, is frequently the climax of the novel that leads to suicide as the denouement. Though these trends were common and widespread, other themes connected to the depiction of suicide in early modernist writing reflected writers' explorations of universal European literary conventions of the period.

Exploring Philosophy Through Suicide in Hebrew Literature

Though Gnessin had used the familiar depiction of unrequited love in *Etzel*, in his earlier text *Beyntayim* (1907) suicide is used as an expression of nihilistic futility and the act is meaningless and purposeless. Bialik, Berdichevsky, and Brenner have used suicide to explore philosophical ideas about the nature of man, the collective, and natural law. Berdichevsky presents suicide as part of the natural law in his works on "Be-Emek" and "Et-Korbani." In Brenner's *Around the Point* (1904) the protagonist commits suicide as an exploration of nihilistic ideas about reason propounded by Schopenhauer's claim: "it is quite obvious that there is nothing in the world to which every man has a more unassailable title than to his own life and person."[62] During a period of great upheaval for the European Jewish community which was in a profound state of transition both Brenner and Gnessin wrote about the forces of disintegration at work on society.[63] Heavily influenced by Schopenhauer's view of suicide, these writers sought to explore in their texts that

which Schopenhauer had explored in his philosophical essays; his opposition to a religious moral framework forbidding suicide, he argues,
is an invention of monotheistic clergy and not even a reflection of the
texts from which they draw inspiration. Instead, he proposes that the
discussion of suicide should be subject to an analysis of pure reason. In
his most famous essay on the subject he concludes:

> Suicide may also be regarded as an experiment — a question
> which man puts to Nature, trying to force her to an answer. The
> question is this: What change will death produce in a man's exis-
> tence and in his insight into the nature of things?[64]

Bialik drawing on this discussion sought to find an explanation outside
religion but based on a framework of social obligations in "Megilat Esh,"
in which he explores the questions of communal and personal suicide.
His work reflects on the medieval martyrology tradition in which whole
communities facing the possibility of *hillul hashem* took their own lives
rather than risk rape, torture, and murder. This work, like "Davar," considers the state of the Jewish nation internally as an institution, and exter-
nally in relation to the non-Jews among whom Jews were living.

Forerunners of the more expressly political suicides explored later in
this book can be seen in works by Aharon Reuveni and Asher Barash in
which suicides occur within a text that is concerned with representing
the political, social, or ideological situation within the *Yishuv*. Reuveni's
Shamot (1925), the third part of the trilogy about Jerusalem from the period of Ottoman rule to the British Mandate, concludes with the suicide
of the healthy hero, thereby challenging the socially expected conventions that the *Yishuv* built mentally and physically strong individuals in
opposition to the characterization of the destructive forces of Eastern
Europe that created weak, sickly, deformed individuals. This imagery
is very similar to the anti-Semitic stereotypes found within the general
European press of the period.[65]

Not all texts written even during the State of Israel interact with the
national narrative, as can be seen from the construction of the narratives,
the context, and the content of the fiction. Avigdor Hameiri's use of suicide in "Hamsin" in *Haguf Hageoni* (1980) occurs in Israel, while *Eish
u-beito Nimhu* (1969) by Asher Barash reflects an earlier age of Hebrew
writing. The protagonist commits suicide after he fails to set up a home

and a family in Tel Aviv. His death reflects his disillusionment with the promise of the first Hebrew city. Both the rejection of the soldier-pioneer hero and the ideological city of Tel Aviv become frequent themes in literature written in Israel and each of these subjects will be looked at in detail in the coming chapters. Suicide as a response to the Tel Aviv ideology is explored more comprehensively through the works of Yaakov Shabtai and Etgar Keret in chapter 4.

Suicide in Hebrew writing is a metaphor, employed frequently in different ways to invoke a diverse array of themes, including a crisis of faith, the difficulty of life after the Holocaust, and abandonment by a lover. Nevertheless, these themes reflect universal trends, which are not particular to Hebrew literature, even when found within its writings.

A transformation took place in modern Palestine in which suicide in literary texts reflected a unique direction, different from that of the modernist European Hebrew writers. It ceased to be a comment on Jewish obligations toward God and instead became a way to comment on loyalty to the national enterprise. Moving away from the martyrology literature of the Middle Ages in which suicide was depicted as an expression of loyalty to God, modern Zionist depictions were secularized. Despite the absence of God and religion, Hebrew fiction continued the conventions of representing sacrifice, using the martyrology style evident in medieval literature.

In the early nationalistic depictions the medieval model of martyrdom was adopted especially in the choice of subjects; for example, Samson continues to be used in the texts, just as he had been a symbol adopted in the past, but instead of pious scholars dying for God, soldiers were depicted dying for the state. David Fishelov in his discussion of popular representations of Samson discusses the repeated use of this biblical hero in a modern secular context as a synonym for bravery, heroism, and national sacrifice. However, in a later text such as *Hitganvut Yehidim*, Yehoshua Kenaz expresses the notion that man's life now belongs to the state, in his depiction of a group of soldiers. One man cuts himself shaving and is asked: "Why do you cut yourself like that? Are you trying to commit suicide? Forget it! You're IDF property now. Any attempt to destroy IDF property is an offense against General Routine Orders." Suicide is now seen as a crime against the state and not against God.

The short story by Amos Kenan (b. 1927) at the beginning of this book is paradigmatic of the shorthand used by Israeli writers to evoke a stable of tropes, conventions, and images that resonate for the Israeli public. Employing a sparse style, the story is only a page long after all; Kenan touches upon historically recognizable Zionist ideals, establishing Danny as the archetypal Zionist figure, only to destroy him in a pointed critique that challenges the very values that have been evoked throughout the narrative. The ideology of the "new Jew" prized youth and socialist ideals, and Danny, "even as a child," exemplifies these qualities: he liked being part of the "group," was "sociable," and sings along with his peers. More than simply representing socialist camaraderie, Danny is engaged in *Shira Be-tzibbur* (communal or public singing), an activity whose performance ritual emphasized Hebrew identity, and was a favorite activity among the socialist pioneers, passing into a kind of cultural folklore within Israel. Communal singing by men and women was often accompanied by communal "folk dancing" a national variant that drew on Eastern European traditions, and emphasized the collective and "togetherness." The lyrics represented the land, nature, and national projects. Both Zionist songs and dances were adopted by youth movements, taught in schools and practiced widely in common spaces, including festivals, kibbutz dining halls and school gyms. These enterprises created a localized culture particular to the new Hebrew (the sabra), which marked the pioneers in Palestine as different from Diasporic Jews with their traditional *nigguns* (religious songs and melodies from Eastern Europe) and gender-segregated singing and dancing.

Danny's participation in a youth movement represents his ideological inculcation into Zionist society. Originally formed at the beginning of the twentieth century, "Zionist youth movements were established to promote Jewish immigration to Palestine. Later they spread in Israeli society and functioned as one of the most important agencies of immigrant absorption and integration."[66] The rules of Israeli society were learned through the youth movement culture.[67]

> The pioneer youth movements, more than any other framework, played a decisive role as the first stage in the Sabra's path of sponsored mobility since they prepared the Sabras for their future roles. As movement members, the young Sabras practiced personal responsibility for others, team work, and demo-

cratic procedures such as meetings, debates and elections. They were equipped with the social resources necessary for social advancement—Sabra slang, folklore, cultural knowledge, and personal connections.[68]

Danny not only participates in this organ of acculturation, but "serves" in it, as one would serve in an army unit. The language of participation in the story is derived from Israeli society's most prominent social organ of national identity and pride, the military. While it is written long after the establishment of the State of Israel, and uses these well-established Israeli semiotic codes, the story is set in the pre-state period, starting in Eastern Europe, presenting Danny's Zionist engagement and his subsequent immigration to Israel.

Even while in Europe, Danny is given a secular education that highlights his identity as a new Jew in contradistinction to what for thousands of years had maintained Jewish identity—religious observance, and education within the cheder and yeshiva (religious institutions). This new form of education teaches him to participate in the collective and to see himself as a single cog that may only be fully realized within the larger machinery of the particular political movement, within Zionism more generally, and within the greater concept of the Jewish people. "He even excelled at writing songs for the collective. He emphasized the petty egotism of the individual and in opposition pointed to the magnificent developments achieved by social groups." Not only does Danny passively receive these sociocultural lessons, but he himself becomes a pedagogue, further disseminating their messages.

Danny the loyal Zionist participates in the *Aliyah Bet*, the illegal immigration to Palestine, organized by the Haganah. Though imprisoned at detention camps, as were thousands of others, part of the mythology of the struggling pioneer, he finally makes it to a future in which he goes to war. Whether serving with the British in the Jewish Brigade, or alternatively with the Haganah as many Jewish soldiers who migrated to Palestine before 1945 did, Danny's military service is an iconic rite of passage. Early military experience played an important role in Zionist history, training Jewish soldiers for the fight for independence (1948) following the Second World War. Danny serves in the army and he is a member of the kibbutz, the socialist agricultural organization whose ideological importance far outweighed its physical and financial contribution to the Zionist immigration. Every move that Danny makes is dictated by his role within the collective and his sense of group identity. "When everyone left he left. When everyone went to war, he went too. When everyone obtained a discharge, he got discharged too," and so on. Only when Danny is abandoned by the group, and is entirely alone, does he commit suicide. His death indicates a challenge to the national institutions of the kibbutz and the army, the tropes of the Zionist historical narrative such as illegal immigration, and incarceration in the detention camps in Italy and Cyprus, and to an ideology that promoted service to the nation.

The patterns that often precede a suicide in literature are clearly identifiable such as his increasing silence, isolation from the community, abandonment, and depression. "The whole evening he wandered alone in the streets and didn't meet a soul. It sent him into a deep depression. For that reason, he killed himself." But his emotional breakdown is read in light of his previous social engagement. Thus the manner of his death is served up in the same satirical tone of the rest of the story, and ultimately privileges the individualistic nature of his death; an act that separates him from the collective. It is the only action that marks his difference, and therefore his identity outside the nationalist narrative.

Historical changes to the centrality of the Zionist narrative led to a change in the representations of suicide in Hebrew literature. As Kenan's story demonstrates, no longer a noble and heroic sacrifice in battle representing a modern notion of martyrdom, suicide was increasingly represented in antiheroic forms in spheres that implied futility or selfishness. The presentation of Danny's suicide is ambivalent, and the distinction between heroic self-sacrifice (martyrdom) and unheroic (self-interested) suicide that had characterized earlier periods of Jewish thought are blurred. Destroyed by the very collective that should have protected him, Danny's death evokes not sympathy, but indignation and anger toward a society that could have both instilled these values and could have abandoned him after having done so. These new depictions of suicide responded to the models and imagery of previous writers, but often upended accepted conventions. The next five chapters of this book consider the ways in which the ideals of Israeli society could be challenged and overturned through the image of suicide, exploring the cultural meaning of this powerful image and its changing role in Israeli literature.

The Construction of This Book

I have predicated this work on a number of notions: (1) The writers explored here engage predominantly with the national narrative. (2) This narrative has a language of images that are recognized by Israelis and scholars of Israel and can be obvious or oblique but hold a significant position in the formation of Israeli identity. (3) Through Israel's history this narrative has changed and developed, but its language and imagery continue to resonate for the Israeli public. (4) Writing in Israel is often dialectical, and can manifest as an intertextual relationship.[69] By reusing images that already have a recognizable meaning a new meaning is provided, as a result of which this new material and significant cultural components can also be reused or subverted. This process creates layered cultural components that are used to build national narratives. (5) This writing is literally, politically, morally, or socially significant. As Gover has said:

> Typically, political discourse is said to have little to do with the more general morality children are taught in school. In Israel, on the other hand, political and moral discourse are never distinct. People learn to think politically and morally simultaneously, in regard to referents, images and conceptions that are deeply and persistently moralized.[70]

This fusion of morality and politics has created a heightened awareness of the productive aspects of literature. The language of Israeli Hebrew literature "has to do work of a higher order than is normally required of other linguistic cultures where literature appears distinct from the subjective conditions of writing, reading, and discoursing — that is, from society."[71] There is no distance established between the text and the audience.[72] As a result, Israeli Hebrew writing can never be seen simply as a matter of technique because it always has the potential to be a significant moral, political, or social tool. Furthermore, authors are consciously aware of the role or responsibility of the text in Israeli society. Thus the appearance of suicide is not subject to purely aesthetic judgments, but also to evaluations about its wider meaning in a social, moral, or political context.

Given the conditions of Hebrew literature, and its place within society, the image of suicide must invariably function as part of these layered meanings which form a dialogue with both previous literature and with society. I have chosen a selection of texts by male and female writers, published mainly since the state's establishment in 1948, and almost up to the present (2009), in order to demonstrate the widespread representation of the image of suicide as a tool with which to represent and sometimes criticize the national enterprise.

I use only texts in which the characters die by suicide. I have excluded works in which, despite extensive discussion about suicide, the characters do not die. I justify this decision because a psychosociological explanation is provided by scientists, sociologists, and medical professionals[73] differentiating between those who attempt suicide and succeed, and those who attempt and fail.[74] Therefore, different issues arise in discussing those who survive suicidal thoughts or suicide attempts, issues that are outside the scope of this book. I have also chosen to exclude texts directly related to the Holocaust, texts that fall into the category of Holocaust literature, or texts written in the area of second-generation Holocaust survivor literature. Despite the richness of the material on suicide available in the field of Holocaust studies, my interest lies with exploring the relationship between the allegorical nature of suicide in texts and the statements that these images make in terms of Israel and Zionism. Texts dealing with suicide and the Holocaust have a different ideological agenda, as issues of personal loss, the personal experience of the writer, and a response to atrocities and trauma tend to be the focus of these works. Suicide in these texts is not an allegorical image (serving as an opportunity for using the image as a tool about other social or political issues) but is instead figurative; interested in suicide and its relationship to death and psychological pain. As I explore in chapter 6, literary suicides that are an extension of the life of the author can be examined by means of the theories that currently exist in this field. My culturally dependent approach offers this discourse a way of conceiving the role that suicide may have to play within a text, and this may be relevant to an analysis of these works if the distinctions are not clear-cut. There is a scholarly tradition of examining literary uses of suicide in relation to the author's own life experiences and suicidal inclinations. Though I deal with the theoretical implications of this work in the final chapter of this book, the applicability of these ideas is material that remains outside the scope of the fiction examined here.

I address the issue of suicide from two perspectives. Scholars of suicide in literature may be surprised to discover that suicide has a culturally sensitive and, in the case of Hebrew literature, a political value. This will not be a surprise to scholars of Israeli literature, who might confidently argue that *all* Israeli literature is to some extent political, and that writers, since the early years of the State of Israel have been writing against the national narrative. However, readers of Israeli literature may in turn be surprised to discover the importance of the image of suicide, the extent to which it has been used, and the nature of its use in the texts. As this book demonstrates, suicide can exist as a tool for making a dramatic political statement which can only be read by placing the character's death within the contextual framework of the text and the society which produced it. Examining suicide in its literary and cultural context, not for its own sake, but for its statement about society argues for a culturally relevant reading of the image, separate from the life of writers or readers. Reading in this way situates this research within a comparative context for reading Israeli literature, locating it within the broader sphere of world literature, and offering the possibility of new ways of considering suicide in literature.

CHAPTER 1

Samson's Suicide:
The Sabra-Soldier Hero

The foundations for the reuse of the Samson image in modern Hebrew (and later Israeli) culture can be traced through the evolution of a nascent Jewish nationalist identity in Palestine and one of its central myths, the *sabra:* "young and robust, daring and resourceful, direct and down-to-earth, honest and loyal, ideologically committed and ready to defend his people to the bitter end."[1] This figure of the native-born Jew pervaded Jewish culture in Palestine and during the early years of the state, becoming a recognized symbol of the new nation. The new Jew was a "quintessentially masculine farmer and warrior — [who] was meant to replace the pale, weak, intellectual, sensitive and victimized Jews of the shtetl."[2] The image that had begun with the *halutz*, the pioneer who arrived from Europe to work the land, evolved into the figure of the sabra, the native born to the land and an icon of the Zionist narrative.

Even with the first images of the *shomer* (guard), the pioneer had been associated with militarization and defense of the land. As the image of the sabra evolved from these roots, the idea of the soldier hero was socially encoded alongside other expectations for the native-born new Jew. From its establishment in 1948, a series of wars dominated the country's identity, as well as its resources. The centrality of the army, militarization, and the soldier within the nation-building enterprise is evident not only within the encounters themselves, or even within the ways in which war shaped Israel's political agendas, but in the explicit construction of the notion of precisely what it meant to be an Israeli — both at home and abroad, and culture reinforced these perceptions.

The willingness for personal sacrifice was encoded in the creation of the sabra-soldier myth, an image that had begun in the pre-state period and was enforced in society, literature, and popular culture. Only with the changing political landscapes following the Six-Day War did a crack in this invincible armor begin to appear. By the late 1970s it had become clear that within certain circles criticism of this major national narrative had begun to manifest, a criticism that was rapidly fueled by the increasing tensions between the Israeli military establishment and public opinion. One frequently employed symbol of this heroic soldier narrative was the figure of Samson. Drawn from the biblical narrative, Samson was epitomized by the self-sacrificing nationalistic ideal. Though much has been said about the popular and widespread use of this image in Israeli society and culture, I contend that it was not solely his heroism, strength, and symbolic identity as the new Jew that marked this biblical figure for reuse in popular forums, but that his final suicide (martyred sacrifice) underpinned the drama of the Samson narrative. Just as the use of a Samson image in medieval literature and memorial culture evoked heroism, in its modern context this dynamic warrior modeled ideal *Jewish* behavior. However, the symbolism of Samson-like soldiers willing to sacrifice themselves for the modern nation-state altered as attitudes toward sacrifice for the collective changed. The heroism of the Samson myth collapsed, and subsequently was inverted, becoming a powerful tool for criticizing the Israeli military hegemony and a society that encouraged a culture of death. This chapter traces a literary history of the changing narrative of the archetypal Samson.

Samson Judges

Modern literary texts draw heavily on the explicit narrative of the biblical Samson and the emblematic imagery of the story. Samson's life is narrated from conception to death in the book of Judges, chapters 14–16. His barren mother promises the angel who foretells his birth that he will be a Nazarite. As such he is dedicated to God until he is released from this pledge. He must avoid alcohol and refrain from shaving, or cutting his hair. During the course of the story Samson performs several feats of strength and heroism, including killing a lion, setting fire to fields of crops by tying three hundred foxes in pairs with torches in their tails, and killing a thousand men with the jawbone of an ass. When trapped in Gaza, Samson carries the gates of the city on his back to escape and when bound by chains and ropes he breaks free. In addition, Samson sets riddles, thereby demonstrating wisdom as well as strength, and he is described as a Judge of Israel. His virility manifests during the course of the story through his marriage, his visit to a prostitute in Gaza, and his romance in the Valley of Sorek with Delilah who then cuts off his hair. After losing his strength he reasserts his faith in God, regains his strength, and finally dies by pulling down the temple of Dagon in which he is standing in order to kill the Philistines found within.

Samson's act of suicide, clearly denoted by the biblical figure's declaration "let my soul die," was interpreted in the rabbinic tradition as an act of heroism and martyrdom, and fed religious Jewish iconography, particularly during the Middle Ages.[3] Samson featured in poetry and statues that represented martyrdom and self-sacrifice for God.[4] This image evolved in the modern period, bypassing the religious symbolism to instead represent nationalistic self-sacrifice. Zionist readings of Samson portrayed this heroic sacrifice as an act for the modern political nation of Israel, in other words: the State.

Why Samson?

Samson's mythic qualities set him among a small group of biblical figures reused repeatedly in modern narratives.[5] David Fishelov outlines three characterizations that are usual among the more popular biblical figures in art and literature. (1) The character is at his or her pinnacle, either in power, beauty, cunning, love, leadership, or courage, and influences the group within the narrative. (2) There is a tension or contradiction within the character and with the events of the narrative. (3) The narrative, and the role of the character within that narrative, have a universal quality such as courage, love (for a woman, for a parent/child, for God), man's weakness (envy, jealousy, hate), or the tension between the ruler and those ruled (whether that leader be a king, an enemy tribe, or God). These narratives and the hero at the center of them have a universal appeal beyond the framework of this individual episode. As Fishelov has shown, these are the characterizations for mythological and archetypal characters in general (Cain and Abel, Hercules, Oedipus, etc.). Certainly, Samson embodies all three of these principles. He is strong, handsome, and cunning. He is committed to a Nazarite life but he likes women and pursues violence, suggesting a contradiction between his character and his fate. The universal element of the tale, along with courage and heroism, is the subject of love and betrayal relayed through the stories of his first wife and later his lover Delilah.[6] Hence Samson has historically played a popular role in artistic representations; in European art and literature with its Christian influences these depictions often focused on themes of loss of faith, treachery, and women's betrayal. In this tradition, Samson was often considered a Christlike figure dying for the sins of others. Within Jewish culture there was a greater focus on interpreting Samson's story as a parable of man's weakness and his need to repent. Samson's suicide was understood as an individual's sacrifice for his people, which supported medieval ideas of Jewish persecution (with Samson signifying martyrdom).[7] Later in Jewish and Israeli culture Samson signified military sacrifice for other Jews who now constituted the nation to be protected.

> The account of Samson's death by choice is an example of supreme sacrifice so common among members of the world's military forces. . . . While some would not consider such a death a suicide, it must be included within the broad definition.[8]

By the early twentieth century, Samson was among a host of biblical characters whose heroism accorded with the sabra ideology of the early and mid-twentieth century that actively created legendary champions who would inspire Jews as well as sustain a sense of national identity and an ongoing obligation to militarization.[9] These heroes were a rejection of Eastern European stereotypes of passivity and weakness, and privileged images of physical strength and combat. They were also constructed to reinforce Zionist ideas of the connection to the Land of Israel. While certain aspects of the biblical narrative were ignored, such as Samson's Nazarite status, other aspects were prized, such as Samson battling enemy forces to protect the land, his virility, and women's devotion to him. This paradigm accords with the cult of fallen soldiers described by Yoram

Bilu and Eliezer Witztum, Yael Zerubavel, Oz Almog, and others, which "looms high in the Israeli foundation myth" of the valiant soldier and his heroic death.[10] The mythification of dead soldiers has "emerged as a cardinal value in the patriotic ethos of modern nation-states," so that the sacrificial death of soldiers is considered an honor.[11] Subsequently, by rewriting the image of suicide, transforming the heroic image into one of futility, modern writers were able to critique a society that had supported earlier myths of self-sacrifice.

Jabotinsky's *Shimshon*: Lothario, Combatant, and Revisionist

Ze'ev (Vladimir) Jabotinsky's version of Samson was fundamental in shaping early Zionist conceptions of the new secular hero. Born in 1880s Odessa, Jabotinsky took up Zionist activity following the Kishniev pogrom of 1903. He helped found the Jewish Legion in the First World War and later became head of the Haganah, the Jewish force for self-defense in Mandate Palestine. From 1921 onward, Jabotinsky was a member of the Zionist Executive and one of the founders of "Keren Hayesod." After a series of policy disagreements on the direction of the Zionist movement, he seceded, eventually founding the New Zionist Organization to conduct independent political activity for free immigration and the establishment of a Jewish state. The three branches of Jabotinsky's power base were the political wing; the youth movement Betar; and the military arm, the Irgun Tzvai Leumi, established in 1937. Together they undertook schemes for illegal immigration, bringing tens of thousands of Jews to Palestine. Banned by the British from reentering Palestine after departing for a lecture tour in 1929, Jabotinsky lived the rest of his life in exile. In addition to his extensive political and military activity, Jabotinsky was a writer, journalist, and translator who advocated the adoption and dissemination of the Hebrew language. His literary writing reflected his political interests.

Jabotinsky's ideological novel *Shimshon*[12] rewrites the biblical story, functioning within an Israeli literary tradition, identified by Yael Zerubavel as one that gives historical depth to "the glorification of dead combatants" by linking their narratives with other "narratives of courage."[13] Jabotinsky's Samson is strong, clever, and wise. Drawn to resemble his biblical namesake, he has long hair and is a champion who lacks restraint with women. But, unlike the biblical figure who is distinguished by his Nazarite status, a promise his mother made when she was miraculously blessed with a child by an angel, this new Samson's difference is erased; his birth is noble but not wondrous and he is therefore intended to seem universal. Samson is a hero who may emerge victorious from every situation, but he must also be willing to sacrifice himself for the collective. This model of Samson as the "national freedom fighter" is in line with David Fishelov's contention in *Gilgulei Shimshon* that heroic militaristic biblical figures were most prevalent in societies where a nationalist ideology dominated.

First serialized in Russian, Jabotinsky's novel resonated among the pioneers in Mandate Palestine on its publication in 1927.[14] "It was translated immediately into Hebrew and rapidly entered the 'bloodstream' of Hebrew literature and Hebrew culture in the land of Israel."[15] The Samson narrative echoed the sacrifices being demanded of Jews in Palestine caught up in the Arab riots of 1920–21 and later 1929. Parallels between the biblical story and the present were inevitable and readers were encouraged to believe in these similarities. Examples include the rule of Jews in the land, then by the Philistines and now by the British (and Arabs), and the impression that Samson's tribe, unique in its rebellion, was going against the general tide of Jewish behavior, just as these young Zionists, or perhaps even more particularly these Revisionists, were doing at the time.

Jabotinsky's novel retained the major thematic plot structures of the original biblical story but his moderations removed the elements of mysticism, and particularly God's presence, from the text. Repeatedly he gave logical explanations for unusual phenomena: if the biblical Samson's foxes were live animals with torches tied between their tails let loose on fields of crops (*Judges* 15:4–6), Jabotinsky's foxes are less extraordinary, though no less dramatically the name of Samson's gang.[16] This Samson resembles Robin Hood with his own set of merry fighting men. Though Jabotinsky's Samson smote "a thousand Philistines with the jawbone of an ass" (Judges 15:15), as the biblical hero had, this new Samson was responding to a single foe, a general named Thousand.[17] This change is explained through the introduction of a new character, Machabonai the chronicler, a fictional addition to the story, who is said to have misrecorded events, to heighten the mythical aspects of the story. Significantly, although Samson's feats are strong and heroic, they remain an achievable reality for any good warrior. Thus a move had occurred since the martyrdom of the late Middle Ages whereby Jews were no longer to be passive victims, but rather armed and able combatants. In Jabotinsky's novel, Samson's death continues to embody the values of heroism. His sacrifice is seen as an honorable event, something he does to redeem and to rescue the Jewish people. Samson's death is not incongruous with the heroism that he had previously exhibited. In his final act, he brings down the Temple, killing more Philistines with his death than he had during his entire life. Just as this suicide is the defining act in the biblical story, in Jabotinsky's version Samson's death is the culmination of the ideals by which he has lived. David Fishelov suggests that the very act of choosing suicide marks Samson as a hero.

> We are after all talking about a hero who finishes his life by committing suicide. Although it is a heroic suicide which involves terrible revenge on his enemies, it is nevertheless an act of personal sacrifice. This aspect is also part of the New Hebrew culture.[18]

It is this sacrifice of the personal for the collective, rather than the number of Philistines killed, that contributes to the notion of heroism that becomes part of the legend. The way Samson dies intensifies the importance of the acts he performed while alive.

The symbolism of heroic, self-sacrificing death played a central role in the iconography of militarism both before and after the establishment of the state, reaching its zenith with the soldiers who fought and died in the War of Independence. These men were described as a "silver platter" through whose sacrifice a state was created and maintained.[19] The deaths of soldiers were "aggrandized as heroic self-sacrifice, a superhuman embodiment of the Zionist collectivist ethos according to which, in extreme situations, sustaining the endangered life of the collective should take precedence over individual survival."[20] The sacrifice, through the representations of death, became as much a part of the total image of the Samson-like soldier hero as the facets of bravery and devotion. Thus Samson's narrative was in line with the expectations of military sacrifice that would develop within the fledgling Zionist reality. A culture of heroism burgeoned, with a recognizable pantheon of dead soldiers as part of the nationalist ethos in which: "Death in combat was nevertheless exalted as the apotheosis of life — a moral will to preserve the existence of the collective and the individuals constituting it."[21] The commemoration of soldiers "warranted them a symbolic immortality in repayment for their sacrifice"[22] and reinforced the values for which the soldiers gave their lives.

Jabotinsky suggests that Samson is immortalized for protecting the collective, but offers a contemporary explanation nuanced to deal with the social and political issues of the day. In pulling down the Temple, his Samson not only kills the Philistines who threatened the Land of Israel but also kills Delilah. This second aspect is an innovation in Jabotinsky's text; Delilah is pregnant with Samson's son and she uses this unborn child as a threat against the Jewish people.

> It will grow strong like its father and I, since my milk has turned to poison, will teach it to hate its father's race. And so out of the judge and protector will come an enemy and destroyer.[23]

Jabotinsky uses this image to attack assimilated Jews in Eastern Europe. He suggests that children born of a union between a Jew and a gentile will reject Judaism and, more significantly, the Jewish nation. For Jabotinsky, Samson's death symbolically protects more than just the lives of Jews under attack by enemies; it also prevents the corruption of Jewishness through assimilation. Samson's death remains heroic, a magnificent display of strength, but its meaning has changed; no longer a defense of God's honor, it is now a man's sacrifice for his people.

Samson, Foxes, Delilah, and Popular Culture

Jabotinsky's novel was extremely popular and well known. David Fishelov argues that the Cecil B. DeMille film *Samson and Delilah*, starring Hedy Lamarr and Victor Mature, was based on this novel. Moreover, other uses of the Samson image appeared in Israeli society during the pre-state and early state-building years. Avot Yeshurun wrote three poems under the title "Samson's Strength," Yaacov Fichman wrote love poems comparing his affection for his Philistine and Jewish lovers, Leah Goldberg wrote a collection of poems called "Samson's Loves," and Uri

Avneri wrote the popular song "Samson's Foxes" as an anthem for a commando unit bearing that name serving in Gaza. Many of the depictions of Samson's heroism were used in other Israeli images and artifacts, and Fishelov outlines a catalogue of popular cultural images in Israel that drew from the allusions to Samson's strength. Other images from the story, such as the lion, became extremely popular and could be found on brands of tobacco, and even luggage, denoting the power and strength of the item. This iconic character remained a popular reference in Hebrew literature, frequently associated with military struggle and the fight for independence. In *My Michael* (1956) by Amos Oz, Jabotinsky's novel is referred to directly by the elderly Revisionists visiting Hannah Gonen while her husband is away in the army. In *Requiem for Na'aman* (1978) by Benjamin Tammuz, the soldier Uri compares himself to Samson fighting for his motherland. On another occasion, the term Samson is slang for a heroic soldier: "I told him before we left, didn't I. He didn't agree. He wanted to be a Samson? Fine. Words are superfluous" (*RN*, 129).

Other synechdoche were drawn from passing references to minor episodes in the Samson story, serving as a cultural shorthand for heroism, militarism, sex, lust, wisdom, betrayal, and combat. The weight imbued in these images became part of the larger framework of heroic terminology associated with soldiers: "Consequently to a certain extent there was a tendency in Israeli literature and culture which encouraged identification with the image of Samson as the chief representation of strength, fighting and heroism," which in turn informed the Israeli social sphere, and the attitudes to militarism and heroism.[24]

The Samson Poet Generation

The victorious depictions of this Samson soldier image that I outlined above which appeared in Jabotinsky's *Shimshon* and in popular culture, and as discussed in the work of Fishelov, demonstrate an idolization of Samson within the Israeli discourse. This in turn, gave way to a generation of poets raised on emblematic portrayals of the soldier hero who had internalized these expectations of heroism and self-sacrifice but found them troubling. Nathan Zach (b. 1930), Yehuda Amichai (1924–2000), Haim Gouri (b. 1923), Anadad Eldan (b. 1924), and Amir Gilboa (1917–84) were among this soldier-poet generation. In works that adopted imagery from the Samson biblical narrative they explored the disharmony between national expectations of sacrifice and heroism, and their own experiences of war. By transforming images from the Samson narrative, these poets were able to confront accepted national ideals in public ways by using imagery and recognized allusions in the cultural discourse. Their poetry wrestled with the status quo precisely because of the high reputation these poets held as sabras. The poets were raised in Mandate Palestine, and had served as officers during the 1948 War of Independence, and several of the wars that followed. Known as the Palmach generation (though they did not all serve in this particular paramilitary group), the poets were educated and shaped by the "socialist Zionist ideology that dominated the value system of the Yishuv."[25] Later they also served the nation as statesmen, journalists, and academics, and were celebrated within Israel for their poetry, which was often read at national ceremonies, canonized in literary publications by the IDF, appeared in school literary anthologies, and for which the poets received many honors and awards.

The purpose of their poetry was the memorialization of the war dead and in this sense their writing became a restatement of the myths of Israeli soldiers' heroism.[26] "These men represented this generation because the fallen were [their] contemporaries, had grown up in the same environment [as they] had, and had been educated with the same values that had been instilled in [them]."[27] They were part of the generational nucleus described by Oz Almog as "the leading group that served as a behavioural model for the entire generation."[28]

In poetry by this generation, Samson's strength became a motif of destruction, and was frequently linked to militaristic images. The soldier became a synonym for Samson with the image of fire presented as a metonym for the hero. Robert Alter argues that "Samson . . . is quietly but effectively associated with a verbal and imagistic motif of fire, the various cords that fail to bind him are likened to flax dissolving in fire when he snaps them with his strength."[29] "The thirty Philistine men threaten his first wife with death by fire if she does not obtain for them the answer to Samson's riddle."[30] This use of fire suggests power and danger, but also a short-lived quality. Willing to go to war for the Jewish nation, even at the cost of their own lives, these poets adopted the image of fire associated with Samson and militarized it. Their poetry connected Samson with a modern army whose legendary covert units were based in Gaza and the Negev. Hence, literary imagery and military reality were effortlessly correlated, and poetry developed ideas and images already prevalent in Israel. Following the Six-Day War, the mythological image of Samson the soldier flourished in Hebrew poetry. "Shimshonai" ["My Samsons"] (1968) by Haim Gouri is an example of this trend.

> Look, my Samsons are returning, the gates of Gaza on their
> shoulders:
> Passing, they smile at blind sentries
> Hyssop. Wind. Crickets.

> Look, my Samsons are returning, their Delilahs at their feet;
> They move along my boulevards.
> I'm awake.

> Look, my Samsons are returning, the memory of lions in their
> hands;
> Marching barefoot,
> In the street there is no sound and no fire.

> Look my Samsons are returning, the frogs of the Vale of Sorek
> in their ears;
> They make their way, they always make their way,
> When was it that I last carried the gates?

> Look, my Samsons are returning, the feast's sacrifice in their
> teeth;
> And the ropes torn, and the riddles solved,
> My first grey hairs.

> Look, my Samsons are returning, no nails in their eyes;
> Returning to me from Gath,
> After the fire.

> Look my Samsons are returning, to the thicket of their nights
> luminous with fox fire.

In this poem, the Samsons are soldiers seen carrying "the gates of Gaza on their shoulders." In an echo of the biblical story, these captured gates are a metaphor for the soldiers' victory. Equally, this is a visual image suggesting military equipment being borne on the shoulders of the marching soldiers. This militarization is carried into the language of this poem and throughout words have dual meanings. The "*sdera*" in "*sderati*" can mean both "boulevard" and "military column." The line "In the street there is no sound and no fire" refers to flames and also to gunfire. The final fox-fire reference can refer to the destruction left in the soldiers' wake, as well as rifle fire in the background.

This image of fire can also be witnessed in Amir Gilboa's "Shimshon Ha-Gibor" [Samson the Hero] in which the desire "to burn everything" is both a cleansing and a self-destructive act. Self-destruction is so integrated with the image of Samson that when he brings down the temple of Dagon, though there is no actual fire in this climactic scene, fire has become a metonymic image of Samson himself. "A blind, uncontrolled force, leaving a terrible swath of destruction behind it, finally consuming itself together with whatever stands in its way."[31] In a militarized context, this destruction is magnified to include the damage the Samson-solider leaves in his wake. Nevertheless, this poem did not serve as a critique of war, but only as an observation of military devastation.

Eldan's poem "Shimshon Korea Begadav" [Samson Rends His Clothes] continues this fire imagery, represented by the sun sinking into the sea.[32]

> When I went
> To Gaza I met
> Samson leaving, rending his clothes
> On his flailed face rivers streamed
> And the houses bent to let him pass
> Like saplings great trees were torn up and clung
> in the tangled roots. . . .
>
> The tramp of his strides tore my tears.
> Samson went hauling a tired sun.
> Fragments of suns and chains sank
> in the Gaza sea. . . .

This Samson is leaving Gaza crying, demonstrating his horror and sadness. The annihilation of the city is described elegantly, as the houses and trees move out of Samson's way, symbolizing the soldier's strength but also the agony he experiences in using this power. By contrast, the soldiers seen leaving Gaza in Gouri's poem are lit up by the destruction behind them, recalling Alter's description of Samson's symbolism as both fire and destruction. The devastation that remains, which is the responsibility of the soldiers, is an ambiguous image since it offers an indication of their success, while simultaneously challenging the morality of militarized action.

The anaphoric structure of Gouri's poem, with each stanza beginning "Look, My Samsons Return," suggests a military formation, providing a marching rhythm and a mechanical tone. Though these men are well-ordered heroes, and the gray-haired man describing them shares some kind of kinship, highlighted by the first-person narrative viewpoint, his age indicates a distance from these mythic ideals. This is reinforced by the command to "pay attention" in the *Hine'i* of the opening lines of each stanza. Ironically the reader is distanced from the Samsons, feeling the old soldier-narrator's frustration, when he asks, "When was it I last carried the gates?" He is at once desirous to emulate these model soldiers and conscious of his inability to do so. He wishes to be like them, while recognizing that carrying the gates is a great burden.

The man looking on in Gouri's "My Samsons" also symbolizes the bereaved parents of soldiers. In the tradition of the period, families were expected to accept the sacrifice of their children for symbolic and material rewards.[33] Furthermore the family, as well as society, were identified with the dead through the national and communal connections: school, youth movements, army units, the kibbutz, and so forth, thus securing the nation's imagined community and linking sacrifice both directly and indirectly with the state.[34] In the biblical tale, Samson removes the city's gates only after he is imprisoned by the Philistines in Gaza. Detaching the gates is the only escape, and they symbolize his remarkable physical strength and ultimately his capacity to obtain freedom. By reusing this image, the gates of Gaza become an emblem of the Jews' new freedom in the new state, which has been provided by the soldiers who bear a moral and emotional weight that ennobles their efforts.

The 1948 poet-soldiers, according to the imagery in these Samson poems, came to see their task as a biblical act of redemption. The internalization of the modern Samson soldier concept became so widespread that biblical and modern experiences became intertwined in the fight for statehood. This connection with reality was magnified further through the use of the place names Gaza and Hebron, which relate to the biblical tale and also to battlefields during the War of Independence and the Six-Day War.[35] Other intertextual allusions force the reader to connect with the intertext. For example, Gouri's poem does not explain why the gates of Gaza are supported on the soldiers' shoulders. It is our knowledge of the original story, in which the hero takes the city's gates to escape imprisonment, which provides meaning for the later representation of the image.[36] We, the readers, understand that in bearing the gates the soldiers are pursuing freedom and furnishing the liberation of the nation.

Yet this masculinity is also brought into question in the poetry of the Palmach generation. In the poems "Samson" by Amichai and "Samson's Hair" by Zach, the established metaphors for Samson imagery are employed to explore the expectations of physical prowess as soldiers and as men. Like the image of fire, Samson's hair is repeatedly used to denote the myth of his strength. In Amichai's poem the cyclical act of a regular haircut destroys Samson's strength. "Every fortnight / I go to have my hair cut. / Every fortnight / My strength leaves me." While in Zach's poem "Samson's Hair," hair is associated with inexplicable power.

> I've never really understood Samson's hair:
> its immense latent power, its Nazarite mystery,
> the prohibition (perfectly understandable) against talking
>   about it,
> the constant fear of losing its locks, the endless dread
> of Delilah's light caress. . . .[37]

The "Nazarite mystery" suggests that it is impossible for any man not involved with the inner secret, in this case literally anyone not a Nazarite, to conceive the secret's magnificence or the strength that comes with the hair. Zach extends this metaphor by inventing a prohibition about discussing the hair, as though the promise of strength is unreliable. With something so important to guard, Samson can never relax. He is in "constant fear" and suffers from "the endless dread."

In Zach's poem, Samson is contrasted with Absalom whose hair is his beauty, not his strength. "But I have no trouble at all with Absalom's hair. / Obviously it was beautiful, like the sun at high noon." Ahitophel, Absalom's general, who looks upon this hair in the poem, also commits suicide in the biblical story, and this reference to another soldier-like figure's suicide emphasizes the link between militarization and suicide.[38] Samson's hair, which is the secret of his strength, marks him out as a hero. In contrast, Absalom's hair does not have ennobling properties. While escaping from King David's forces his tresses are caught in over-hanging branches and he is captured and killed. Zach depicts Ahitophel bewitched by the tresses, whereas Samson is aware of their strength, but not their beauty. Ahitophel is "conniving, cold," and jealous. His infatuation with the hair marks him as different from Samson and prevents him from being considered a hero. The Samson soldier, a successful military archetype, is distinguished from other men who appeared to have similar attributes but less military success. As with Zach's poem, biblical texts became a vehicle for expressing nationalist ideology by valorizing and channeling the strength of the collective. Military sacrifice is presented as the highest honor in a struggle for the correct ideological cause. Samson was on the right side of the struggle in the biblical text but Ahitophel was not. Hence, the Samson image is also connected to a sense of high moral judgment.

The poets increasingly challenged these clear tropes of power and valor. Often, the image of virility associated with the biblical and early Zionist Samson was inverted. In "Samson" by Yehuda Amichai, the act of haircutting is a kind of invasion. While his hair is grown he imagines that he is filled with prowess. He laughs at his enemies, "destroy[s] their temple," and "nothing happens. Not even light injuries." But when his hair is cut, it is a symbolic castration; his masculine strength and power are destroyed. According to Glenda Abramson: "Amichai's Samson is . . . impotent. Every fortnight he goes to have his hair cut and consequently loses his strength. Yet when his hair grows again this returning power goes unnoticed."[39]

Images of sexual strength dominate depictions of Samson. These are often tied to descriptions of Delilah as the symbol of femininity. In Gouri's "My Samsons" the Delilahs fall at the Samsons' feet and in Zach's poem "Samson's Hair" sexuality is demonstrated by "Delilah's light caress." By intimating that Samson is responsible for his own castration, the poets hint at a metaphorical impotence felt by modern soldiers. In doing so, they distance themselves from the dominant celebratory depictions of military mythology.

Although the images of Samson are often powerful and moving, they are not always exclusively about strength and prowess. In Eldan's "Samson Rends His Clothes" the hero is composed of contradictions. Although he is strong, his power is a burden. Here Samson's hair is a metonym for strength, "And among the roots locks / of his hair," but the hair is among the roots of the trees, as though the loss of strength or the inability to control the use of his force positively causes the pain. Amichai's "Samson" is fated to repeat the same patterns, taking a passive role in his destiny, thus alienating the reader, whereas the Samson of Eldan's 1971 poem inspires pity. Eldan's Samson, unlike those in Gouri's "My Samsons" who left victoriously, is seen leaving Gaza "rending his clothes," a sign of mourning.[40] "His pain" and his tears, "on his flailed face rivers streamed," indicate the horror of war and the sadness of the heroes forced to witness it. This hero destroyed the town of Gaza, but the trees and houses leaned out of his way as though helping him, rather than being trampled by him. Despite fulfilling his duty, demonstrated in his exit from Gaza, this Samson's tangible pain deeply affects the witnesses: "The tramp of his tread tore my tears."

In all of these poems Samson has become an antihero, and there is a clear ambivalence toward both the expectations of a soldier and his duties. Nevertheless, this Samson continues to embody the traditional iconography of the biblical and pre-state Samson. Although in Eldan's poem Samson continues to fulfill his responsibilities, he does so with a heavy heart and without joy.

Unlike previous images of fire, the disappearing sun suggests that the light that once fueled the actions of this Samson has passed: *Shimshon halach gorer shemesh ayefah / Shivrei shmashot ve-shorshot shaku* (Samson went dragging a tired sun / Fragments of suns and chains sank / in the Gaza sea). The sibilant alliteration in these lines generates an immediate association between *Shimshon*: Samson, and *shemesh*: sun, such that Samson embodies the fire and the light. The sun's power is fading and cannot sustain the Samson soldier indefinitely.[41]

Gilboa, in questioning the mythic expectations of Samson through strength and sexuality, also challenges other identifiable tropes in the Samson story—chiefly the desire to die for the nation. In "Samson the Hero," Gilboa invokes the new Jew imagery that fetishized youth.[42] His satire of the expectation of sabra sacrifice is played out in the meditation on age within the poem; as a child he hoped to die at seventeen and a day, thereby signifying the attendant expectation of heroism, which is then contrasted to the eighty-year-old Samson at the end of the poem.

The reader is aware that the biblical Samson died before old age. But the real man of Gilboa's poem lives on: "At eighty he stopped growing up and in the forgetfulness of his hours he mused like a newborn child" and in his old age he suffers "forgetfulness" and "sleeplessness," things unknown to the biblical Samson. The references to carrying the world on his shoulders like Atlas, or carrying a cross like Jesus (who is hinted at in the idea of dying at thirty-three), demonstrate a tension between himself and the mythic heroism of his predecessors who bore the weight of their burdens on their shoulders. Unlike the biblical figure, this Samson man does not move the gates of Gaza, which are "still asleep in the ore," suggesting either that they have not been lifted from their hinges, or even that they have not yet been fashioned into gates and are still in their raw state of iron ore. The hero, who fails to carry the burdens of the nation, also fails to merit the delights of Delilah. Nevertheless, in denying his role in the heroic pantheon he remains safe from her acts of betrayal. The physical strength integral to the legend does not belong to Gilboa's Samson, who is all too human. Furthermore, he wishes to remain so, identifying with the desire to have a family and grow old, rather than to die as a young man.

There is a paradox in the presentation of Samson who comes to symbolize the new breed of powerful and successful soldiers, and his eventual demise. Although these poets believed in the soldiers' Samson-like role shown by their participation in war, often as officers, yet their rewriting of the Samson character conveyed the dilemmas and situations of the modern man. They represented their own life as the life of Samson, but if in this alternative life they had inevitably lived differently from the constraints of the biblical narrative, then it is this personal experience that they chose to represent. The relationship between the poets and their internalized image of themselves as Samson is a complex bond. Their experience as fighters is validated by their role as soldiers; they too have fulfilled the model of the heroic fighter. But this act challenges their understanding of the ideal hero; since, as that hero, they suffered fear, guilt, and sadness — aspects of Samson's character that escaped the biblical narrative. The Palmach generation's poetry demonstrates ambivalence toward the expectations of the soldier myth.

The poets retain a suspicious relationship with the image of Samson. They do not question his existence or his legitimacy but they find it difficult to rationalize this view of themselves, or at least of the soldier fighting for the liberation of the Jewish nation, and their own experiences as that warrior. They are forced to negotiate between the accepted imagery of Samson and their own experience. The conflict between the reality of this strength and courage, and the ideals they feel that Samson, and in this case they as Samson, ought (because they have been ideologically educated to believe that they ought) to maintain, are illustrated through the motifs of Samson's life. The potent sexual imagery often represented by hair and by Delilah, which demonstrated man's weaknesses, the representation of strength shown through hair and loss of hair, the aging process, and the image of fire, are all used to indicate this disparity between the myth and the reality.

The poets ground their reuse of the biblical images in real-life locations and exalt many of the traditional ideas of the Samson myth, yet they raise important moral and political questions about the legitimacy of existing as such a champion. They ask what happens when the real Samson, not the figure of legend, grows old, when the mundane events and the beauty of daily life, such as the wedding of a child, are affected. Consequently, they undermine the heroic soldier suicide myth. These poets emphasize simple beauty in contrast with the nationally ascribed images of beauty that relate to noble sacrifice.

The strength with which Samson is credited becomes an ambiguous image. Although able to perform feats when required, usually in a military sphere, the new Samson has become impotent or incapable of resisting temptation.[43] Eldan's Samson moves with strength and purpose but is mourning and crying. The depth of detail indicates the routine and mundane aspects of life. He is not a hero, he is pathetic and his shoes squeak. Amichai's Samson cannot prevent his fortnightly haircut. Gilboa's Samson cannot control the loss of memory that comes with old age. The poets do not abandon the legend nor do they reject it, but even when suggesting kinds of weaknesses, they noticeably steer away from the figure's suicide. Although not overtly stated, the dramatic tension in the writing comes from the way the Samson figure is living in the poem, and the knowledge of his impending destruction. Tension is created between Samson's fate in the intertext, with which the reader would be familiar, and the depiction of these soldier-poet Samsons. Suicide and self-sacrifice remain the unspoken subtext of these poems. The myth has been replaced by an antihero image — but the antihero still has the obligations of the myth — he must sacrifice himself for the collective. The same poets who reinforce the myth presented by an earlier generation, by virtue of the ways they live, also create ambiguities through their poetry about the values of heroism.

Destroying the Samson Image

Though the Palmach generation continued to write into the 1980s and 1990s, in general their popularity diminished as they were superseded by a new generation of writers in the late 1960s and 1970s. The *Dor Ha-Medina* (Generation of the State) writers, mainly born and raised in the early years of the fledgling state, were educated in the shadow of the Zionist founders' legacies. This new generation inherited a set of recognizable cultural attitudes toward the soldier narrative that still held firm in Israeli society. Hence a repertoire of tropes representing this soldier narrative in general, and its articulation through the Samson narrative in particular, held significant cultural capital. Through their writing they began to offer an alternative response to the traditional, established hegemony. At the same time a "systematic trend associated with the devaluation of the myth of heroism was underway."[44] When the myth of heroism could no longer be maintained, attitudes toward soldiering began to change.

In "The Way of the Wind" Amos Oz inverted the expectations created in the public cultural discourse on heroism in order to rage against the national attitude toward heroism and self-sacrifice. He not only challenged this narrative, but also railed against the founding fathers who had, with such expectations, failed their sons. Though the story of Abraham's binding of Isaac is often used to illustrate this breakdown in the national legacy, here Oz draws on Samson, suggesting not just the father's sacrifice, but the son's complicity and agency in the act of suicide. Whereas once Samson had represented the sabra ideal and a celebration of national ideology, inverting the image and questioning Samson's objectives could challenge the sabra and the national narrative he was expected to illustrate.

Historical changes in Israel following the Sinai Campaign (1956) led to the first transformations in social attitude toward the military, and this can be seen in the change in the depiction of Samson. For a decade after the Sinai Campaign, there was no large-scale outbreak of hostilities between Israel and the Arabs, but neither was there a decline in tension. Fighting occurred along the Syrian and later the Jordanian borders, Israeli settlements were shelled, and agricultural workers in demilitarized zones near borders were fired upon. The role of the soldier became increasingly indeterminate as civilian clashes and border defense replaced clearly defined wars that could feed the mythology surrounding Israeli narratives about the sabra soldier. Jerusalem remained divided during this period, with the city often isolated from other centers of Jewish occupation. Amos Oz's short story "The Way of the Wind" appeared in 1965, during this period of tension, at a time when the army's unquestioned authority began to face challenges. The story's reappearance in a second, more popular issuing of the collection in 1976 had even greater resonance in the Israeli psyche.[45]

In 1967, the Six-Day War that had led to the unification of Jerusalem and was seen as a great victory introduced new morality questions into Israeli society. As occupiers of territory, Israelis had to confront the responsibility accompanying power. Furthermore, the war of attrition (1969–70) with its shell bombardment at the Egyptian border and the surprise attack and televising of humiliated captured Israeli soldiers during the Yom Kippur War (1973) radically redefined attitudes to the military from this point onward. The soldier-poets' ambivalence toward military expectations in 1948 and 1956 reflected a desire to accommodate the challenge between ideological depictions of life as a soldier with the expectation of sacrifice and hopes for a personal future. By the end of the 1970s, this ambiguity had been eradicated because the mythical depiction of soldiers faced mounting challenge in Israeli society. Attacks on civilian targets, the establishment of Palestinian terrorist groups, the insecurity of borders, and the difficulty of maintaining order in conquered territories undermined the mythology of the uncontested strength of the Israeli army.

"The Way of the Wind" reflects the attitude of confrontation that developed in the wake of the Sinai Campaign. It contains many of the elements found in the rewriting of biblical narratives by the New Wave, who contested the mythological constructions of Zionism of the previous founding generation.[46] Set on a kibbutz, Oz presents the story of a father, a staunch member of the kibbutz and a leading academic light in historical Zionist discourse, named Shimshon (Samson) and his son Gideon.

Shimshon, the father, represents all that the previous generation of "Samsons" venerated. He embodies the Zionist national narrative. He lives on a kibbutz, the symbol of the return to the land and the collective, he was a soldier, he is extremely virile, and he is concerned with writing a Zionist history. Shimshon possesses a mane of white hair, reminding us of the biblical Samson, and piercing blue eyes, part of the canonical imagery of the new Jew in Hebrew literature of the 1930s through the 1950s.[47]

> The name of Shimshon Sheinbaum needs no introduction. The Hebrew Labour Movement knows how to honour its founding fathers, and for decades now Shimshon Sheinbaum's name has been invested with a halo of enduring fame. For decades he has fought body and soul to realise the vision of his youth. Setbacks and disappointments have not shattered or weakened his faith, but rather, have enriched it with a vein of wise sadness. The better he has come to understand the weakness of others and their ideological deviations, the more ferociously he has fought against his own weaknesses. He has sternly eliminated them, and lived according to his principles, with a ruthless self-discipline and not without a certain secret joy. (JH, 42)

This parody of the successful pioneer ironically highlights the qualities considered essential to the perfect Samson model of the new Jew. Perseverance and fighting spirit have made him manipulative and he exploits the weaknesses of others. Now isolated, he enjoys a sense of superiority dictated by a lack of moral values and absence of emotional life. For Oz, the mythic ideal sabra is a hollow construction. Shimshon's work, "ideological productions," meant that he "sacrificed the warmth of a family home" (JH, 43) while ironically, he rejected family life in favor of promiscuity. Shimshon refuses to acknowledge his illegitimate children, thereby suggesting that his liaisons have been meaningless and that the Samson hero is unable to father progeny who will grow into his likeness.

> His personality attracted women just as it attracted disciples. He was still young when his thick mop of hair turned white, and his sun beaten face was etched with an appealing pattern of lines and wrinkles. His square back, his strong shoulders, the timbre of his voice — always warm, sceptical, and rather ruminative — and also his solitude, all attracted women to him like fluttering birds. Gossip attributed to his loins at least one of the urchins of the kibbutz, and elsewhere, too, stories are current. But we will not dwell on this. (JH, 42–43)

Even though this Shimshon is compatible with the legend, Oz's description is satirical, identifying those elements that made the legend of Samson an ideal, and suggesting that the ideology was mistaken. This story indicates the breakdown in the strength of the soldier/hero/founder imagery. Samson, whose child in Jabotinsky's novel would have been strong had he lived, is, in Oz's novel, feeble and pathetic. The only legitimate son, Gideon, is portrayed as the ultimate failure for the Samson generation. He is an inadequate and ineffectual boy, not the expected offspring of such an icon.

> Gideon, however, turned out to be something of a disappointment, not the stuff of which dynasties are founded. As a child, he was always sniveling. He was a slow bewildered child, mopping up blows and insults without retaliating, always playing with candy wrappers, dried leaves, silkworms. And from the age of twelve he was constantly having his heart broken by girls of all ages. . . . He did not shine at work; he did not shine in communal life. He was slow of speech and no doubt also of thought. (JH, 45)

Gideon is weak and frequently attacked but he does not retaliate or attempt to defend his reputation. He is associated with nature, like the

Samsons that we have seen previously, but while their connections are to lions, jackals, asses' bones, and fire, Gideon is linked to the flimsy, delicate natural phenomena of dried leaves and silkworms. Unlike the earlier, polygamous Samsons, as in Gouri's poem "My Samsons" where Delilahs fall at their feet, any girl can break Gideon's heart. The criticism of Shimshon exists in his final failure to contribute meaningfully to the Jewish nation despite his own rhetoric. Furthermore, his son Gideon cannot support or protect the Jewish people. Despite being named for another biblical hero, famed for his own military prowess, he is a poor soldier, and he cannot shoulder the mantle of political Zionist responsibility, which is his birthright, showing him to be a failure in communal life. Oz is attacking the tradition of Samson and the Zionist legend.

In this example, the old heroic Samson has given way to the representation of a frightened, childish man-boy. This new "soldier" is not interested in the collective, writes bad romantic poetry about the mundane, unlike the nationalistic poetry of the previous generation, and starts the day by shaving, a symbol of the total rejection of the Samson ideal. By cutting his hair, he is making himself weak. Significantly, Oz's representation of Gideon is only imbued with dramatic tension because of its contrast with previous generations' representation of Samson.

The events of Oz's story are set around Independence Day, a key image in the association of the state and the Samson figures that have created it. The intended military celebration, with paratroopers jumping out of a plane as part of a display, becomes a farce because the celebratory jump is overshadowed by Gideon's death. Gideon has joined the paratroopers, one of the most prestigious units, in order to make his father proud, despite his mother's disapproval. When the group jumps out of the plane for the display, Gideon wants to attract the attention of his father and demarcate his difference from the rest of the group. Even this act of differentiation suggests a breakdown of the universalist and duplicable aspects of Samson's myth evident in Gouri's poem "My Samsons." Gideon opens a second parachute and is caught by the wind that eventually blows him onto electricity wires, where he is caught dangling. After a number of embarrassing interactions with kibbutz members, and particularly his father, Gideon commits suicide.

Oz parodies a society that suggests military heroism as the pinnacle of existence. Gideon's attempt to realize the heroic dreams of his father is not compatible with his own desire to express independence and individuality. In his attempt to assert his right not to be subsumed within the collective, he endangers his own life by opening the extra parachute to attract attention. This powerful scene demonstrates the breakdown of several ideals that had been part of the sabra narrative. The myth that the kibbutz creates brave soldiers is shattered. The belief that Samson's generation was working for the benefit of its sons is also questioned. By choosing the paratroopers, Oz identifies an image in the collective consciousness that symbolizes heroism, and then disputes the meaning imbued in that image by making Gideon, a soldier of that unit, a failure in terms of national ideology. The reader's sympathy for Gideon makes him an antihero, and therefore an effective instrument with which to criticize the national ideology.

At the crucial moments in Gideon's life, Shimshon the father has failed his son. We learn that this has happened in the past when he ridiculed Gideon for his relationship with women, and for his non-aggressive hobbies, such as writing poetry. This also happens when he betrays Gideon's mother by ignoring her wishes to ban her son from entering the paratrooper unit. Finally, Shimshon fails his son when Gideon becomes trapped on the electricity wires by refusing to support him. His criticism is rational, but this does not help the son who needs emotional support. Shimshon accuses his son of cowardice.

> His father's eyes filled with blood as he roared:
> "You coward, you ought to be ashamed of yourself!" (JH, 54)

Despite the efforts of the kibbutz and the military to rescue him, Gideon is totally isolated. It is at this stage that Gideon realizes he can remove himself from this situation. He can commit suicide.

The suicide of Oz's antihero stands in sharp contrast to the attitude toward images of military suicide represented by all of the previous generations of Hebrew writers explored here. His sacrifice is not noble. It neither destroys enemies nor offers revenge. He is not tragically killed at the height of battle, but during a display of national pomposity. At last, suicide has become a symbol of individuality. The image can no longer be read as a religious or symbolic act of redemption, it is not even an act of sacrifice for the collective, and with this literary climax Oz makes his most significant political statement and his sharpest critique of Israeli society.

Yaakov Shabtai in *Zikhron Devarim* (*Past Continuous*, 1977), a novel depicting the decline of Israel during the 1960s and 1970s and the collapse of mythic ideals about Zionism, also addresses the image of the failed soldier. He satirizes the national attitude toward death in a military context, and its presumed heroism by offering an unheroic death. Ariyeleh, a soldier in the army, commits suicide. "He shot himself in the mouth with a pistol and was found two days later in his car on a dirt road between orange groves not far from the sea dressed in a leather suit and a floral shirt and a yellow tie" (*PC*, 135). He is not wearing battle dress, his act of suicide is mentioned only in passing, and there is no heroism and no psychological explanation for his death. Furthermore, his mother, Yaffa, unable to comprehend this act of futility, falls back on the mythic portrayals of soldiers' deaths. She wishes that her soldier son Ariyeleh had been killed in the army rather than dying the way he had, by shooting himself. She does not lament his death; it is only its form that shames her: "If he had only been killed in the army at least" (*PC*, 136).

Natan Zach takes up this quote, and asks about Israel's obsession with suicide in literature and its rich military association, where suicide becomes a metaphor for military self-sacrifice, and a form of nationalistic martyrdom.[48] But in a society where "service and performance in the armed forces and reserves have been the key to professional success outside the military," it is clear that service in the IDF is in the main seen as honorable, and if necessary a worthwhile form of sacrifice.[49] A study of the IDF has shown that soldiers who have served in the elite combat units are likely to report that "they had learned the value of camaraderie, deepened their understanding of Israeli society, and heightened their link to the land."[50] The power of suicide images is more significant because it challenges precisely those views that are still considered the norm in Israeli society today.

The soldier-pioneer of Israeli nationalist ideology and his heroic death had been an illustration of the ultimate sacrifice every man owed to the state. Yet within four decades, in literature at least, Samson had become a symbol of the futility of struggle and national ideology, and the tool of political opposition. The noble image of suicide always associated with military prowess and national dedication has become the image of the isolation and abandonment of the hero. The representation of suicide and its role as a political literary device had been defeated.

With this change came the collapse of the iconic, self-sacrificing soldier committing suicide for the collective. Yaffa's lamentation of her son Ariyeleh's disreputable death reflects traditional social attitudes that echo Samson's symbolic acclaim in Israeli society. However, it is precisely the manner that Shabtai uses to represent this death that serves to challenge these national values. The deaths of Ariyeleh and Gideon mark the change of direction that literary suicide takes in Hebrew literature in the following two decades, and the collapse of the military's prestige.

CHAPTER 2

The IDF: Training Base Four with All the Cripples

The armed forces may socialize soldiers to national norms embedded in the military's manpower policy, which determines who serves, at what level, and in what capacity. Second, the armed forces may bring together individuals of various ethnic, religious, and socioeconomic backgrounds in common cause and in a collaborative spirit, providing a suitable environment in which to break down communal barriers, as the "contact hypothesis" would suggest. Third, whether through socialization or intense contact, the military may alter the views of future leaders who later use their positions of influence to spread their revised definition of the nation.

The formation of the Israel Defense Forces (IDF) in May 1948, under Prime Minister David Ben Gurion, represented the unification of disparate Jewish paramilitary groups, with a range of political and military functions. Sometimes working with the British, and sometimes working against them, these different organizations had operated within Mandate Palestine (though their roots could be traced as far back as the *Shomer* [Guard] forces in the late nineteenth century during Ottoman rule of the region). In addition to protecting Jews in Palestine and battling against the British regime, many of these groups operated to bring immigrants from Europe (both legally and illegally). Following the end of the Second World War they helped rescue and relocate Holocaust survivors. By the time of its institutionalization, the status of Israeli military forces was already well established, indicative of the revolutionary change that Jews experienced, moving from "a condition of powerlessness and vulnerability to one of empowerment."[1] The soldiers, who had often operated in secrecy and belonged to choice units garnering legendary mythology, were the nascent state's elect. They symbolized all that the new country venerated, and in the succeeding twenty years, as Israel experienced continued hostility with its neighbors, the soldiers' sacrifice, and the ongoing military victories in a series of wars, cemented the IDF's status in Israeli society.

The commitment demanded from individuals who are willing to die for the nation through the military machinery, and the very real material rewards following army service that society bestows on those who serve, marks the IDF as a rite of passage. Historically, this reinforces the military's central position in the nation's life. Popular perceptions of military participation created the sense that "when a member of a family serves, the whole family is recruited."[2] Just as "Jewish freedom fighters, soldiers, policemen and spies were quickly mythologized as soldiers of the dream,"[3] the institution itself feeds the nation's hunger for a pantheon of heroes.

Hitganvut Yehidim (*Final Exercise*, 1986,[4] published in English as *Infiltration*) is a novel set in 1950s Israel, about a military unit of conscripted recruits of an inferior medical grade. In this book, Yehoshua Kenaz explores a number of ideological expectations about the IDF's mythical reputation through the character of Alon. These myths include the belief that Israel's army fought as the weak, the few, and the morally right, against the strong, the many, and the morally reprehensible. The moral superiority of the Israeli army is predicated on the belief that the army protects the defenseless and does not attack the innocent. Mercy is shown to prisoners. Acts that appear to contradict law are undertaken because the Israeli army observes the moral high ground, and soldiers are always conscientious. Becoming a soldier assumes commitment to comrades, a sense of honor, belonging, physical prowess, pride, and self-worth, qualities corresponding to the Nietzschean concept of the *über-*

mensch, a superman. As such, this elite military corps is the guardian of the moral imperative.

In the previous chapter, I explored the development of the sabra in the mythic representation of the soldier-hero figure Samson and the changing depictions of this image in modern Hebrew literature. The expectation that soldiers are willing to sacrifice themselves for the collective is not particular to Israeli society. Émile Durkheim argued that a soldier commits acts of suicidal bravery, willing to die for the nation because of his wholehearted commitment to the project that the fight represents. He termed this kind of heroic suicide "altruistic," arguing that it resulted from the high degree of social integration into the national project that soldiers experience. Belonging creates the obligations of sacrifice where necessary and personal interest is forfeited in the best interests of the collective. Military organizations rely on this assumption about soldiers' loyalties and the state depends upon this devotion and strength. Hence, death in battle has been portrayed in heroic terms, thereby sanctifying sacrifice and affording it (and the soldier's family) social and cultural capital. For Israel, the very act of the nation's survival was dependent on the soldier's willingness to participate in the collective need. Nonetheless, as I demonstrated in the previous chapter, suicide in a framework that abandons this call to heroism represents a rejection of the ideological expectations toward soldiers and, as I will demonstrate in this chapter, by association the institutional position of the army. Moreover, in Hebrew literature the army itself has become a metaphor for the state.

Throughout *Infiltration,* Alon represents the Israeli national ideals, and hence his suicide near the end of the novel focuses attention on the expectations of these myths — it is precisely because his death is a personal act rather than the by-product of a military action, that questions can be raised. The challenges to expectations surrounding the Israeli military that come about through the depictions of physically inferior recruits allows Kenaz to contest the myths of strength, heroism, and virtue that encompass popular conceptions of the IDF.

Kenaz demonstrates that the ideological construction of the *Über-mensch* is a dangerous course of action, setting as it does a seemingly impossible ideal. The *Untermensch* of his novel, the weaker inferior social outcasts that belong to training base four, basic training for substandard conscripted soldiers, believe many of these myths. They perceive themselves to be social pariahs because they do not meet the physical, social, ideological, linguistic, or cultural standards of the army. Yet, throughout the novel Kenaz shows that many of these men do achieve the traditional standards of a devoted soldier. As with Alon's crisis and subsequent suicide, in failing to recognize their personal transformation they undermine the notion that the military serves as a melting pot inculcating the national myths, creating the sense of camaraderie and collectivity, and socializing the recruits to the nation's values. Thus *Infiltration* challenges the military myths in Israeli society.

Kenaz's novel, set in a period in time during which the Israeli military enjoyed a period of uncontested glory, was written long after this heyday had come to an end. Significant transformations within Israeli society and the military had affected attitudes toward the IDF. "By the time of the 1982 invasion of Lebanon, many Israelis were thoroughly alienated from the core principle that their country used force only when there was no alternative."[5] This process of degeneration can be traced through changing attitudes toward the commemoration of national heroes who died serving the state, and a questioning of the military operations in which soldiers might lose their lives. This chapter lays out those issues that have been key in eroding the army's mythological status within Israeli society, exploring the military's position from its early incontestable status as a foundational pillar for the new state, through changing Israeli experiences of war during the latter half of the twentieth century. Moreover, the significance of powerful groups opposing the Israeli military including the Four Mothers, and the rise of the peace movement that ultimately culminated in the Oslo Accords, destabilized the army's hegemonic governance. Kenaz's text presents a literary exploration of the national folklore associated with the Israeli military, and the price that such myths have demanded.

Weakened Status of the Soldier

Hanoch Levin's theatrical review *You, Me and the Next War* produced in the late 1960s, and his cabaret *The Queen of the Bathtub* in 1970, were satirical attacks on "the tendency to elevate the narrative of war or idealize or spiritualize Israeli military force."[6] Levin was speaking against the sacrifice of the nation's children, discussing the reality of death, and crucially attacking what he perceived to be "the false appeal of the grandiose, abstract visions invoked to legitimate such losses." In doing so he was striking at the heart of the national predisposition to idealize death in battle. Despite evidence to show that among soldiers Levin's attitudes were already increasingly common following the 1967 war, at the height of the war of attrition (1969–70) no one was quite ready for this public attack.[7] Heated demonstrations by the audience and the political establishment were nothing compared to the actors' refusal to play in the roles and the performance was canceled. It wasn't until the Yom Kippur War (1973) that the attitude in Israel toward the military and the role of the army in society began to be questioned more publicly. As Ya'akov Yadgar has shown in his analysis of the press between 1967 and 1997, "the Yom Kippur War . . . undermined some of the essential foundations of Israel's national image"[8] which, in turn, led to a "forceful political and cultural expression in the 'trend' of 'shattering' national myths."[9] This process has affected "significant segments of Israel's intellectual elite, followed by other groups within the wider society."[10] Kenaz's depiction of an army unit reflects this changing response in perceptions of the Israeli army in society.

Yoram Bilu and Eliezer Witztum record that this transformation can be identified through an altered military approach to mental illness and war-related mental illness.[11] Despite the vast quantities of documents available on the 1948 War of Independence, the records of mental illness among soldiers are almost entirely absent from medical reports of that era, a matter that appears to Bilu and Witztum to be a gross omission.[12] This shortage of information is due to both organizational as well as ideological reasons. A limited number of official psychiatric units and professionals who could identify and diagnose cases of mental illness made it relatively easy to ignore such reactions to war, or to label them as moral problems related to "cowardice" or to "lack of motivation" instead.[13] The increased identification of such cases and the improved systems in place to deal with soldiers who suffer from mental illnesses can be identified in line with "the historical review of combat stress reactions in Israel since 1948 [which] has disclosed a systematic trend associated with the devaluation of the myth of heroism."[14] Accordingly, cases could be diagnosed in increasing numbers as it became possible to recognize those cases in social terms. Alternate literary depictions of the army are a demonstration of this trend.

Commemorating the Dead

Rituals of commemoration for the dead constitute one of the primary ways that society manipulates military myths. A nationalistic suicide, one in which the individual sacrifices his life for the collective, is an idea common in nationalist discourse.[15] In turn, the process of commemoration for fallen soldiers is designed to reinforce the national entity, affording those who die in a military or nationalist context special honors, particular burial places and memorials. There has been extensive discussion about the ways in which dead soldiers have been used physically and metaphorically as a tool for building a national ideology and for encouraging citizens to identify with the national landscape.[16] This historical background to the depiction of the army in Israeli society has been challenged by more recent events. A move to destandardize military commemorations threatens the control the army has had over the symbolic capital in soldiers' deaths. Moreover, while it was soldiers who represented the majority of war casualties for decades, representing a single monolithic age (and gender) demographic, the impact of suicide bombs on the civilian population during the 1990s reframed the model of the Israeli martyr, altered the demographic of those dying in Israel for the sake of the nation, and separated the deaths from the army, its institutions, and its control over commemoration. This dramatic increase in the number of civilian casualties also weakened the central position afforded to military deaths in the national framework. As Michael Feige has noted, in the 1990s more Israelis died in terrorist attacks than in military operations, and even these operations were rarely on a battlefield but were instead the result of "guerrilla acts and incidents."

> While combat soldiers are generally young Jewish males, secular or religious, the random diversity of terror victims includes women, children, elderly, the ultra-Orthodox (*Haredim*), non-Jewish guest workers, and so on. *The issue of commemoration*

practices has required a redefinition of Israeli heroism and national sacrifice.[17]

The bereaved families demanded commemorative systems for their loved ones who had not been soldiers, because they wished to have their "sacrifice be acknowledged in a manner similar to those who fell in battle."[18] Families, finding national systems to be inadequate, created their own. According to Feige, this has meant a redefinition of social hierarchies of commemoration that had previously placed soldiers' deaths at the pinnacle. Those parents of soldiers who died in wars also began to commemorate their sons outside the national framework of "sacrifice and socially sanctioned mores of commemoration characterized by depersonalization and standardization."[19] These new methods have served to highlight the individuality of the victims, emphasizing the identity of each fallen person. Death has been reframed socially, with terror victims continuing to be commemorated institutionally in terms of sacrifice for the nation, while private individuals have sought to challenge this view of death.

The *yizkor* books, commemoration volumes produced by the army and national institutions such as the kibbutz, designed to be the central memorial device after the early wars of the state, had been made available by publishing companies, organizations that were predominantly controlled by national movements.[20] They too had enforced an image of the soldier that was in line with ideological Zionism: a heroic soldier, a part of his community, a loyal Zionist. According to Nurit Gertz, this type of activity was about the "mythologization of the fallen sabra" which through the act of commemoration, in turn, "mythologized the entire sabra generation . . . linking his exemplary figure to the exemplary figure of his comrades."[21] Former soldiers working in the kibbutz, the publishing houses, and other national institutions had a stake in being linked to their heroic, dead comrades. In the same vein, the bereaved whose loved ones died in terror attacks from the 1980s onward emulated these same commemoration patterns which had traditionally denoted military sacrifice. In utilizing these recognizable tropes they were able to include these other victims in the national pantheon once reserved for soldiers.[22]

The arrival of cheaper and accessible modes of commemoration such as the Internet has meant the loss of the army's monopoly "or at least their hegemonic influence . . . on the direction of commemoration and the formation of cultural meanings associated with heroic death in Israel."[23] This resulted in a loss of control over the way the army is viewed in society. A proliferation of websites commemorating the fallen allowed each soldier to be memorialized in the way that his family saw fit, further separating the army and other national institutions from the process of commemoration and the symbolic capital it afforded them. Yet as Liav Sade-Beck demonstrates, even these radical new processes, which offered families opportunities to create new forms of commemoration and protest, in many ways fell back upon the conventions of earlier forms, in order to maintain their children's positions within the hierarchies of national commemoration.[24] For victims of terror, applying the same patterns of commemoration (and particularly the ease of Internet access for this purpose) further disenfranchised the army of its ability to select those who would be commemorated and from controlling the manner of remembrance.

Different groups have found new methods of commemorating victims, though these too have become formulaic. Two trends related to this transformation in memorial culture seem evident: on one hand the kinds of ceremony and memorial have changed, and secondly the attitude to the army, service, and war (that is, the desire to die in battle on the orders of the army) has changed. New tropes of commemoration have emerged from the previous rhetorical tradition, and though different from those of the past, they continue to create new models of standardization that erase individuality in exchange for viewing these deaths as heroic, and serving the nation.

In addition, a change in public attitudes toward the army, seen in the challenge to military commemorations, is also evident in the rise of antiwar movements, the reduction of the IDF budget, and the increased numbers of soldiers refusing to fight.[25] In 1978, following the visit of Anwar Sadat to Israel, 348 reserve officers in the Israeli army called on Israeli prime minister Menachem Begin to make peace with Egypt. The public letter that these officers signed became the manifesto of a left-wing grassroots movement: Shalom Akhshav (Peace Now). Unlike other peace groups, Peace Now was not pacifist. In the main, the movement's campaigners were soldiers who continued to carry out their active duties, but in their letter they called for a lasting peace and a return of territories won by Israel following the 1967 war. In the early days of the movement, women were not allowed to participate precisely because they were not active fighters in combat units. In producing soldiers who were willing to question military authority, and seemed unwilling to die for the nation, "Peace Now challenged the very core of Israeli myth from which it itself had arisen."[26] The officers who made the protest could do so precisely because they were held in such high esteem in Israeli society. As Michael Feige shows: "for the first time it was implied that Israeli soldiers' willingness for heroic sacrifice was conditional and could not be taken for granted."[27] Due to its wide influence and size, Peace Now was vehemently attacked in its early years by government supporters. But the Lebanon War (1982) was a turning point for peace activists. Soldiers were among those who protested against the violence in Sabra and Shatila that had been perpetrated by Lebanese Phalangists when they entered two Palestinian refugee camps in Lebanon that were under IDF control and massacred the populations within. Peace Now supporters continued to perform their military duties throughout the 1980s and 1990s, but there were other forms of resistance which rejected all military involvement.

A total of 467 soldiers were arrested during the Lebanon conflict of 1982 for refusing to fight, and were labeled deserters. Another 300 soldiers were imprisoned during the first Intifada for the same reason. By 1993, the Oslo Accords and the awarding of the Nobel Prize for Peace to Yitzhak Rabin and Yasser Arafat in 1994 demonstrated the hope for peace that had been building within Israel. In turn Peace Now was inculcated into the mainstream, with concerts like Shalom Haver (Peace Friend) producing the first musical album to knock "Songs of the Six Day War" from its record position as the widest-selling musical album of all time. The assassination of Prime Minister Yitzhak Rabin in 1995, moments after he had sung "Shir LaShalom" ("A Song for Peace") an anthem of the peace movement, and the copy of the lyrics found in his pocket stained with blood, became iconic symbols of the struggle for peace in Israel. Despite the widespread goodwill toward a two-state solution during the early 1990s, by 2000 changes in government policy were among factors that led to the rise of a second Intifada.

In 2002 a new movement arose using the same language and style of protest used by Peace Now in its earliest days. Yesh Gvul (There Is a Limit), an antiwar movement of soldiers who refused to serve for ideological reasons (also known as refusenikim), demonstrated attitude changes toward the army among citizens in Israel. This movement was couched in the language of Israeli ideology and the importance of sacrifice — national suicide — and yet these men rejected the basic ideological principle of national conscription: serving in the army for the benefit of the state.

> We, reserve combat officers and soldiers of the Israel Defense Forces, who were raised upon the principles of Zionism, sacrifice and giving to the people of Israel and to the State of Israel, who have always served in the front lines, and who were the first to carry out any mission, light or heavy, in order to protect the State of Israel and strengthen it. . . . We hereby declare that we will not continue to fight this War.[28]

Although there were only 504 signatories, less than 2 percent per 1,000 conscripts in 2002, these conscientious objectors indicate an unbefore seen evidence of (progressively widespread) opposition.[29] Along with public declarations were other, quieter examples of the refusal to serve, people who did not ascribe ideological reasons for not fighting but simply failed to turn up for duty. A total of 2,616 deserters were recorded in 2002, five times more than the number of refuseniks, and a 40 percent increase over the 1,564 recorded deserters the previous year.[30] It had become increasingly evident that the stigma attached to being labeled a deserter or a coward was no longer a sufficient deterrent in a number of cases. In addition, a rise was recorded in the number of soldiers suffering from combat-related mental illnesses, indicating public acknowledgment for this condition, another sign that the self-sacrificing noble hero image was being shattered. However, the greatest indication of change in attitude is that the Israeli government only imprisoned a fraction of these deserters, fearing that a crackdown would spark a wider revolt in the ranks.

The soldiers' refusal to serve was often tied to issues of having to serve in the occupied territories, and for both regular and reserve soldiers this reduced the "luster of service." In addition, an increase in the number of training accidents, and the presence of illegal drugs, reduced parents' confidence in the army and they began to question the institution's interest in their children's well-being. Though the economy had grown, it was still significant that funding for the military was reduced from around 45 percent of the national budget in 1984 to 22 percent by 1995 and "occasional lapses of professionalism and discipline" influenced a decline in morale; such as in 1994 when a platoon of Israeli soldiers in southern Lebanon ran away in the face of a small Hezbollah attack.[31]

Internal changes in the army can also be witnessed in the destandardization of military headstones that occurred in the 1990s. Some of these changes had begun with the Lebanon War, which led to a change in Israel's commemoration practices, signaling the beginning of the "individualization of bereavement."[32] The previous formulas for wording had been state approved, allowing no room for personal messages on tombstones thereby emphasizing the nationalist implications of soldiers' sacrifice. "Death becomes public in that it is expropriated and made the public property of extensive sectors of the population."[33] In Israel, the graves of soldiers are usually set apart from those of civilians. They are either located in a separate place, such as the military section of a civilian cemetery, or in special military cemeteries. Graves are uniform and draw materials from the local landscape. In many places the headstones are "carved from Jerusalem stone, each bears the same simple statement regarding a fallen soldier."[34] The graves are similar in composition and each has a holder for a memorial candle. The tombstone is of local material and the body of the grave consists of a rectangle of stone that is raised above the surface of the ground. The inscription bears the name of the dead, his or her age, date of birth and death, the parents' name and place of origin. The stone also bears military information, the soldier's rank at death, military number, and the symbol of the IDF, the only variation in the inscription concerning the context of death. However, recently individuals have argued for more personalized messages such as "beloved son" or "faithful husband" to be included. In the early 1990s, a test case at the High Court challenged the army's standardized gravestone style following which it became possible for families to add personal messages to military headstones.[35]

Thus, the central position of the army in Israeli society has been weakened from several directions. The opposition to military attacks, maneuvers, and acts of aggression led elements in society to question the position, authority, and purpose of the army. The image of the strong heroic soldier had been weakened, as the fiction and poetry examined in chapter 1 demonstrates. By the 1970s, writers like Amos Oz and Yaakov Shabtai had challenged the mythologized representations of soldiers found in the literature of earlier generations. Later, the increasing numbers of soldiers recorded to be suffering from mental illness, involved in protest movements, or simply refusing to fight undermined the incontestable militaristic rhetoric of heroism that had been such a feature of the past. Moreover, combatants no longer belonged symbolically to the state and the national collective alone, as families began placing personalized messages on the graves of soldiers who died in action, or commemorating the soldiers outside a national, ideological framework. Meanwhile, the increasing number of civilian deaths meant that other sectors of society also claimed a share of the national glory in dying for the collective. Death for the nation remains a central trope in commemoration in Israeli society, but the belief that only soldiers in the army are the people who are sacrificed is no longer preserved.

The Army: Metonym for the State

Yehoshua Kenaz explores and, in turn, reinforces the idea of questioning the mythological status of the army. The army as a tool of Zionist ideology had always provided a means for cultural absorption. The new immigrants to the state in the 1950s and 1960s, with their cultural, linguistic, historical, and ideological differences, could learn to reject their past in order to become suited to the new ideological and social conditions in which they lived. This melting-pot myth envisioned the army as an incubator for assimilating the new citizens. Yet, *Infiltration* challenges the notion of the army as a unified and unifying entity. This novel presents a version of the reality of life in the army in the 1950s; a period during which many of the myths about the army and the state were created. During this formative period, the previous history of individual pre-state paramilitary groups was erased, and instead supplanted by the heroism of the IDF. This image of unified national heroism is reinforced in the text, in a comparison of Israeli units to *The Three Musketeers*. These characters, who feature in several novels by Alexander Dumas, narrate the stories of an elite French palace guard, lauded for their commitment to one another. Kenaz plays with the ironic construction of myth by highlighting the fictionality of this text, and by offering a literary reality at variance with it. Those soldiers encountering Kenaz's alternative military experience believe the Israeli myth to such an extent that they are unable to reconcile it with the reality they experience. They continue to search for the dream, believing in their own defectiveness since they cannot experience the Zionist narrative in a way they believe is correct—a reality which does not exist. By setting the novel between wars, indicating a period of relative tranquility with no massive immediate confrontation with external forces, Kenaz is able to reflect on the internal divisions in the army and by extension within the state. Suicide indicates the breakdown of an individual in the novel, shattered by his inability to reconcile these apparently contradictory visions of the military.

By choosing the army, Kenaz has chosen an experience that resonates in the lives of most Israelis. Mandatory national conscription exists in Israel; traditionally most members of Israeli society, male and female, are conscripted at eighteen. Consequently, the image of the army and the experience of basic training have associative significance. By choosing to portray a unit of noncombatants, who are sickly and weak, Kenaz contests the popular social image described by Alan Mintz as "Ashkenazi male heroes whose experience is defined by the great issues of national destiny."[36] Participating in the Israel Defense Forces (IDF) is considered a primary rite of passage that "initiates one into full membership in the Zionist civil religion," and as Mark Aronoff has shown, "it is the single most important test, particularly for males, for individual and group acceptance in the mainstream of Israeli society."[37] Kenaz contests this traditional image by presenting recruits who are physically "cripples. Defective combat-worthiness! Medical Grade B!" and are not solely concerned with "the great issues of national destiny" (I, 7). Kenaz's conscripts have minor disabilities, such as heart murmurs and epilepsy, which allow them to undergo basic training in order to serve in the army in desk jobs, thereby confronting the heroic soldier image of physical prowess leading to a combat role, which had traditionally been part of the Israeli national identity.

The myth of the fighter is the only hero with which these men are taught to identify. Kenaz demonstrates that in their eyes, physical strength is the only acceptable measure of manhood and they, as the weak of

Sparta, to whom they compare themselves, have no right to exist. Believing physical weakness has prevented them from fulfilling the national obligation to fight for the army, Micky, one of the principal characters and a former football star, indicates the magnitude of the physical humiliation these soldiers experience, by drawing parallels between Greek military states and their own homeland.

> "In Sparta," said Micky, "they used to throw the sick, weak, crippled babies out onto some mountain, so that they would die of hunger or so that the wild animals would eat them. Because they wouldn't grow up to be good soldiers and only be a burden to society and weaken it."
> "In Sparta they were smarter," said Micha the Fool. And he explained:
> "That's a rhyme."
> "In Israel," said Micky, "they've invented Training Base Four for the same purpose. That's where they chuck all the invalids and it's all much more humane. They even play soldiers with them, to give them the illusion that they're worth something."
> (I, 23)

Convinced of their failure despite the position that these recruits will eventually hold in the army, they continue to see themselves as physically worthless. Micky suggests that any bandit would be able to annihilate these pathetic trainees. For youths at the brink of maturity, this criticism of their abilities extends beyond their position in the army, to include the larger dimension of their contribution as men to Israeli society. If they are failures in the wider context of the army—since they cannot get into a regular unit—then they are also unlikely to be successful in other spheres. Since these men see their lives as a failure to achieve the demands of masculinity in their society, by extension they consider themselves also sexual failures.

This connection between the military and sexual prowess was explored through the image of Samson in the previous chapter. The term for weapons in Hebrew is *Klei Zayin*, "which is slang for the male [sexual] organ, and this linguistic connection seems to reinforce the notion that by carrying a gun a boy becomes a potent male."[38] For boys at the end of puberty the failure to manage a gun, fear in the face of violence, and a sense that they could be easily conquered in battle create genuine concern about their identity as men. The discussions about strength among the youths contain this subtext of virility.

> "That gang's a suicide squad," said Zackie. "They're not afraid of anything. Their captain's a guy called Abu Yussuf who swore to his mother to kill one Jew a day at least, and if a day passed without him killing a Jew then he wasn't a man. They went into an orange grove next to Nes-Ziona and killed the workers. They tied their legs together on top of their heads and chucked them into a hole in the ground. That's how they found them. Then they went somewhere else and killed some more Jews. No one'll catch them."
>
> "Don't worry," said Alon. "We'll get them. We'll get the ones who send them here." (I, 23)

By tying the men's legs above their heads, they are exposed sexually as well as physically. Here the workers in Nes-Ziona are portrayed as emasculated. They are not real men because they have been uncovered and are unable to defend themselves. In contrast, the recruits boast that soldiers are real men. Kenaz's portrait rejects the traditional model of soldiers with Delilahs falling at their feet that Haim Gouri constructs in his poem "My Samsons," thereby posing questions about social expectations of sexuality among the soldiers. As the invalids of Sparta, Kenaz's soldiers consider themselves to be like the exposed workers. Only Alon believes that the soldiers are *we* and not *them* and he includes himself among the soldiers: "We'll get them." Alon's strong identification with national myths is connected to his kibbutz upbringing marking him out as a sabra, and he differs from the other members of the unit who are either from urban homes, or new immigrants from Eastern Europe (Holocaust survivors) or from Arab countries (*mizrachim*). In staking out his masculinity to the group, Alon announces, in contrast to most of the other soldiers, that he has a girlfriend.

Divisions within the unit represent the diverse nature of Israeli society and the rifts between individuals previously forced to unite under the Israeli collective of the 1950s, with its Labor-Zionist focus. In *Infiltra-*

tion, Kenaz conveys the claustrophobia of a military unit and its inherent friction, which is intended to mirror the claustrophobic nature of Israeli society. The recruits' lack of privacy and confined living conditions further aggravate the already present ethnic and cultural tensions, and the pressures of basic training push the soldiers to their mental and physical limits.

Kenaz creates a microcosm where "everybody knows everybody else. There aren't any secrets" (I, 189). This group serves as a symbolic miniature for a macrocosm, which is the State of Israel. As Hannah Hertsig suggests:

> Kenaz managed, with the prodigious hand of the artist, to give meaningful expression, a nihilist such as him, to something that may be called here "Israeliness." The Israeliness is examined, dispersed by its causes, and is caught as an object of fancy and revulsion . . . Israeliness is also a "wide metonym" for the concept of "the collective," on the foundation of its meanings which branch out, and cover more and more contemporary spheres.[39]

According to Hertsig, the macrocosm or collective, which is the State of Israel, is more than just a political entity. It is part of the identity of each person living in the state — a state of being which she calls "Israeliness." Kenaz's model of a military unit, with its myriad differences, presents the opportunity for the men to voice different social and ideological issues about the state. Thus, while all are Israeli, each character represents a different social or political group that is part of a greater whole. Rakefet Sela-Sheffey has suggested that this sense of Israeliness disregards "ethnic origins, classes, genders, beliefs or whatever other factors of distinction" and is "meta-discursive" so that although on certain other occasions Israelis would split radically on issues of identity, on other occasions, "these people may also find it natural and worthwhile to provide a shared notion of Israeliness."[40] The unit's final cohesion speaks to this ultimate *Israeliness*. Alon's suicide represents his inability to recognize Israeliness as an amalgamation of the differences in Israeli society and the transcending nature of communal beliefs, and instead sees the fragmentation as a failure of the Zionist ideology with which he was raised.

What Is It to Be an Israeli?

The ideal soldier, represented by Alon, is a native-born Hebrew speaker whose interests include national songs and Labor Zionism, represented by the kibbutz on which he was born. He identifies unquestioningly with the army and the kibbutz. These two national institutions were a staple of mainstream Labor-Socialist Israeli ideology. Alon accepts the myths unquestioningly, which reflects his conviction that his identity is solid as he is connected to the nation — and this in turn provides him with a sense of belonging — leading to his self-assurance at the start of the novel. He accepts the myth that it is always possible to conquer the enemy since he trusts in the State of Israel and the power of the army. He is committed to the ideal that every soldier should sacrifice himself for the collective if required to do so, and he represents the essence of Zionist youth. When a senior officer gives his opening speech, the other characters are bored or cynical; in contrast "Alon's head [is] bursting with visions of heroism":

> The captain's deliberate voice droned on monotonously, and to Alon his words sounded like the glorious verses of an ancient epic, told by the elder of the tribe to the young warriors sitting in a circle at his feet, calling silently on the spirits of their ancestors to come and inspire their hearts and empower their arms for war. (I, 53)

Melabbes, a recruit in the unit and the narrator of this section, represents individualism and the desire to remain separate and aloof from the collective, often at the cost of isolation. Though Melabbes finds Alon's beliefs comical, he is inspired by Alon's passion for those beliefs.

> In these moments I saw him shaking off the dull weight of the cloddish earth, the savage and exhausting sadness of the interminable arguments with Micky, and soaring back into his true element, the bright blue skies and far horizons of legend. (I, 53)

Yet, the depiction of Alon undercuts the Zionist heroism that he appears to represent. By choosing to center his novel on a "training base four unit" — "with all the cripples" (I, 7), Kenaz dispels the myth of the strong heroic soldier. Alon does not belong to the hegemonic elite to which he aspires because he is, in fact, in an inferior unit. He does not feel comfortable within the kibbutz, where he is mocked. His interest in art separates him from his kibbutz compatriots. His failure to become a paratrooper and his appointment as a military policeman further indicate his inability to conform to the heroic ideal, as does his abandonment by his kibbutz girlfriend. Melabbes's comparison of Alon to Don Quixote is a comic satire on the illusion of a chivalric romance. Alon's girlfriend, like his battles, is an imaginary construction; these are myths he has devised but which are unrealizable. Alon's girlfriend has a shadowy existence. Their relationship is revealed as an act of idealization on his part, while we learn that she is never truly committed to Alon's artistic vision. Eventually she leaves him. While criticizing Alon, Melabbes is also explaining the power of ideology in nation building. Kenaz demonstrates the seductive potency inherent in belonging to a national group. Though Melabbes is interested in narratives, he regards them as separate from reality, in contrast to Alon, who identifies absolutely with mythic images and heroes.

Even Alon, the character closest to the model of the strong heroic soldier, is unable to fulfill the military expectation. He is terrified, evidenced by his decision not to leave the base despite a weekend pass, because he is afraid of facing his family and the woman he wishes were his girlfriend. He is even too afraid to send the letter he writes.

> Why did I stay here over the leave? Alone in this sad, empty building? Without anyone I can talk to. Instead of going home, seeing her, seeing my mother, the friends I love? Confronting them and being what I really am. With all the defects. Instead of facing up to the problem I ran away from it, I escaped to an army stage set to play at soldiers. Between the truth and the pretense, I chose the pretense. How long will I be able to keep it up? One day the act will have come to an end. And the worst thing is, that I've begun to believe these lies, these false hopes, myself. (I, 249)

The terrifying reality is masked by belonging to the army and fulfilling the mythic role being a soldier represents. Yet, during his patrol of the perimeter on an exercise on the base, he is frightened by the shadows, undermining this expectation of heroism. In a blind panic, he fires his rifle, demonstrating a loss of control and dignity, the watchwords of a soldier. He is not afraid on the *Hitganvut Yehidim*, the final exercise of training, despite the rest of the unit's terror because he believes that the task is ideologically justified. Embracing the army's routine gives him confidence and a feeling of safety. It is when this final illusion of the army's supremacy and his place within it is shattered, illustrated by the brutality of his commanding officer toward him, that he commits suicide. In his concluding scene, Alon learns he has been assigned to the military police; a position that is considered undignified in the heroic code of the successful kibbutz soldier. His dream of military glory is crushed and following this final and ultimate humiliation, Alon decides to commit suicide, and he shoots himself on the following page.

The betrayal of Alon's ideals can be seen when his commanding officer talks to the unit before each man is assigned his permanent duty at the end of basic training. The officer exhibits his disdain for the kibbutz — highlighting the gap between the model soldier who supposedly should have been produced by the kibbutz according to the rhetoric of the period, and the shocking reality — by pointing to Alon, the failure and kibbutznik, to illustrate his argument.

> "When I was an instructor in the paratroopers, I had a lot of kibbutzniks there. I never understood why they were so full of themselves. True, they've got some good fighters among them; a lot of them are physically fit. But no more than among the kids from the towns and the moshavim. Besides, you've got quite a lot of screwballs too. What's wrong there, in the way you live, that produces so many nuts? You were supposed to produce the finest, the elite! The ideal Israeli. What happened? What went wrong?" (I, 563–64)

Through this speech, Kenaz demonstrates the ways in which the state has betrayed the individual both in creating a deceptive myth that did not resemble the actuality, and for exposing the individual who believed in this dream to mockery.

At the start of the novel the recruits discuss the legendary construction of an ideal unit. Kenaz's ironic depiction satirizes the men's desire to meet the ideal without critically questioning it.

"In every platoon of recruits there was one sexual pervert, one who went crazy and one who tried to kill himself. We've got our pervert and we all know who he is. And we've got more than one crazy here already. So all we need now is the platoon suicide."
(I, 178)

Thus, it is the dysfunctional individuals within the unit that ironically signify both the soldiers' bonds and the unit's cohesiveness. Part of the mythological depiction of a real unit is fulfilled by Alon's suicide. Like other units, the soldiers develop many of the qualities described in the military rhetoric. They do become strong, heroic individuals; they form a bond as comrades, but are unable to overcome the gap between the expectations of their own situation and the imagined reality. Alon's belief that in this unit "nothing's for real" is a tragic perception. He undermines the success of the unit when he claims that the unit is pitiful because "in real units there's folklore, there's group spirit, morale. People are prepared to die for each other." The men are identifying themselves as an inferior group since at the start they see themselves as "pathetic" and not as "a real unit" (I, 178). When one of the soldiers presents this picture of the ideal unit with its required suicide, he is asking whether they will ever achieve this homogeneous sense of belonging. Kenaz is ironically depicting the cost of belonging to the national project. Later Alon kills himself in response to the rejection he suffers at the hands of symbols of Israeli society, such as the platoon commander and the kibbutz members. His feelings of alienation and isolation from the one group that is significant to him, the Israeli collective, lead Alon, who is the embodiment of ideological Zionism, to fulfill the role of the suicide in the unit, thereby making the group fit the ideal model. In his act of suicide, Alon has finally achieved his ambition of ideological integration. However, with the act of suicide, Kenaz demonstrates the wider hypocritical military and social expectations of duty and integration.

Alon's death is not the only mention of suicide in the novel. The death of Uri Ilan, an Israeli spy caught in Syria, who committed suicide rather than betray his comrades, stands as a model of patriotism. As a figure of popular folklore, Ilan is yet another example of the model heroic suicide that Alon fails to achieve. Rather than die in battle serving the collective, or commit suicide in a manner considered heroic in this period, Alon's death is a symbol of futility. Like Ilan, tortured by his Syrian captives, Alon has been tortured by the institutionalized prejudice of the military, and the impossibility of living up to the mythic ideals. Micky, Alon's closest friend in training, posits the view that personal choice and conscience, that is to say, the opinions of the individual, separated from the requirements of an ideological society, are far more important, contrasting Alon's belief in the ideology of togetherness. Micky argues with Alon declaring his own disinterest in heroic behavior and rejecting mutual responsibility. "If he was a traitor or wasn't a traitor it's none of my business, and believe me I don't give a damn. It's his own affair. He doesn't owe me. He doesn't owe me a bloody thing!" (I, 56). Micky is divorcing himself from the expectations of the collective, thereby devaluing acts of national heroism.

Just as the model of heroism is questioned, so too is the belief in the Israeli army's moral infallibility. Kenaz achieves this penetration into military mythology by separating the army experience from the experience of war. The only battle these recruits face is with the institution of the Israeli army and its cruel officers. While the vicious sergeant turning unskilled men into a powerful fighting force is a common literary trope, the brutality of the officer in *Infiltration*, and the myth that the army is righteous and does not abuse the weak, is destroyed. One example of this is the treatment of Alon, which leads to his suicide. Another example is evident in the case of the cruel treatment of Avner because he is a Jew of Arab origin, indicating racism and segregation — in contrast to the idea of unified Israeliness. A third example can be witnessed in the treatment of Miller, the German Holocaust survivor who is so brutalized that he dies on the final exercise. There is even the question of whether the new recruits are being shot at by the officers with live ammunition.

> I didn't believe the story about the blanks. At moments like these anything was possible. They, hiding up there on top of the hill, were capable of anything. Death too had become a matter of no importance. The mysterious goal justified this means too. This was the last illusion, really the last. (I, 494)

The officers have become the *Übermenschen* of Nietzschean construction. Believing they are gods beyond the normal boundaries of morality or justice, they judge that the end justifies any action, in this situation making Israeli soldiers fit the mythological model and destroying those who fail to reach this standard. This is evident in their treatment of the soldiers when they are shooting them. They have the power of life and death and sit in judgment over the other soldiers. The power God has over life and death in traditional Judaism has been usurped by the new gods of the Israeli army:

> "Why do you cut yourself like that? Are you trying to commit suicide? Forget it! You're IDF property now. Any attempt to destroy IDF property is an offence against General Routine Orders."
> (I, 159)

The only crime in this new secular religion is to betray Zionism. Alon's suicide is therefore a rejection of the IDF. By damaging military property, he is indicating that he no longer has respect or a sense of obligation for the army.

Fitting In as the Unit's Suicide?

Uri Ilan's suicide and the suicide combat units at Nes-Ziona are all examples of martyrdom and sacrifice for the collective, resembling the suicides of early Samson soldiers. However, Kenaz undermines these acts of sacrifice by presenting them in a novel whose very heart questions national obligations and responsibility. In these cases, suicide is a means of defining personal identity. But this novel also uses the image of suicide to represent the abdication of responsibility. When Zero-Zero is awakened and cannot get back to sleep, he considers death as a way of escaping the unpleasantness of his current situation. "'Those two bastards' — he pointed to the door — 'fuck their mothers, woke me up and now I can't get back to sleep.' He whimpered soundlessly. 'I feel so bad. Why can't I just die and get it over with already'" (I, 197). The promise of death offers release and escape from the terrible Israeli reality that he experiences. Yet Zero-Zero does not commit suicide. The promise of a better future, divorced from institutional expectations, represented by his wife and unborn child prevent him from being overwhelmed by his desperate situation.

Kenaz contrasts Alon's suicide with Avner's thoughts of suicide to develop the idea of the limitations of ideological thinking. Avner's suicidal thoughts, which he later rejects, are motivated by feelings of depression and isolation. His possible suicide was not motivated by ideological or national factors, and in turn, this is backed up by his rejection of suicide as an option. In rejecting suicide, Avner and Zero-Zero display maturity and demonstrate acceptance of their personal identity and social position.

> "We set out again and Avner said: "That was the first time I wanted to kill myself. I didn't know how to do it, and anyway it was terribly important to me to see how they reacted, how sorry they'd be, how they'd regret it, how they'd realize their mistake, blaming me for something I didn't do: *Why didn't we believe him? He was telling the truth!* It was a form of revenge. To die and remain alive, and make them come and beg my pardon, make them suffer."
>
> ". . . what was right yesterday's wrong today, we're getting leave, we're not getting leave, we're good soldiers, we're bad soldiers."
>
> "And every day you forget what happened the day before," said Avner. "Every minute you have to readjust yourself." (I, 190)

Avner explores suicide as a means for revenge. Although he contemplates the possibility, he abandons any plans he might have had to kill himself and assimilates the idea into resolving issues of his own identity: "every minute you have to readjust yourself." In Avner's eyes, existence is a process that is continually evolving. Alon lacks the ability to define and redefine himself every time he is confronted with different perceptions of reality. Avner, in embracing this quality, learns to define his individuality, and is therefore able to reject suicide. Enduring the officers' cruelty indicates his freedom from the army and his ability to withstand the negative aspects of ideology, while developing his own sense of self.

Betrayal

Kenaz further demonstrates the limitations of ideological thinking in contrasting Alon's relationships and Avner's relationships with others. Loyalty is a principal quality that soldiers ought to possess, as Alon notes.

The acts of betrayal that take place throughout the novel question the soldiers' loyalty network, and through this Kenaz exposes another myth about the army. Soldiers cannot and do not protect each other in the novel. This constant theme, betrayal and the absence of loyalty, becomes a regular tension in the soldiers' friendships. Micky refuses the obligations of loyalty for Alon, despite previously being invited to witness his friend's most personal feelings and hearing about Alon's intimate romance with Dafna. Alon's most treasured possessions, the nude pictures he has drawn of Dafna symbolize his emotional inner world, and he wants to share this secret with his friend. But Micky is troubled by this total exposure and declares that there is too much one can reveal to a friend: "There are some things you should never show a stranger, and a friend's a stranger too." The refusal to see Alon or to think about him in the brief period after he is severely injured but before he dies, is Micky's final betrayal, signaling Alon's total loss of identity, and so the last link symbolically tethering Alon to life is cut. The inner dimension, Alon's art, had been his only expression of personal identity; in rejecting his artwork Micky is rejecting Alon, and Micky cannot and will not offer Alon any other existence.

Friendship, which is not under military control, is a precious and rare connection, disparate from ideological expectations. The allegiances that the soldiers form with one another in training are out of necessity, but their constant flux and the possibility of betrayal undermine their value. Moreover, these relationships cannot save the soldiers from suicide. Friendship, which promises transcendence, is highlighted in opposition to military camaraderie. Micky snubs Alon's overtures of friendship, betraying him at the final moment declaring "There are limits to friendship, the borderlines between the self and the other" (I, 568). By doing so, another myth about the military is exposed by Kenaz. The model of a unit's allegiance to its members is shattered. Micky refuses the responsibility for his friend suggested by the military commander. The senior officer appeals to Micky: "You're his friend, you were always together. Don't you know?" but Micky denies this obligation, "I wasn't here" (I, 569). There is time between the announcement of Alon's suicide attempt and his eventual death from his wounds, but Micky not only refuses to visit him, he will not inquire about his condition. In his mind, Alon is already dead.

Perhaps he's already dead. Dead or alive — he's already dead to me. Strange, that apart from the dull, oppressive fear of the constant threat inside you, there's no sorrow for the dead man himself, no pity, no anguish at parting, no sense of loss. Perhaps just a hint of anger at the insult of the body, the insult of this ridiculous, contemptible death. (I, 568)

Micky's final abandonment of his friend is an act of betrayal that further signifies a challenge to the myths of army life. His response indicates a broader pattern of betrayal that Hertsig identifies throughout the novel. According to her, each of the characters plays both the role of betrayer and the role of the betrayed.

In section 4 "The Cannons' Roar," a blinding betrayal takes place, whose results are intimately connected. Micky betrays his best friend Alon — he does not trust in him at his most difficult moment, resulting in his suicide. We only need to see that in the final section there is no solution to the clear fact that each character is, in turn, betrayer and betrayed, and furthermore, it emerges that refraining from action, or taking part in an event blindly, is considered betrayal.[41]

Avner also experiences this betrayal from Melabbes; however, through his belief and commitment to friendship he experiences redemption. Avner's changing attitudes toward friendship reflect the characters' personal changes as they undergo training. At first he uses acts of kindness as material for later bargaining, "If you were really a good friend — you'd go and get me some black coffee" (I, 44) and later "Try to act like a friend." Avner falls asleep on guard duty, warning Melabbes that he has an obligation to keep him awake, but Melabbes, leaving him to sleep, allows him to be caught by a commanding officer. Avner imposes responsibility for his well-being on Melabbes, leading Melabbes to feel resentment about the situation. "I said to myself that this too, like the personal confessions, was his way of forcing intimacy and involvement on others" (I, 44–45). Melabbes feels no loyalty and objects to the responsibility placed upon him. The pinnacle of Avner's development as an adult is reached when his newfound respect for women meets with his reformed attitude to true friendship.

Avner displays his growing maturity in his increasing regard for women. Avner represents the mythical portrait of male sexuality embodied by the Samson figure. He constantly manages the different women thronging for his attention. The reader is told that he previously rejected a girl he made pregnant: "when he found out about it he buggered off and didn't want to have anything more to do with her. She had a breakdown, . . . He ruined her life" (I, 130). During the course of the novel the reader witnesses Avner's affair with a married woman. However, by the end of the novel he has ceased his affair and apologized for his behavior to the girl who had become pregnant. On meeting Ziva, a new woman in his life, he takes her hand and feels an overwhelming connection. "Look, we meet at a moment when I'm beginning my life as a man and my whole world is collapsing under my feet." "For a second he had the peculiar feeling that he was both self and other at the same time, and that what she saw in him was no less true than what he really felt or thought about himself." "Something deep, spiritual, connects us to each other" (I, 323). Avner is "beginning [his] life as a man"; he has passed through the army, where he started as a boy at the end of youth and has developed an attitude of responsibility and of compassion. Avner's women are no longer passive objects experiencing Samson's attention unquestioningly, or worse, vixens willing to betray him. Instead, Ziva is depicted as an intelligent, sensitive woman, no longer the two-dimensional representational victim of the soldier's gaze. Kenaz is demonstrating the complexity of society and human relations and thereby challenging the myths' limitations. Avner's previously callous attitude to women has metamorphosed into respect while his attitude to friendship becomes a reward, a loss of boundaries, and a willingness to accept friendship without demands.

Avner demonstrates that friendship and national ideals are in conflict. He argues that one can only feel for the individual and not for the whole of society. This opinion is in contrast with Alon's view of the world. It is because Avner values the individual and tries to connect with people that he is strengthened and he matures. This maturation process is also seen in Micky as his obsession with soccer dwindles:

> "Today I can't even work up enough interest to go and see a soccer match or read about it in the newspaper. I'm not interested in meeting guys from the team. Before it was almost my whole

world. And now it's over. As far as I'm concerned it's over. I'll find something else I can be good at without fears or restrictions."
(I, 109)

In their youth, their identity was defined through their passion for soccer and women, respectively, and became central pillars of their identities. In their journey toward adulthood they throw off these childish illusions, and learn to survive without them, while Zero-Zero overcomes his suicidal feelings because of the importance he places on his family. For each of these three characters personal experiences transcend their need for national belonging. As individuals, they are not dependent on Zionist myths, but can choose their own paths. Their development is contrasted with Alon's failure to complete this process of emotional growth.

Silence and Death

Kenaz represents the connections fostered by ideology and relationships through talking, while the disconnectedness of social and actual death happens in silence. As with *Requiem for Na'aman*, *Mr. Mani*, and *Closing the Sea*, novels that will be explored in the coming chapters, silence signals approaching death.

"I'm not going to be in the military police."
"So what are you going to be, in your opinion?"
Alon was silent. (I, 564)

Having been rejected by his superior and given the disgraceful posting to the military police, Alon refuses to comment. This contrasts starkly with the heated debates that he has conducted throughout the novel with Micky. Silence not only precedes death but also conveys the image of death. Those who are associated with death later in the novel are often described as silent, so that the representation of silence serves as a sign or premonition. Alon appears in the images of death from the first scenes of the book with "his totally silent voice" (I, 26), and before his suicide, "what heavenly silence, calling the soul, which cannot reach her" (I, 561). This contrasts with the noise generated by the ideological arguments and the constant thronging of the group, confined in a small space on the base. This theme of silence recurs throughout the narrative; for example, the unit falls silent when Miller dies while on the troop movement, the final exercise at the end of basic training. For a moment, the death of an individual is more powerful to the group than the usual rhetoric and ideological quarrels (I, 488).

Yet, having presented a series of arguments against the army, Kenaz does not reject the institution entirely. Following Alon's death, Micky tries to cut himself off from feeling the pain that comes with the loss of his friend. Having abandoned Alon, he still feels grief and guilt. He takes part in the military parade and becomes part of the collective venerated by Alon. Ironically, he is comforted by the sense of belonging provided by the activity of communal marching. He has at last decided to belong to something greater than himself, just as Alon had demanded from his friend. By identifying with the national institution — the army, he rationalizes Alon's actions, thereby providing meaning to the suicide for himself.

> The mechanical repetition of the complicated superfluous movements on the parade ground already seemed completely ridiculous, not to mention the yelling of the CSM and his curses and threats. But Micky felt that he had to take it seriously. Something in the automatic movements and wheeling's of the body in obedience to the barked commands, something in the rhythmic stamping of the feet and the uniform mass movement of those drilling with him relieved the oppression in his heart. Every ounce of energy and concentration he devoted to the precise execution of these stupid exercises seemed to him to detract from the weight of the fear in the depths of his being. (I, 569)

By belonging to the collective, he is protected and comforted. Nevertheless, Micky sacrifices his identity and individuality in this process, just as Melabbes had done at the parade at the start of the novel:

> I was overcome by the sensation that I was losing the possibility of hesitation and choice and control over my actions, and operating within the framework of some grand plan, step after step, according to a scenario that had been determined in advance. Thanks to this sensation, in all its extraordinary clarity and un-

expectedness, I had been enabled, on these very rare occasions, to taste the taste of freedom, and to realize that it was not simply a wish and a promise but a real and actual event. (*I*, 47)

According to Kenaz, the institutions of the state, such as the army, have produced officers devoid of humanity, creating unrealizable myths of strength and heroism, and have, in the process, sacrificed those too weak to defend themselves. Yet, the army has also created a sense of belonging; it has offered homogeneity to widely differing individuals, thereby constructing Israeliness, and has educated the soldiers in national values. Belonging in this novel offers the opportunity to transcend personal fear and pain for a higher cause. In turn the individual is destroyed when he becomes subsumed into the cause. But for those who are able to find personal distance in individual hopes and dreams, and even in humor — as Micky looks on at his commanding officer, seeing the absurdity in his orders and the responding troop movements — then there is a purpose in belonging to the collective.

The close of the novel, where Micky has explicitly chosen to belong to the greater national ideology, is imbued with hope through the birth of Zero-Zero's son. However, the incongruity between the characters' earlier bids for freedom, during their challenge to the ideological status quo, and their tacit acceptance of the national infrastructure in their final march at the parade, is paralleled by the birth of Zero-Zero's son. Instead of representing a new start for future generations, free from ideological constraints, Zero-Zero trusts the mythic portrayal of the army. He fails to see his own horrific experiences as representative of the reality for all soldiers, instead believing that his son, because he was born a sabra, will be able to confront Israeli society and succeed where he could not. The ideological image is so dominant that even when the men encounter a reality vastly different from it, the fiction about the army remains intact. In this, the state has proved more powerful than the individual.

> "I've got a sabra son," he said, "a sabra like them," and he pointed to a few of our number. "He'll be like the kids who grow up here from the beginning. He'll talk Hebrew like them. He won't know no foreign language, only Hebrew, and he'll sing their songs. Here it's a good place for kids to grow up. They turn out

better looking, healthier, strong. I won't call my kid any of those lousy names from over there, Lupu, Shmupu, Berko, Shmerko. I'll give him a sabra name, one of them new names, not loser's names. What a crazy world, I'm telling you, that I've got a sabra kid! I'll bring him up like one of them strong, nice-looking kids, so he'll fit into this country. So he won't be shit like me.

"Never mind he won't lack for nothing. I'll give my soul, my lousy life, to see he grows up right, like a sabra, not like a loser."
(I, 592)

Kenaz demonstrates through the difference in attitude between the historical period in which the novel is set and the one in which it is written, the changing mythology of the Israeli army. The sociological presentation of military suicide is inverted, with the act of suicide no longer heroic, but a rejection of the military institution and the mythology constructed around the army. By the close of the novel the recruits have become soldiers, loyal to one another, heroic, brave, strong, but the final failure of the mythology is evident in their incapacity to recognize the fulfillment of every task that has been set before them. Unable to identify their successful assimilation into the army and by extension Israeli society while, still believing in the reality of the dream, the men remain with an incongruous hope. Zero-Zero believes that his child, because he is born a sabra, will be able to fulfill the mythological expectations of Israeli society. Yet it is Alon, the sabra with his sabra name, who commits suicide in the novel.

Kenaz questions the veneration of the military in Israeli society and of course, by extension, the inviolability of other institutions held sacred in the socialist Zionist framework of the state-building years. He can do so only by working within the recognized tropes and socially accepted ideals. Despite his powerful critique of the system, Kenaz does not reject or abandon the Zionist vision. The majority of the characters survive with positive futures within the Israeli collective. They do not reject the nation or the army. Alon's suicide is powerful because though we are given his psychological breakdown and social abandonment, it is the role his death plays in the historical and of course literary context that provides the greatest level of poignancy. In dying, Alon abandons the possibility of an optimistic future — one signified by the more or less happy ending of Melabbes, Zero-Zero, and Avner.

CHAPTER 3

Unfortunate Suicides: Rewriting Narrative

The present shapes the past: the interests and needs of the present — or, more bluntly, politics and ambition — mold and make use of the past in order to influence the present.
—ALEX WEINGROD

The teaching of history [is] a legitimate tool of the state for implanting national values, even at the price of the selective use of historical evidence.
—ELIE PODEH

The "drive to construct the new national Hebrew culture" was a deliberate attempt to create a unique Jewish identity in Palestine.[1] Narratives of heroism accompanied by "commemorative strategies" used rituals that connected a traditional Jewish past with a national present as a means of shaping the Hebrew nation and its identity.[2] Culture was of primary importance in enhancing this mission. "The Hebrew literary establishment was a major agent in the formation of 'the Zionist narrative,' that is, the system of narratives, symbols, and attitudes which the Zionist movement generated, wittingly or unwittingly, in its attempt to mobilize the Jewish population in both the *Yishuv* and the Diaspora, for actions leading to the creation of a Jewish sovereign state in the ancestral homeland."[3] Through all forms of cultural production, the shaping of collective identity and collective memory remained a focal point.

The creation of national narratives in the move toward a Jewish national homeland in Palestine and its realization in a political form as the State of Israel have been well defined in Israeli society and in recent years have received much scholarly attention. In line with other national movements, Zionism engaged in the process of creating "complex strategies of cultural identification and discursive address that function in the name of 'the people' or 'the nation' and make them the immanent subjects of a range of social and literary narratives."[4] Nurit Gertz has shown that the numerous narratives that "appear and reappear in variations according to the specific event taking place at a given time and the system in which they occur" can be called master narratives in Israel, "all-encompassing models by which people are asked to live and die."[5] These narratives have the power to transmit ideological messages, in subtext, if not in text, and these become a "particular Zionist reconstruction of Jewish history" in which collective memory is sculpted in the name of national history.[6]

This chapter builds on Yael Zerubavel's study of the ways in which "the Zionist periodization of Jewish history and its portrayal of symbolic continuities and discontinuities . . . designed to enhance its vision of a new national age, and conversely, the Zionist vision of the future was, to a great measure, shaped by its reconstruction of the past."[7] Her work, along with that of Michael Feige, Nurit Gertz, Maoz Azaryahu, Yoram Bilu, and others, has established that the use of commemorative rituals, geographic sites, and calendric days which had been an inherent part of the Jewish tradition were reemployed in the service of the modern nation, thereby anchoring the new in the old. Nevertheless, as Zerubvael reminds us, counter-memory becomes a way to disrupt an acceptance of the culturally constructed historical narratives. The Zionist national narrative was itself a disruption to the Jewish Diasporic past. Thus counter-memory functions dialectically, articulating the hegemonic and politically motivating meanings of the narrative, only to discredit them, and highlighting that which has remained hidden, edited, and absent.

While early Zionist history has ascribed a powerful role to literature in the creation of the Zionist master narrative, the invention of tradition in the modern age has also faced its strongest critique within the novel. Timothy Brenan claims that "the epic was that genre the novel parodied in its nation-forming role. . . . where 'beginning,' 'first,' 'founder,' 'ancestor,' 'that which occurred earlier,' and so on are . . . valorized temporal categories corresponding to the 'reverent point of view of a descendent.'"[8] The three novels considered in this chapter preserve this idea of epic with its expectations (and details) of heroic deeds and events of national (or cultural) significance, yet they do so in order to undermine the culturally constructed narratives of heroism and the markers conceived to be significant in the history of the nation. Thus the master narrative's attempts to represent the past in a "story-like" fashion, in order to provide a general notion of a shared past as a unified group moving together through history, with its perceived linear conception of time, is radically disrupted and undermined by portraying nonlinear time, cyclical histories, counter-histories, and postmodernist literary devices highlighting the very ways in which narrative is constructed.

Nor is the master narrative a static process; rather, as Gertz demonstrates, narratives metamorphose in a constantly changing dynamic which reflects changes within Israel's own history and conceptions of itself: "constantly changing relationships between them are based on the view that a culture is a totality composed of the systems operating within it, all struggling for power, prestige and hegemony. The texts formed in — and by — a society are weapons used in these struggles. Texts that were central in one period are shunted to the sidelines in another, and vice versa. In this process, the narratives embedded in the texts go through greater or lesser adjustments in content and structure to adapt them to their new status."[9]

As the first two chapters of this book have demonstrated, contesting narratives and symbols within Israel did not occur as a result of any single major moment of crisis. Rather, a series of smaller changes within the Israeli reality over a period of the state's existence have led to waves of transformation. It might reasonably be argued that even as we recognize the exclusion or overlooked experience of one group in Israeli society, forced to suppress their individual or group narrative in favor of the collective rendition of the past, and even seek to redress this imbalance; we may simultaneously fail to observe the mistreatment of another group, until they too call for our attention in accordance with changes in society at large. This chapter considers three historical novels written in different time periods over the past thirty years, working within a framework of counter-memory whose different narrative agendas reflect wider changes in Israel's capacity to accept and integrate conflicting narratives, or at least to acknowledge their existence.

Benjamin Tammuz's novel *Requiem Le-Na'aman* (*Requiem for Na'aman*, 1978) brings to the fore Jewish narratives from the late nineteenth to mid-twentieth century, including the settlement of Palestine, that were at odds with the Labor-Zionist master narrative. *Mar Mani* (*Mr. Mani*, 1990) by A. B. Yehoshua explores the ontological framework of linearity that dominates the Zionist narrative, with its strong Ashkenazi and European origins thereby highlighting the absence of Sephardim from the discourse of national history, including those living within Palestine during the nation-building years. Alon Hilu's novel *Ahuzat Dajani* (*The House of Rajani*, 2008) reinscribes the previously suppressed Palestinian narrative onto the Zionist narrative of late nineteenth-century Jewish pioneering. The novels by Tammuz and Yehoshua use cyclical time and the family saga as a contrast to the collective, and demonstrate through the use of memory voids between generations, the false nature of a continuous and complete narrativization of the past. Hilu achieves a similar objective by juxtaposing the diary of a speculator and agronomist acquiring land for interested European Jewish organizations in nineteenth-century Palestine with the written musings and stories of an Arab boy living on a family estate near Jaffa. Despite differences, the three novels share a quest to restore the absent to the nation's narrative. They do so in their treatment of content, sharing themes such as silent protagonists, madness, unexplainable compulsions, and repeated and often ritualized suicides; and they do so in their treatment of form, deconstructing the very process of narrative itself in a postmodern disruption of the realism that they appear so painstakingly to create. All three novels contest history, arguing that there is no final and knowable truth.

The coalescence of the Zionist national movement from a series of disparate though similarly operating groups and ideas to a unified organization is traced to the First Zionist Congress convened and orchestrated by Theodor Herzl in Basel, Switzerland, in 1897. This is part of the construction of a national identity through the filtering of the past and the establishment of iconic markers (flag, anthem, language) that Benedict Anderson has shown to be integral in the process of creating a nation.[10] The birth of Zionism, the adoption of "HaTikvah" as the anthem (later to become the national anthem of the State of Israel), and the organization's flag in blue and white with a Star of David (and a lion that later disappeared) established the movement's foundations. With its plans for a sovereign Jewish territory, this moment marked the beginning of the construction of the national narrative. In turn, literature which sought to construct these political imaginings in realistic terms drew from this particular nationalist discourse. "From its beginnings, most Israeli literature has centered on the lives of Ashkenazi male heroes whose experience is defined by the great issues of national destiny."[11] A set of iconic tropes such as the pioneer (*halutz*) and *shomer* (guard) explored in chapter 1, and notions of soldiers' sacrifice and the importance of the military, arose to support this ideological narrative, which could only be arrived at by filtering out counterclaims and personal narratives that were at variance with this dominant articulation of history.

The image of suicide in novels that confront the nation's historical narratives is a symbolic reflection of the author's rejection of this accepted depiction of modern Jewish history with its incontestable structure, and a challenge to the ways in which aspects of history are selected and commemorated in a process of canonization that excludes competing or conflicting experiences. As with the previous chapter, suicide is an act of extreme individualism by which the characters reject the social expectations they face and demonstrate a refusal to subsume personal identity beneath national identity. These suicides are acts of autonomy and highlight the nature of personal narratives. This chapter focuses particularly on the dichotomy between the public and private conceptions of Israeli-Jewish history. In peeling back the layers of narrative structure, this chapter also touches upon a secondary element, that of the Arab-Israeli conflict, and the erased history of Palestinian society.

Nevertheless, the writers construct these novels with characters often outside the "great issues of national destiny," not purely as a vehicle by which to build history as a straw man to be knocked down, but rather to demonstrate that despite the essential truths of a strong historical background, other competing truths depicted through the characters' complicated lives must find a place in the nation's conceptions of itself. These novels are not anti-Zionist, since they do not reject Zionism, but they suggest that Zionist ideology has excluded other competing narratives — stories that should not be forgotten. Furthermore, "the fact that national events are so strongly connected with the lives of the characters in these novels leads us to think that these are not only stories of individuals but stories which also depict Israeli life as such."[12] By using literature to criticize the national narrative, the authors are also criticizing the state thereby commenting on the society in which they live.

Tammuz and the Reclamation of Non–Labor Zionism

In *Requiem for Na'aman* suicide is the pivot for the story of four generations of the Abramson family. The novel traces the lives of this family from the first Zionist immigrants to Palestine at the end of the late nineteenth century, through the creation of Tel Aviv in the 1920s, the First and Second World Wars, to a decadent generation in the 1960s and early 1970s. The characters are divided between those who are builders, engaged in developing the Zionist project, and those who are dreamers, rejecting Zionism and the land. Characters in the first category include Ephraim the patriarch, who is a citrus farmer; his son Aminadav, who moves to Tel Aviv and opens a brick factory; and his grandson Oved, a soldier in the Haganah. By contrast, the dreamers — including Bella-Yaffa, Ephraim's wife, who misses her Russian home; her son Na'aman who moves to Europe; and Oved's brother Elyakum, who travels through Europe, disappearing for some time — are unable to make a home in the Land of Israel. All three dreamers eventually die: the first two by committing suicide, the third in a suicide-like act of military bravery. Those who commit suicide in this novel are depicted as unable to assimilate effectively into the dominant ideology of Labor Zionism. They long for Europe and reject Israel. Independently of one another they disappear into the imaginary world that they have each constructed in order to avoid the Israeli reality. Within the framework of the novel, their acts of suicide indicate the final break between the Zionist reality and the safety of the fantasy. Within the broader context of the narrative, these suicides indicate a desire to evade Israeli society, whose corruption suppresses the voices of those who challenge it.

The novel uses a literary model of repeating cycles that must eventually be broken in order for the characters to stop committing suicide. In *Requiem for Na'aman*, the cycle begins with the patriarch Ephraim Abramson, known by the diminutive Froyke-Ephraim, and the disappearance of his wife Bella-Yaffa, who he hunts for unsuccessfully. He organizes search parties and travels through Europe trying to locate her. To do this he becomes an international representative of the citrus growers' cooperative, which demands that he encourage investment in Zionist projects throughout Europe and speak about the need to immigrate to Palestine at an event in London. Precisely because of his wife's rejection of Zionism, which is contrasted with his passion for it, he is unable to understand her and can therefore never learn that she has killed herself. Her suicide provides the focus of the novel as a meta-framework that raises questions about the reasons for a person to commit suicide when apparently contented and having fulfilled the Zionist dream. Realizing that she does not like the ideological expectations imposed on her by her father and husband, and instead prefers the "open spaces, golden fields and avenues of slender trees" that her father calls "a false charm, a vanity of the Gentiles," Bella-Yaffa understands that she can no longer survive. The "cedars of Lebanon" in "the land of our fathers" that both men admire repel her, and this evident physical distance from her home and emotional and ideological distance from the national project leads her to commit suicide (RN, 3–4). As she says moments before death, "I love the dream more than I love you. . . . I am a soul struck off from the book of life." The book mentioned here refers to the Jewish belief that God inscribes a person's fate on the Jewish New Year in either the book of life or the book of death. As a symbolic reference, this book also serves as a metaphor for the mainstream Zionist narrative from which, by her rejection of Israel, Bella-Yaffa is excluded. Her suicide cuts her off from the traditional Jewish God, and from the modern god, the state. Bella-Yaffa's death may be considered a betrayal of the nationalist narrative, yet Tammuz, through the omniscient narrator, satirizes the blind adherence to Zionism and the failure among Zionists to understand those who would disagree.

Tammuz suggests that there is a second allegorical meaning attached to the use of suicide. He believes that the act causes a break in the link between the living and the dead. Ephraim's search also becomes a figurative journey to find and repair this link that was broken when his wife committed suicide without leaving an explanation for doing so. The couple's son Na'aman becomes an important part of this narrative chain when "Froyke-Ephraim sensed and understood that Na'aman was his mother's son" (RN, 16). Later, "Froyke-Ephraim, who had not seen his son for a year, was still struck by the boy's resemblance to his mother; and sitting in the darkness on the deck, he thought about that other voyage, when he had sailed with Bella-Yaffa from Odessa to Jaffa, thirty years before" (RN, 25). Na'aman corresponds to the depictions of his mother. They share a gentle nature, otherworldliness, love of music, and the desire to travel to Europe. The suffering that each experiences in Israel and that leads to their suicides ties them irrevocably.

Even before his death, Na'aman ceases to exist as an independent individual and becomes the connection between his father and his missing mother, symbolizing the erosion of his personal identity and linking him to his mother's rejection of Zionism. In turn, this also offers the reader prophetic insight into his imminent suicide. Abramson's correlation between his wife and son culminates in the realization that his wife committed suicide as he learns of Na'aman's suicide.

> About a month after the outbreak of the war Ephraim received a letter from France, . . . a message that Na'aman had put an end to his life. Ephraim Abramson held the letter open in his hands, re-read it several times, closed his eyes and said to himself: They're both dead, then, both the mother and the son. They are writing to me here that the mother is dead too. There can be no doubt that this is what they want to tell me. (RN, 39–40)

By living in Europe he has made a physical break with the Land of Israel; by dying in Europe, Na'aman is also disconnected from Israel and Zionism and is disinterested in his father's work promoting Zion in the Diaspora. In dying alone, he signifies his emotional and psychological break with human beings, an isolation evaluated in sociological terms as a break with the fabric of society. This represents his rejection of the more acceptable narratives of pioneers and their children born in Israel who are loyal to the land. He also becomes a missing part of the narrative since his death remains unreported for some time. His existence is shadowy in the family chronicles, with his relationship to other members of the family clear only to the reader. Na'aman, after whom the book is titled, plays a small role in the story, but it is the significance of his break with the Zionist enterprise, emblematic of the unknowable void, that makes him central to the novel. His suicide leaves a gap in the past, which the other characters cannot piece together. This contrasts with national narratives through which past events are framed within a coherent interrelated sequential account, and with the Zionist narrative in particular which frames the events in the *Yishuv* and Israel as of central importance, while European Jewish history is relegated to the margins.

Zerubavel has argued that the selective relationship between memory and forgetting is an integral part of nation building, and just as Na'aman remains a forgotten part of the family saga, existing outside the frame of the nation, Bella-Yaffa, the granddaughter of the first Bella-Yaffa, symbolically becomes the keeper of the family memory. She is the only person who hears her Uncle Herzl's words muttered quietly at his father Ephraim's graveside, and she remembers Herzl's words, "all the days of her life," suggesting that memory, rather than recorded history, plays the more important role of chronicling a family's past (*RN*, 139). She is made aware by an old Arab man, her servant's husband, that the summerhouse has a legend about a woman who had arrived in the middle of the night and then died. Unexpectedly she has learned the true fate of the first Bella-Yaffa, though for her this becomes a shadowy legend, not a historical certainty. "Bella-Yaffa wrote these things in her copybook and one day — she said to herself — she would compile all this folk material into one small volume, but not for publication" (*RN*, 141).

Although Bella-Yaffa serves as a family archive, since she is aware of the history and secrets of members of the group, she chooses not to reveal this information, keeping it private and refusing to publish her personal family history or her poems. Her response is in marked contrast to the public recording of history, and signals her identification with the personal, family realm. Her awareness of the family history remains limited. She understands that she is named after an older Bella-Yaffa, who was an ancestor and Ephraim's first wife. She also understands that Na'aman was important to the story of Ephraim and Bella-Yaffa, but she never clarifies his relationship to the family and assumes that he was Bella-Yaffa's lover.

> It was not I who invented Na'aman, but my great-grandfather. Or perhaps Na'aman was not an invention, but flesh and blood. This is something I will never know nor does it make any difference. (*RN*, 158–60)

The younger Bella-Yaffa has confused insight. She is unsure of Na'aman's existence, wondering if he was real and died, or if he was a figment of her great-grandfather's imagination. Her hesitancy over his existence and his suicide may be read as a fragmentation of the link between the living and the dead, which Zionist history assumes is clear and continuous. Since the younger Bella-Yaffa can never make a clear connection between Na'aman and the truth, so can she never put him into context. Both Bella-Yaffa's suicide and Na'aman's prevent the younger Bella-Yaffa from knowing the truth. Suicide disrupts the connection between generations in these novels, serving as a reminder that the creation of national narratives and their coherence is a false, artificially imposed construction of the past.

The second Bella-Yaffa, like her namesake, also abandons the nation though she can no longer flee to Europe as her ancestors had. She is too sick to be in the army or to stay at the university, thereby symbolically abandoning the nation's institutions of both defense and culture. The illness is part of the eccentricity she has inherited from her great-grandmother and so she is forced to stay at the summerhouse, the burial place of this matriarch, which has a special magical power for the young Bella-Yaffa, thereby linking the two women. When she recovers, she does not return to the university, and instead teaches herself. She speaks Greek, Latin, English, French, and Arabic; she learns about weeds and flowers from the Arab servant's husband, and at the house she "read more in one year than she had absorbed in her three years of study in Jerusalem" (RN, 140), showing that her inner personal world is stronger than that of institutions or mass culture.

Her response to the accepted ideological framework is played out repeatedly among other characters throughout the novel. When Ephraim disagrees with the kibbutz movement, Tammuz satirizes the many nuanced ideological stances and opinions held in pre-state Palestine, thereby providing an alternative reading to that of the monolithic Labor-Zionist pioneer-hero.

> By the middle of the Twenties the Jewish population in the Land of Israel was already divided into two clear camps: the bourgeoisie and the socialists. All the other divisions, which after many years formed thirty-six political factions fighting against each other in flaming fury, outwardly, and making deals with each other under the table, inwardly — these were nothing but tu-

mors, like cancerous outgrowths, of those two camps: Ephraim
Abramson on the one side, and Karl Marx on the other. (*RN*,
54–55)

The derision that appears in Tammuz's writing toward the breakdown
of ideological structures that hold the Jewish people together is matched
only by his scorn for institutions and individuals who have abused ideology for personal ends. Ephraim's work as a farmer and his need for
financing after the First World War are contrasted with the money available for the ideological pioneering kibbutzniks. The Labor-Socialist kibbutzim received money from special national funds, allegedly because
they were creating a new society that was not profit-hungry. Ephraim
is angry and cynical at the explanations given for this unequal distribu-
tion of resources. The false supposition that there are different kinds of
Zionists and therefore some more worthy than others of aid displays the
corruption of ideological frameworks. Ephraim is not eligible for funding
because, according to the banker

> the farmers who had come at the end of the previous century —
> they were farmers, like all farmers in the world; whereas the new
> ones, who had come after 1905 and had established the com-
> mune Daganiah, were idealists. (*RN*, 49–50)

Ephraim is outraged at the treatment he receives at the hands of the
banker. He represents a counter-voice to the agricultural idealism attributed to the kibbutz movement at the price of dismissing other agricultural endeavors which also developed out of a love of Zion. At a meeting
of the citrus growers' association, Ephraim offers a criticism of the kibbutz, arguing that the new ideology is corrupt and false.

> A person who has tried his hand at idolatry, at Social-
> Revolutionism and Bolshevikism, until the Gentiles came and
> kicked him in the buttocks, pardon me, Your Honors; such a
> man, when he comes to the Land of Israel to live without wed-
> ding canopy and ceremony, and tells us stories about how he has
> no need for money and no desire for property, and he is purity
> itself and sleekness, a creature not of this world, a seeker of the

good of the entire world, on condition that he be given loans from special funds, on easy terms of credit or preferably on no terms at all; such a person is called an idealist. (RN, 50)

Tammuz's alternative voice to Zionist history presents the kibbutz movement as an act of opportunism rather than deep-seated ideological beliefs. Tantamount to heresy, this criticism of a sacred topos of Israeli culture is contrasted with Ephraim's brand of Zionism; however, this evocation of counter-memory is further disrupted in his wife's suicide, as a result of which she rejects all forms of Zionism.

This satire of Zionist politics lies at the heart of *Requiem for Na'aman*, occurring repeatedly, highlighting both its false premise and functioning as a vicious attack on the method of using nationalist ideology as a way of controlling individuals. Meshulam Ha-Gelili is a caricature of an ideologue and kibbutznik. He inspires Elyakum, Ephraim's grandson, to abandon his grandfather's farm: "This man was working assiduously on preparing a program, from which members of the kibbutzim would be able to recognize what their aspirations were and how to behave according to principles set for them" (RN, 66). We soon discover that Ha-Gelili's actions are not motivated by high ideals, but by the rich rewards that his position gives him. Leisl, Elyakum's girlfriend, warns him that Ha-Gelili is corrupt and corrupting.

> "That spiritual father of yours has been divorced twice, and now he's getting all his girlfriends pregnant, one after the other . . . he sends them to the Histadrut Trade Union Health Service in Jerusalem to have an abortion . . . he writes them covering letters . . . on Kibbutz stationery." (RN, 77)

Ha-Gelili's sexual corruption undermines his political service, which in turn, is used to manage his dissipation. The Histadrut, the Israeli trade union for all workers established in 1920, claimed 25,000 members or 75 percent of the Jewish workforce in Palestine by 1927. It became one of the most powerful institutions in the State of Israel, functioning not just as a trade union, but also in its nation-building role it became the owner of a number of businesses and factories, eventually becoming the largest employer in the state, owning the country's second largest bank, Bank Ha-Poalim, as well as providing a comprehensive health care system. Ideological initiatives and national institutions, represented by Ha-Gelili, become merely the vehicles by which he manages his love life. Elyakum, an idealist, refuses to believe such a damning condemnation of his friend. Since he cannot imagine a world of corrupt moral values, it is impossible for him to accept that other people would abuse systems based on principles. Tammuz highlights the innocence and naïveté of individuals seduced by Zionism at the expense of moral independence. Elyakum's charge that matters between a man and woman are outside the purview of ideology is ironic given Ha-Gelili's appropriation of ideological symbols in order to manage his affairs. Elyakum's ensuing suicide in the course of duty as a soldier reveals the inadequate preparation for those seduced by national institutions and serves as a protest.

Elyakum's innocence symbolizes the lost individuals who believed in a Jewish home, but were unable to form a strong persuasive argument for their beliefs and were therefore swept along in the ideological machinations of others. At his brother's wedding Elyakum makes a speech about Israel and the importance of development, expounding upon his love of the land and his Zionist commitment: "think for yourselves and answer me: was it worth it to come to swamps and malaria and murders, in order to be lawyers and to work in a bank?" (RN, 62). Ephraim approves of his grandson's words, although he thinks that they would have been weightier if the boy actually worked the land. The irony becomes immediately apparent when it emerges that Elyakum's statement is motivated by his recent involvement with the kibbutz, thereby demonstrating that he is working the land, but within the movement Ephraim most opposes. Elyakum becomes a study in ideological blindness, rejecting the land at his grandfather's farm for the kibbutz land which he is persuaded is ideologically superior.

Elyakum is parodied as he goes from movement to movement. After joining the kibbutz partly through the influence of Ha-Gelili, he is then betrayed when the older man sleeps with Leisl. In response he rejects Zionism, and this connection to his grandmother foreshadows his later suicide. To escape Palestine, he leaves for England where he falls in with communists. Their behavior and beliefs are mocked in a vicious critique of communism that marks the marginalized place this ideology held in the Zionist collective consciousness. He returns, a qualified teacher of Marxist theory.[13] Finding no satisfaction in communist doctrines, Elyakum is then reabsorbed by the state, becoming a devoted follower of the national ideology and the need for personal sacrifice. By frequently falling in with different belief systems, his recent recommitment to Zionism is presented as yet another false philosophy. As an officer, he becomes excessively dedicated to the state, eventually dying for the nation. His military suicide, the result of highly ideological devotion, a phenomenon described by Émile Durkheim and analyzed in the previous chapters, is yet another method by which Tammuz rejects Zionism by challenging the cost that this devotion demands.

The pathos of Elyakum's suicidal death is undercut with a cynical parody of the national attitude to the death of soldiers. Tammuz satirizes the formal processes of commemoration and Elyakum's desire to belong to a community by highlighting the large numbers of casualties and soldiers who died with him. The "power of belonging" Elyakum is looking for in his passion for ideology is provided in his death.

> At the end of 1948 the number of war victims reached five thousand. And the dead left behind them bereaved parents and war widows. And in these large numbers there was the power of belonging; and from the power of belonging the road is not far to succumbing to fate. And from having succumbed it is only one step to the frozen face. Not to cry. Not to break. Those who fell did not fall in vain. Not like those millions of Jews who died in the crematoria. Here we know what we are being killed for.

Ridiculing the sense of belonging created with the vast numbers of fallen soldiers, Tammuz mocks a society that had a brutal response to the Holocaust and that creates a hierarchy of values toward kinds of death, whereby the deaths in Europe are depicted as senseless in comparison to the deaths of soldiers during the War of Independence. Tammuz repeatedly demeans heroic sentiment created at the expense of the individuals who suffer. This is as true of his portrayal of Ha-Gelili, and the women impregnated by him who are directed to have abortions, as it is for Elyakum who dies in battle.

Acts of naming in this novel symbolize the process by which national narratives are constructed through the process of selection, offering power over events in the past. Tammuz demonstrates that this labeling, an act of national appropriation, cannot change the status of an item. Bella-Yaffa spends her time at the summerhouse working on a dictionary focused on naming realia. In the work she is doing with Bieberkraut, her former teacher, she is searching for the essence of being, and believes that the true name of an item will provide an explanation of this concept. Eventually, she learns that the purpose or role that an item has, and not the name given to it by people, provides the item with meaning. As the Arab worker says in reference to a weed he has been fighting for fifty years, "what do I care what its name is? . . . even if it had no name, cursed be it" (RN, 220–21). After fourteen years of work, she burns her research, signaling a break with this need for power over other things. Tammuz indicates that the creation of national narratives is engaged with the act of naming history in order to identify and select events appropriate for reinforcing the ideological message. Burning the dictionary is another departure from a process of formalization and control.

In a similar sense, the novel contrasts personal visions with national dreams. The former indicate a shadowy individualistic world, secret from the eyes of others. The younger Bella-Yaffa frequently has dreams and visions, which increasingly distance her from actuality, making the real and the unreal confused in her mind, just as her great-grandmother's dreams are a place to act out suicide fantasy. By expressing her devotion to the dream, the first Bella-Yaffa indicates her imminent suicide, and Na'aman is described as "a disembodied soul" (RN, 22). When the second Bella-Yaffa dreams about the first Bella-Yaffa, whom she never met, she sees a version of the past that she could not have witnessed, and as a result becomes increasingly confused about her identity.

> One night Bella-Yaffa saw Ephraim Abramson galloping on a horse among the hills, and beckoning to her to join him. Soon the rider caught up with another galloping horse, on which a woman was riding. When he approached the woman he saw that it was Bella-Yaffa. The dreaming Bella-Yaffa looked at the Bella-Yaffa who was on the horse and saw that indeed it was she. Ephraim Abramson reached out his hand and felt the face of Bella-Yaffa on the horse, and Bella-Yaffa the dreamer said to him "How do you know that Bella-Yaffa is Bella-Yaffa? Perhaps here a question mark is needed?" (RN, 218–19)

In this vision, Bella-Yaffa had been dreaming about the death of the first Bella-Yaffa and the search that Ephraim made for her when she disappeared. It is when she awakes from this vision that she burns the papers. Although this may seem like a kind of insanity, Bella-Yaffa has complete clarity; she understands that their research into the true name of nouns is futile after so much time. The research has reached only the letter *Bet*, the second letter of the alphabet.[14] This is also the first letter of her name, indicating that you can never really define a person; just as she remains elusive, even to herself, she is aware that life, people, and events cannot be categorized, labeled, evaluated, and defined. After this moment of destruction, Bella-Yaffa starts walking to the wadi, and increasingly her dream world and reality become confused. This is illustrated when she says to a passing Yemenite, while on foot, "I am going to my home, and Na'aman is expecting me there, and I have no need of a donkey. I am riding on a horse" (RN, 228). Na'aman is dead, she does not know who he was and she has never met him. Her insane ranting exemplifies her breakdown as she becomes increasingly untethered from the rational world. Menucha Gilboa in reference to *Requiem for Na'aman* talks about the hereditary legacy of destiny and madness.

> A dynasty was born of boys and girls, where the madness passed amongst them, from generation to generation, as though it were a legacy. Even if we do not call this phenomenon insanity, but *specialness* or a curse, or even fate, it still continued to rule through the generations. This is the edict of fate which causes suicide or insanity. And in certain cases this leads to strangeness and eccentricity. Since this is the edict of fate — there is no release from it; . . . with this the author expresses a determinist world view. Determinism is a kind of genealogical curse, that is to say a tragedy that passes through a family, with no possibility of evasion.[15]

But Tammuz shows that this genealogical curse can be broken. By reenacting the first Bella-Yaffa's death but surviving, the second Bella-Yaffa breaks the edict of fate. It is only after this event that the spiritual heir's disturbing visions abate and finally "she sank into a long sleep, a sleep with no dreams" (RN, 228). These personal visions are a way of avoiding the national reality.

In Tammuz's novel, ideological dreams are represented as an extreme manifestation of the power of ideas and the hold these social dreams may have on those who live to enact them. On Independence Day, a symbol of nationhood, the younger Bella-Yaffa comments on the obligation individuals feel to fulfill an unworkable national dream. "You are not guilty . . . you are not guilty. And you know why you are not guilty? Because you are floating and sailing within the dream of other people, who have died long ago. They, the others, have dreamed a dream, many years ago, and you are the materialization of that dream. . . . They could not have known how those dreams of theirs would descend into reality and take shape in it" (RN, 207). The individual's survival can only take place through the acknowledgment of reality, which abandons national ideology and the attendant insane personal visions that are an extreme response to this enterprise.

Requiem for Na'aman's celebration of the individual manifests itself in the personal connection between characters, a connection free of ideological rules. Bella-Yaffa is a spiritual heir to the first Bella-Yaffa, because she rejects all the formal ideology that the rest of the family in some way adopts. Ephraim builds the land, Elyakum dies in the army, even Herzl, who seems to stand aloof, takes part in secret missions for the Haganah. It is only the first Bella-Yaffa who rejects the ideology of her husband and her father and commits suicide. Menucha Gilboa has argued:

> Bella-Yaffa was in her own way a kind of sacrifice that her father offered up to ideological Zionism. With that she also became a sacrifice for destiny and madness that caught hold of her and never left. These two aspects met in the Land of Israel and contributed to her death, her suicide.[16]

She tries to tell her husband of the situation with her final words, but because she is now too upset, and too insane, she cannot communicate her feelings, and only the reader knows how she has become a victim of ideological beliefs. The second Bella-Yaffa is able to reject Zionism without the need to commit suicide, because she can resolve the tension between nationalism and personal identity. By understanding personal history, and abandoning the need for the power to name things, and by rejecting insane visions and ideological dreams, she is able to present a reconciled view of living in Israel.

The legacy of madness that had been left by the previous Bella-Yaffa, breaking the link between the living and the dead because of her disappearance, and the silence surrounding her death, indicates one of the main themes in the presentation of suicide in Hebrew literature. The living are unable to communicate suggesting the disparity between personal narratives and national accounts. In turn dissenting voices are silenced by their exclusion from the canonical construction of national history.

Silence marks the difference between the personal world and ideological rhetoric; the noisy, public speeches in the novel are shown to be empty declarations, while the private world is characterized by silences. At the party in the summerhouse on Independence Day, Bella-Yaffa's conversation contrasts with the public speeches that had been made during the day by the officers and ministers. Usually she lives in silence in the house; thus her quiet words are an extension of this silence, just as her great grandmother's explanation about her death is spoken silently to the reader alone. There is a separation between the public realms of national gatherings, and the private realms of home where silence dominates. Homes signify a feminine sphere — represented by these women, by contrast to the masculine public with its nationalist overtones. This representation of the divisions between male and female also suggest the divisions between male (national) and female (personal) forms of history.

The issue of silence and speech dominates *Requiem for Na'aman*, which is subtitled "A Chronicle of Family Conversations." Ironically, the lack of interaction between the characters and their powerful silences demonstrates the inability of individuals to communicate. When Bella-Yaffa and her husband Ephraim are described at the opening of the book, they are silent together.

> And the woman Bella-Yaffa leans on the porch rail, and is silent, and her husband works in the kitchen, and he too is silent, from experience; and sometime later he comes out . . . and then the woman says, "Look, Froyke, what magic there is all around us, what dreadful sadness." (RN, 2)

The beauty in this scene masks Bella-Yaffa's inability to communicate with her husband and her need to reject his ideological dreams. Just as she cannot say this to him in person, she is also unable to write it to him when she kills herself, and so he is left in silence, not knowing what has happened to his wife when she disappears, or the reason for her death.

This silent power is inherited by Sarah, Bella-Yaffa's daughter, "And she loved Aminadav, her stepbrother, and without a word guided him into loving her. She never made spoken demands, but she always obtained her wish" (RN, 14). Na'aman, who begins to speak only through his music, also inherits this silent communication.

> And so when he was sixteen Na'aman was uprooted from his father's house. In Jerusalem he lived in his teacher's house, and as he had not spoken much with others whilst living in his father's house, at his teacher's house he stopped talking completely, except for what was necessary to ask and to reply in connection with his studies. (RN, 16)

Na'aman remains silent for many years, and the conversation he finally has with his father occurs when Na'aman plays music for his father on the boat during their trip to Europe. This music finally releases Ephraim as the tunes are old folk ditties that connect him to his past.

> "Na'aman," said the father, "why haven't you ever asked me about your mother? After all, your mother vanished from our lives, like a ghost. . . . And you never asked me, even once."
> "We've never talked, Father," said Na'aman from his seat at the piano, not turning his head. . . .
> Again the engine of the ship continued to bear out the time and the silence between them. (RN, 23)

The silence Ephraim shared with his wife is echoed in the relationship with his son, a realization that leads him to abandon the conversation. "He looked at his son and fell silent" (RN, 25). Similarly, Herzl, who is not Bella-Yaffa's son but is brought up in the Abramson house of silence, where Bella-Yaffa had lived before Herzl's mother became Ephraim's second wife, also becomes, like Sarah and Na'aman, someone who contains his thoughts and feelings. "He was a silent man by nature, a man who walked solitary, took an odd comfort from the things that he saw and knew, without telling them to anyone" (RN, 96). This family legacy of silence is passed on between generations and Bella-Yaffa's grandson Oved joins the Haganah where the "obligation to secrecy was a basic principle" (RN, 57). Sarah and Aminadav do not query their son's actions. Only Elyakum tries to question this behavior, but he is scolded by Oved his brother and told, "Do your own work and don't ask questions." At Oved's wedding Elyakum makes an ideological speech about working the land, which is considered inappropriate by his parents. He is out of place, since he does not accept silence easily, and yet he never learns to interact with the social groups around him, thereby finding himself in an enforced silence. "He had not yet found a common language with the other people in the kibbutz" (RN, 66). As Leisl says to Ephraim: "apart from me, he hardly speaks with anyone" (RN, 83). "With time, he stopped speaking" (RN, 111). Elyakum communicates only on a national or ideological level; he is never able to interact with individuals through conversation rather than rhetoric. His immersion in ideological creeds prevents him from establishing normal human relations, thereby serving as a criticism of national dogma.

Oved, who rarely spoke to his brother Elyakum during his lifetime, and fails to acknowledge the silence between them, only speaks out after Elyakum's death. However, this speech is national and political, taking up the mantel of Elyakum's legacy and perpetuates the disconnection between the family members. This outburst is an indication that Oved's pride and ideological principles have been injured rather than a reflection of his feelings for his brother. He considered allowing his brother's death to pass "in silence" to be an act of degradation (RN, 113). But these feelings of devotion were never expressed during Elyakum's lifetime, highlighting the collective's displacement of the individual.

Similarly, Elyakum's own father cannot speak about his grief. "Aminadav never spoke in long or ordered sentences. Nor did he know how to cry, as he did not know how to laugh" (RN, 113). Worried that he cannot cry at his son's funeral, and amazed that Herzl the silent hero can, Aminadav begins to apprehend his own existence.

> Or was this whole thing beyond Aminadav's understanding, because he did not exist at all? For if he did exist he would have known what to do. Aminadav tries to remember something important from his life, but apart from certain difficulties he is unable to recall anything, and he becomes still more alarmed. (RN, 113)

The change of tense from past to present distances the reader from Aminadav's process of thought, indicating the character's increasing isolation from reality and increasing submersion into his subconsciousness.

> Is it possible that Herzl lives and exists in a different form to that in which Aminadav lives and exists? . . . And into Aminadav's heart crept a terrible suspicion that perhaps it had all been a kind of mistaken bargain, and all that was, had been in the wrong direction, or without any direction at all. If Herzl frisks about like this, it means that he knows what he is breaking up about and what for, whilst Aminadav does not know a thing and nobody tells him. Or perhaps they had told him and he had not understood. All this time he had not understood. What did he have there, inside, in his breast? Aminadav listened within himself and suddenly it seemed to him that there was a void. Perhaps it had been full once, perhaps it had been full only two or three days ago; but now, it seemed empty. Absolutely nothing. (RN, 113)

The emotional ties that might once have grounded Aminadav have broken in his nationalist fervor.

The cycle of silence is repeated in each generation. Ephraim, who has now outlived his stepson and grandson, listens to the radio in the hope that the minister will mention them. Ephraim "turned around, to say to Rivka what was in his heart, but remembered that there was no one to speak to" (RN, 118). Although his daughter is in the other room, Ephraim cannot interact with her. The silence hints at madness, and increased isolation, foreshadowing his approaching death.

Tammuz subverts the construction of historical narrative through satire, humor, and mockery. Evidence of this can be seen in the way the war heroes who recount their battle experiences at the Independence Day celebrations are called Hero A, Hero B, and so on. These men remain nameless and without individual identities. They have merged into a more general collective narration of history rather than being individuals with personal experiences. This pattern is used again when Tammuz describes wealthy post-1967 Israeli society in Tel Aviv and the characters become interchangeable:

And thus on a wintry Saturday evening in the year 1968 there arrived at Uri's house seven men of stature and renown—Arik Ron, Ronni Ronnen, Nuri Yaron, Ron Oren, Oren Laron, Uri Renan, and Arnon Shmuelsohn.

This last one was the only one who had not changed his name into Hebrew, because his father had taken care of that in his will. All the others had activated their imaginations on an early rung of the national revival, and had chosen distinctive and different names, each one according to his heart's desire and according to the counsel of bookish friends and people who knew the language. (RN, 181)

Later when these characters are referred to again they no longer even merit individual identities and are called "Ron, Yaron, Laron et al. and also Shmuelsohn" (RN, 183). Tammuz's comic characterization of the characters as interchangeable if not identical depersonalizes the individuals, establishing them as a faceless crowd, an effect heightened in his representation of their indistinguishable gaggle of wives as "Tzippi, Shosh, Shulah, Silvi et al." (RN, 183). Personal relationships have disintegrated and there is no longer a meaningful connection between husbands and wives and in subsuming individual identities in the name of the collective, the state has erased the particular. Though in other frameworks suicide is a way of obliterating identity—when engaged with a discourse of national narratives—suicide actually becomes a way of asserting individuality.

In Israel, part of the nation-building process involved the Hebraization of names.[17] Ron, Yaron, Laron sound the same because their individuality is erased in this communal act of recreation, a satire that reflects the exilic Jews' attempts to re-create new identities as sabras by changing their names.

The profound symbolic meaning of name changing as an important Zionist ritual that represents the disidentification with a discredited past becomes evident when compared to name changing as part of the traditional ritual of conversion to Judaism, and (perhaps even more evocatively) to an old Jewish folk custom of changing the name of the severely sick in order to guarantee their recovery.[18]

Tammuz parodies this trend and the attempt to create a mythic national identity in order to fulfill the expectations of the collective. It is for this reason that Shmuelsohn, who is forbidden by his father to change his name, and thereby erase his past in exchange for a new, falsely imagined present, is also the character who is not destroyed by the ever-changing social trends. Shmuelsohn is identified with a real, solid past, and not only with hollow Zionist ideology and rhetoric. Therefore, his imagined identity as a sabra is not his primary identity.

Tammuz suggests that Ron, Laron, Yaron et al., in subsuming their individuality within the confines of the collective, have lost any sense of pride or identification with the collective itself; their corruption and their abandonment of the collective then follows. At the height of its power, the hegemonic Zionist narrative not only provided a meaningful structure for people's lives, it was, in turn, maintained by those lives. Ron, Laron, Yaron et al. cease to take an interest in the affairs of the state; then they stopped worrying about the threat to national security, and began to separate themselves from national institutions, such as the army. Increasingly greedy, and eventually corrupted by this greed, they no longer identify with the state. Finally, their sense of entitlement alienates them from Israel:

> Come what may, Ron, Yaron, Laron et al. and Shmuelsohn now started sending money to Switzerland, so that at least when they reach old age they would be able to rest from their toil. And so that their old age would not put their youth to shame, a lot of money would be needed in their old age. But from where is much money to be gained, if the price of securities drops or all of a sudden some steakhouse goes broke?
>
> And so it is possible to take something from the party coffer, or exert pressure on contractors and accept what are called bribes. It may not be acceptable, and also it may not be fair, for someone who just takes. But people who all their lives only gave and gave and gave to the nation, to the State and to the party,

why should they not enjoy a little bit for themselves in their old age, in Switzerland? (RN, 134)

Shmuelsohn is saved to some extent because he has not changed his name, suggesting that he has retained a connection with the past, and although he follows along with the rest of the group, at the end he stands apart eventually betraying them to the authorities. Tammuz satirizes the making and the destruction of this class of individuals who no longer feel connected to any kind of ideological framework. This is the opposite extreme to Elyakum, who is consumed by ideological movements because he cannot stand apart from them. The conclusion of the novel indicates that there is hope for the future, and for a Jewish state, but that the manipulation of Zionist ideology will ultimately destroy the state. In challenging the hypocrisy of Zionism from within Tammuz suggests that Israel has a teleological role as a Jewish, but not a Zionist, enterprise.

As we have seen, in *Requiem for Na'aman* Ephraim plays a role that is in opposition to the dominant labor ethic of working the land. He is a farmer and does not belong to the kibbutz movement. The Abramsons are affected by the First and Second World Wars, since in the first instance they have to move to Egypt and then struggle economically on their return, and in the Second World War Elyakum is a soldier. However, the world events are considered unimportant to the family: "The events of the Great War did not touch Ephraim's heart except insofar as they were connected with the Land of Israel" (RN, 43) and "Between one secret night session and the next their lives were led beside still waters, even though all around them the world was going up in flames" (RN, 45). Similarly, the Second World War appears a distant meaningless experience until the Abramson family is drawn into its web.

> Apart from two chance bombings of Tel Aviv, by Italian planes, there were no casualties of the Second World War in Palestine. Like the Abramson family during the days of their stay in Alexandria in the First World War, the Jewish population was ready and willing to wait patiently until the Gentiles would finish killing each other for the reasons known to them alone. And indeed it is possible that the war would have been pictured in this way by the

sons of the Jewish settlement, had not Hitler sought to destroy the Jews of Europe. (RN, 104)

Once Jews become targets of the war, and Haj Amin becomes Hitler's guest, the Jews of Tammuz's novel begin to take a role in world history, but again this is not a unified position, thereby suggesting the diversity of beliefs and historical experiences even of individuals in the same family. Militarization among the Jews in Palestine takes on a serious but comic dimension in *Requiem for Na'aman* with each faction supporting a different organization. The Labor-Zionist mainstream supports the British army and the Haganah (the Jewish Defense Force). The Revisionists call for extreme responses thereby supporting Jabotinsky's Irgun Tzvai Leumi, the breakaway faction that carried out reprisals against Arab attacks. The even more extreme LEHI, a breakaway group from the Irgun, is funded by those who most publicly denounce any Jewish armed response (RN, 101–4).[19] Tammuz also satirizes Arab armed response. Publicly they espouse peace, while privately they fund Najdah, the underground Arab military organization. Neither view is conveyed as a deeply held conviction for the Arabs in the novel; support for Najdah is parodied as a duty undertaken in order to fulfill the command of the religious leader the Mufti, Haj Amin-al-Husseini, to "throw [all the Jews] into the sea" while simultaneously satirizing this leader who "in the meantime had fled the country and settled in Germany" (RN, 103–4). This fragmentation of the military forces with their conflicting messages indicates the clash of national institutions. There is no single unified vision, even within the military response to Zionism, and Tammuz is again reinforcing the message that the hegemony of a single narrative view, like the hegemony of a single national institution, is a mythical construction, differing widely from the lives of individuals within Israel.

Menucha Gilboa argues that Tammuz's conspicuous antagonism to "Zionism and the Jewish authority"[20] is rooted in his Canaanite outlook. This movement advocated a common ethnic past between Jews and Arabs in Palestine, linking the two harmoniously without the need for separate and conflicting nations. Tammuz moved away from this position after an extended stay in Europe while studying at the Sorbonne, and he became suspicious of the possibilities for trust between Arabs and Jews.

After several years of living in Paris, then serving as the cultural attaché to the Israeli Embassy in London and later as a visiting writer at Oxford University, he changed his philosophical attitude toward the Jewish Diaspora experience. According to Menucha Gilboa, Tammuz began to reject the Caananite vision which understood the two thousand years of exile as a pollution of the authentic semite that the Jew had been, and now viewed Jewish Diasporic identity in new ways. For him, being Israeli came to mean incorporating the years Jews had been in exile, with the historicity of the ancient homeland.

> He saw himself as a Diaspora writer like James Joyce. . . . During his post-Canaanite period Judaism became important to culture in all fields, and in Israel he thought that everything had become strangled. Only in the Diaspora is there the possibility for internal forces to open up.[21]

In *Requiem for Na'aman*, Tammuz censures the process by which an Israeli national consciousness was created and this criticism is directed at political nationalism. Throughout the novel he presents another view of the collective — the Jewish people.

> The English also did not know this: that the Jews are a pragmatic people, and they have an important precept that they apply — a man will always try to fit his principles to reality, but if that is difficult, then he will fit the reality to his principles.
> And since the British authorities did not know any of this, their end was that they were kicked and flung out of the Land of Israel; and the story is known. (*RN*, 106)

By separating Jewishness and Israeliness, Tammuz offers an alternative nation that is not a dueling fragmented political entity but rather a people for whom survival, rather than conquest, lies at their core. Thus united, Jews are able to defeat the common enemy.

> The *Haganah* put up a placard "Let our cries be harkened unto from the abysses of quiescence!" and the British were sure that they were hearing "hollow phraseology."

They did not understand that there is a nation among the nations ready to die for its phraseology, both because it had been offended and because it lacked experience in international politics. (*RN*, 106)

Tammuz's writing cleverly undercuts the sentiment of heroism and ideology usually associated with modern nation-building processes by indicating that political decisions were not always made as a result of reasoned calculations by the ruling body, but sometimes by accident or innocent persistence. This use of irony challenges the traditional Zionist concept that the collective acts in harmony for the benefit of the individual. Lev Hakak in summarizing Natan Zach's work *Kavei Avir* suggests that Tammuz and Yehoshua (as well as Yaakov Shabtai and Amos Oz) deal "with madness, suicide, murder, alienation — in sum, with the dreadful aspects of life" because they are demonstrating the disparity between the hopes and dreams of Zionism and the reality of the state in its early years.[22]

> Zionism did not achieve the shaping of a new and healthy human being in Israel; instead, man as reflected in literature is quite ill. The strangeness, the distress and loneliness, the folly and death and alienation in contemporary Israeli prose might be explained also by the struggle between the generations, by the collapse of ideology and values, by the sobering reaction to hopes that were perhaps larger-than-life, by the lack of cultural identity on the part of the second and third generation of Israelis, and perhaps by the fact that literature, in this case, precedes reality and serves as a mirror reflecting the moods, the fears and the yearnings of a new generation.[23]

Tammuz's work is a requiem, a final prayer for the death of the Zionist dream. It communicates the disparity between the ideals and the failure to fulfill these ideals. The legacy of the second and third generation of Israelis seems unrealizable in this framework. However, this new generation also yearns to contribute to Israel, but it must forge a new path, distinct from that of the previous generation in order to achieve this.

Mar Mani and Cyclical Time

Mr. Mani, Yehoshua's most postmodern novel, deconstructs the very act of narrative. Each of the novel's five sections portrays a different moment in time, through a conversation between two individuals; however, only one side of the conversation is given. Each section is framed by an introduction explaining the situation, the relationship between the participants, and the immediate history leading up to the conversation. There is also a conclusion following each conversational section in which the omniscient narrator describes the subsequent fate of the characters. The novel is constructed in a counter-linear fashion moving backward from 1982 to at least 1776, when Yosef Mani was born to Eliyahu Mani, for whom we have no date. The first conversation begins in the late twentieth century and each subsequent section occurs at an earlier period until the final conversation, which is set in 1848, but covers a period further back in time. The theme that runs throughout the stories is the fate of the Mr. Mani that appears in that generation, and each Mani is a relation of the first Mr. Mani that speaks in the final conversation. Many of the Manis contemplate suicide; some of them attempt suicide and succeed, and some attempt suicide but are stopped or die of other means before the act of suicide can be completed.

The family in *Mr. Mani* are Sephardim who have been in Jerusalem for at least six generations, dating back to the early eighteenth century, in contrast to the Ashkenazi immigrants at the heart of the founding Zionist mythology but who only arrived in Israel from the late nineteenth century. In the novel, Zionist history is indicated by major events such as the World Zionist Congress of 1899, events during the British Mandate in Palestine, and the war in Lebanon. These situations form part of the national redemption narrative, through which Zionists declaimed the need for a Jewish home in Palestine. These events are in marked contrast to the private lives of the Sephardi Manis who, without making a public and political declaration about the need to live in Palestine, were resident in Jerusalem.

In this novel, the cycle of suicide is also linked to the past, revealed in Avraham Mani's implication in the death of his son and the impregnation of his daughter-in-law. Concerned that he will not enter *Olam Habah* (the next world), Mani considers whether to take his own life as a way to atone for his crime. His final words, "Is it self-murder, then? Yes? . . . No? . . ." (MM, 363), suggest he is unable to decide whether suicide is a fitting punishment for his acts of murder and incest. Mani returns home to his family "still preoccupied with the thought of suicide and with various possibilities of carrying it out" (MM, 365). Unable to choose, both the uncertainty and the urge to commit suicide become a legacy passed down between generations of Manis. As Alan Mintz has argued, "more than one century later, [it] is imprinted in the genetic code of the Manis."[24] Since Mani's own behavior is unresolved, successive generations are tied to this legacy of guilt and indecision that creates the unexplainable desire to commit suicide in his heirs. The personal destiny of the Manis is stronger than the national enterprise.

Throughout the novel Mr. Mani, the characters conducting the conversation in each chapter observe the Manis' suicidal behavior and see these actions as predestined. Egon, the German speaker of the second conversation, identifies this phenomenon in the death of Gavriel Mani in a cave in Crete:

The whole episode of my lost glasses was simply a pretext for him to satisfy a suddenly surfaced whim to be a prisoner or hostage, bound hand and foot, before he died. Perhaps he needed to atone for some old feeling of guilt. (MM, 107)

In the third conversation, Ivor, a British lawyer sent to handle the same, younger Mani in Mandate Palestine, observes that "looking back on it now, I can't swear that he didn't do it deliberately . . . that he didn't do everything in fact, for the sole purpose of being caught" (MM, 156). Ephraim Shapiro, in conversation four, also thinks that the need to commit suicide is predetermined: "I don't think you have realized yet that this story is not about me. It is about him, Mani" . . . "And I ask myself: if he was already determined to take his own life — if the idea was even then in him like a living seed" (MM, 239). Hagar, the female narrator of the first conversation, provides the key to understanding and identifying this overwhelming compulsion within the Mani men. She is aware that the impulse to commit suicide is linked with the past. "It was a repeat performance. Maybe, I thought, he put it on every night to rehearse his own death until it became so obvious and convincing that he could stop fighting it" (MM, 48). This predestined force is in contrast to the redemptive nature of the Zionist narrative that argued Israel was the result of work and conquest, an explanation that assumes man's dominance over his environment. This is demonstrated by Yehoshua's presentation of the Manis as figures in the shadows of Zionist history.

Although the Manis appear at several key historical junctures, their presence is usually passed over or ignored. Their involvement in these historical events is negligible. Yehoshua cleverly rewrites the convention of the historical novel by placing his characters at the heart of events, but leaving their impact as unrelated or irrelevant. When Dr. Mani attends the Zionist congress in Basel, Herzl collapses. Mani is called into the room, but he does not tend to the Zionist leader, and at the congress, he does not participate in the ideological debate. Mani is not connected to formal history. His interests are personal and he is present to try to raise money for his clinic, a very real enterprise in Palestine. He proves unable to raise funds, though he is offered the loan of a horse and carriage in Europe, perhaps a snub implying that in order to be considered a gentleman (and therefore receive funds), he ought to look like one — an incident that may also be read as racially influenced, since Dr. Mani is Sephardi and his "Eastern" status opens him to the prejudice of the "Western" Ashkenazi Zionists. The clinic is considered nonideological since it is willing to care for whoever needs medical attention, and because it wasn't proposed as a formal Zionist attempt to develop the land. This hypocrisy is highlighted in the hospital's population which includes many of the new pioneers, and in its management, since the hospital is run by Jews; both of these aspects legitimate the requests for funding from the Zionist establishment. Yet its grassroots endeavor which undermines the possibility of European patronage emphasizes the disconnection between the local needs, and the Zionists' visions. It is possible to suggest that the exclusion of the Manis from the Zionist narrative represents the portrayal of the Oriental Jew in the dominant Ashkenazi national narrative, which has failed to recognize the contribution made by the Sephardi Jews in building Israel. Yehoshua is documenting the relations between the recorded history and an alternative *truer* history. More importantly, he is reminding Ashkenazi society not to allow the Sephardi experience to be written out of the national narrative. As with this conversation, each dialogue is framed by a major Zionist event, thereby highlighting the normative presentation of the Zionist narrative, which is then contrasted with the Manis who remain divorced from this experience, and do not contribute directly to it, while simultaneously operating in its shadow. The suicide rejects national ideology and is linked to the proposition that there are alternative ways of reading history.

For Hagar the speaker in the first chapter of the book, but the final speaker in historical terms, who comes to represent the attempt to synthesize and understand history, Mani's predestined suicidal attempts become a tragicomic affair, since the actions are routine and unprovoked and therefore appear ridiculous.

> I walked down the hallway to the back of the apartment, to this little bathroom off the kitchen, because I thought that if everything was happening again, he was probably in there washing himself as part of his suicide exercises . . . There on the terrace . . . was my suicidal Mr. Mani. (MM, 48)

As with Bella-Yaffa in *Requiem for Na'aman*, by connecting the different generations in *Mr. Mani*, Hagar forms a link between the first and the last chapters of the novel. Once Hagar is able to see the situation as part of a greater family narrative, she can recognize the role of destiny, and it is then that she is able to change the fate of the Mani dynasty and prevent further suicides through the birth of her child. Naming plays an important role in both novels, signifying the identification and therefore control of national narratives. Just as Bella-Yaffa links two generations of Abramsons, in *Mr. Mani* several names are repeated across generations — there are three Yosef Manis and two Efraim Manis. Hagar, who is pregnant by the youngest Mani, names her son Roni after her own father. In doing this she figuratively changes the cycle that linked and predestined Manis to follow one another, thereby defying previous patterns. Hagar represents the capacity of the individual to understand that events are part of a much larger framework while simultaneously recognizing that the individual can never really know more than personal experience. National narratives seek to explain the larger framework while ignoring the contribution of individuals to the nation, an idea that both of these novels reject through the image of suicide.

Yehoshua's Hagar and Tammuz's Bella-Yaffa are concerned with investigating the past, and discovering the family history, even though they have only a vague notion of what actually happened. This suggests the disparity between recorded history used in a national narrative, which is accurate, clearly understood, and clearly articulated, and the narratives that are excluded from this canon, becoming vague and unclear. Hagar, who lost her father at an early age, spent a great deal of time with her grandmother "from whom she liked to coax stories of her father's childhood" (MM, 5). She is also aware that Judge Mani was born on Crete, lost his father and was raised by his mother. She makes the connection with the gravestones and she seems to know more about Mani than does his own son. She finds miscellaneous sets of spectacles in the grandmother's room and understands that these are links with the past. But she does not have the details and is aware that even the Manis cannot explain these things to her, evident when Mr. Mani rummages through the drawers of the desk in Efi's apartment and turns to Hagar asking if she thinks they are Efi's, "because he didn't know whose they were" (MM, 30–31).

Only the reader is aware of the intricate details of the story (MM, 99). The spectacles were gathered on Crete by Efraim Mani, who had brought them to Egon the German soldier in exchange for his father's life. None of these spectacles were suitable and so they had been left in possession of the Manis and eventually found their way to this drawer. By amassing information about the past, Hagar functions as a family historian. Her concern with personal records that have no connection to the nation highlights the gap between individual lives and the appropriation of these lives for the purposes of national narratives.

The women at the center of these two novels, Hagar and Bella-Yaffa, symbolize the rupture in the masculine hegemonic tradition, and in their respective ways reject the national project. Like Bella-Yaffa, Hagar rejects the constraints of national institutions, though raised on a kibbutz. Even though she is brought up and protected by the national enterprise, her university application had to be agreed by the kibbutz and the Ministry of Defense, and she noticeably rejects her mother's advice to wait a year; her behavior signals a conflict between the nation with its attendant ideology of collectivity, and Hagar's personal desires. As we learn, her parents, who were models of the nationalist Zionist effort, met while being active in a socialist youth movement. They moved to the kibbutz and Roni, Hagar's father, died in the army during the 1967 war, the war that is seen symbolically as the battle that unified Israel and demonstrated the absolute strength and victory of the Jewish state. Despite this strongly ideological Zionist background, Hagar's contact with the Mani family encourages her to reject the collective and to identify with individualism. When Hagar decides to go to visit her mother on the kibbutz, she does not think of her trip as "coming to the kibbutz tonight, Mother. I thought of it as coming home. To you. To tell you about what happened in Jerusalem" (MM, 11). Later she refuses to go to the formal Sabbath meal in the dining hall. Hagar abandons the kibbutz and its values, as well as the national enterprise that built ideologically motivated communities. Her actions are also a denunciation of institutionalized religion, by refusing to attend the kibbutz ritual meal, while she has found just being in Jerusalem a religious experience. Hagar accuses her mother of turning psychology "into a religion" (MM, 20), certainly for Hagar a false religion; another example of an ideology that has been misused and which she therefore legitimately rejects.

While waiting for the bus to Tel Aviv, Hagar feels an inexplicable desire to visit her mother in Beersheba. She rationalizes the action, since she believes it was triggered when she vaguely recognized someone from the kibbutz. It becomes clear in the narrative that the person she sees, unbeknownst to her, may already have been related to the story of the Manis through his grandfather Ivor. This lawyer, who appears in chapter 3, defended in private the Mani he was meant to prosecute in public. These coincidences of fate reflect an overriding narrative that can be called destiny. Hagar is meant to take each of the actions that she does because she belongs to a greater family narrative, that of the Mani family. These twists of fortune work mysteriously throughout the novels, suggesting a nonrational interpretation of history.

This strange attraction to places throughout Mr. Mani further indicates the role of providence and luck that runs through the story. By offering a mystical or serendipitous account of history, Yehoshua confronts the linear connection drawn in national narratives between people and land, a link which he suggests may simply be coincidental. As I showed in chapter 1, the names of sites that appeared in the biblical story of Samson such as Gaza are conspicuously linked with the importance of those same sites in contemporary Israel, thereby validating modern experience by linking it to a Jewish past. Curiously, the Manis know details about places that they have never been to before. The sudden warmth characters feel toward Avraham's Vineyard, and the attraction Gavriel Mani feels to the Hebron Road, cannot be explained by the characters' own encounters. Judge Gavriel Mani goes by way of the Hebron Road when he visits the kibbutz in Beersheba where his grandson lives with Hagar and her mother. On one occasion, there is an attempt to sell him a horse at a petrol station; however, the road is dangerous and he realizes that it is wiser not to come that way "even though he felt drawn to that route" (MM, 73). The reader learns that his grandfather, while working as an interpreter for the army, had passed through with a Scottish colonel who was looking for the perfect racing horse and journeyed between Hebron and Beersheba, trading horses. His father/grandfather had also used that route when he traveled that way with a party of Jews upon his arrival in the Land of Israel "so they remained there in that no-man's land, south of Hebron on the way to Beersheba" (MM, 179). Judge Mani is subconsciously linked with the past, demonstrating this pattern of cycles. Although the reader is aware of these coincidences, the characters are not, and no meaning is ascribed to these linked events for them. This differs from national history in which the link between places is consciously recorded to create national meaning, supporting the connection that is fashioned between the biblical landscape and the modern nation-state.

Silence is represented as a punishment for sin in *Mr. Mani*, part of the fragmentation between family narratives, because generations are unable to communicate — compared to national history which is organized and passed on. It is only the last conversation, the first one chronologically, in which a Mani speaks. The punishment Avraham Mani seems to receive for being at least complicit if not directly responsible for his son's murder is the loss of the right for his family to communicate. He is condemned to silence. The story is narrated by others so that even the Manis' own identity is no longer under their control, but is subject to the impression of others:

> They literally exist as creatures in a discourse not their own. This sense of being owned by the speech of others, or at least being dependent upon others for their representation, nicely conveys the Manis' failure to make an impact on the world or even to propagate themselves.[25]

The Manis' inability to speak about their own experiences demonstrates the breakdown in communication that is prevalent throughout the novel. Each conversation includes only one voice, just as the story of the Manis is constructed and represented by a figure outside the narrative, so the conversations are also a limited view of reality, as we can only assume or imagine the gaps in the communications. These conversational monologues represent the breakdown of interaction. In the first chapter Hagar's phone message does not reach her mother, the kibbutz member who had campaigned against private telephones. In the fourth conversation there are problems with sending letters and telegrams. The climax is reached when a telegram sent from Jerusalem, which should have read "We are well. Will start home after Yom Kippur," arrives in Poland as just "We are happy," creating a serious miscommunication and engendering panic for Ephraim Shapiro's parents (*MM*, 266–67). In conversation five, the mails are highly irregular and Avraham Mani's messages are also delayed, or become confusing for his correspondents. "Although he had expected to be back within a few months, he remained there for over a year, during which nearly all contact with him was lost," and "the infrequent greetings or bits of news that arrived from Avraham Mani were vaguely worded and confused" (*MM*, 296–97). The reliability of sources in constructing national narratives is brought into question through these communication issues. Moreover, the absence of truth creates tension in the intergenerational relationships, which implies a disruption in the national legacy as it is passed between generations.

In *Mr. Mani*, this silence in letters and in speech comes to signal the collapse of human relations. As the characters become increasingly isolated, they are drawn toward death. In the second conversation, Andrea, Egon's grandmother, "lost the power of speech" when Egon tore up the order she had organized for him, and she resolved not to say another word to her grandson until she had reconsidered the matter, and she died before she had the opportunity to do so. Although they had made up by the morning of her flight home, this silence had become a controlling, unbreakable force, "although she was willing by now to talk to him, she could not think of a way to break her silence." In the final chapter, Rabbi Haddaya has lost the power of speech through a stroke. "He now had to be constantly cared for by his wife, who serves as the link between him and an outside world that still looked to him for answers that it could no longer understand" (*MM*, 297).

> "Now that the two of us are alone, I would be most grateful if Your Grace would kindly whisper a word to me. I am all silent anticipation. What can be the meaning of this great silence of yours?" Is it in truth silence, then? Is señor's muteness decreed? (*MM*, 345)

In *Mr. Mani*, Egon makes his grandmother take a physical tour through history when he takes her on a walk along a hill on the island of Crete to point out where events occurred to him (*MM*, 91–92). He cannot explain his story without physical interaction with the past; but the most he can achieve is stops at observation points that he has laid out for his grandmother, paralleling the construction of the novel that presents single viewpoints, snapshots in time, with only one character narrating an event. It is paradoxical that the reader, who is not walking through Crete with Egon, is able to piece together his narrative, and echoes the ways in which narrative is consciously created through the piecing together of moments in time

Another postmodern literary tool that makes us conscious of the construction of the novel, and by extension the framing of historical events for nationalist ends, is Hagar's sense of being watched. "I wasn't there just by myself but . . . how can I put it . . . as if someone had put me on the opening page of a book. . . . A book. Some novel or story, or even a movie, for that matter" (*MM*, 22). Since she is the figure who appears at the start of the novel, the reader is reminded that history is shaped and controlled. This representation of Hagar in the novel is similar to Egon's deliberation on a fate that led him to jail. "And all at once I felt a peace, because I knew that something bigger and more important than that beastly adjutant, bigger and more important than Thomas Stanzler's dying hand, had landed me in jail" (*MM*, 115). Is it cosmic forces that Egon feels and the hand of destiny, or the character's interaction with the writer, in a self-conscious awareness of the construction of the novel? Each of these methods of literary construction serves to make the reader aware of the nature of narrative and asks the reader to question the composition of stories. Yehoshua is reminding the reader that national narratives are a process of selection and exclusion.

In *Mr. Mani* and *Requiem for Na'aman* the crucial historical events, for both national and world history, appear alongside the lives of the individual characters in the novels. Tammuz's novel, published more than a decade before that of Yehoshua, was innovative for its time. The end of Labor dominance following the 1977 elections offered the first occasion that forced national institutions to confront publicly the alternative voices that had helped create Israel, but had been silenced by the political power of Labor Zionism. Tammuz's work, though radical in its day, was responding to the still barely questioned hegemony of the national narrative. By the appearance of Yehoshua's novel, critical post-Zionist scholarship had challenged many of the recognized nationalistic conventions. Academics and intellectuals had already accepted that these myths were being reconsidered, even if they did not agree with many of these challenges; however, Yehoshua's literary work sought to explore new frontiers of ideology. His work is even more dramatic than that of Tammuz, though it is less satirical.

Yehoshua's characters are more extreme in their opposition to Zionism than those of Tammuz's work. Manis who do participate in history are "grandiose, ineffectual and obsessed in ways that work to undercut the legitimacy of their visionary politics."[26] The second Yosef Mani tries to claim all Arabs are Jews who have simply lost their way. His namesake, the third Yosef Mani, in a similar way, tries to make Arabs politically aware and encourages them to rise up with a nationalist movement as a response to the Balfour Declaration. In both these situations, the Manis have chosen the opposite side of history, supporting a one-state solution and denying the legitimacy of the Balfour Declaration. Instead of supporting Zionism, these Manis have taken the side of the Palestinian Arab population. Generally, however, the Manis live outside history, not taking part in the major formative events in the Zionist master narrative, and are almost unaware of the historical actions taking place around them.

> On the one hand, Sephardim in this novel are portrayed as cosmopolitans whose worldliness has allowed them to remain free of the ravages of ideology and to glimpse options not seen by

others at crucial turning points of history. Yet, on the other hand, they are prevented from making an impact on history — and their very survival is put in jeopardy — because of their abandonment to obsessional notions and obsessional desires. . . . Yehoshua is mixing up the basic stuff of modern human nature and refusing on principle to underscore the presence of some grand design, although many suggestive, and sometimes contradictory, patterns seem to propose themselves readily and without stint.[27]

The Manis' marginalization can be seen, as Gershon Shaked argues, as a means for confronting the constructed narrative of history and thereby dispelling myths as a way of performing "resistance to the ideological assumptions of Zionism."[28] Though *Mr. Mani* charts key events in Zionist history, as Leon Yudkin observes: "The Manis are not, it seems, in the forefront of history, fixing its contours, but are always there or thereabouts, in accompaniment."[29] The story of the Manis, like their suicide, places them in opposition to the national narrative. Throughout *Mr. Mani* Yehoshua is reminding the reader not to accept a single perception of reality, and his literary structures disrupt any inclination to do so. By maintaining a single perspective in each conversation, Yehoshua reminds the reader that he is provided with an enforced or controlled view of reality.

As we have seen, family sagas provide a forum for the presentation of intergenerational conflict, thereby conveying the challenge to history by each successive generation in society, through the symbolism of the text. This is evident in the clash between generations in *Requiem for Na'aman*. The Manis try to rewrite their history in *Mr. Mani* and yet are unable to escape the destiny of their family. Each dialogue is conducted between a younger and an older person, highlighting the intergenerational transmission of history. The conversations are between Hagar and her mother, Egon and his grandmother, Ivor and his senior officer, Ephraim Shapiro and his father and the conversation we do not witness between Linka Shapiro and her mother, and finally the conversation between Avraham Mani and his rabbi, an older man who has played the role of father to him.[30] In each conversation it is the younger person who speaks, representing the future and more abstractly symbolizing the role that each generation has in re-creating or re-presenting the past. Yehoshua is indicating that the process of rewriting narrative is a way of forging a new future, rather than solely accepting the construction of the national past by the previous generation. Though Tammuz and Yehoshua are questioning the construction of narrative, they offer hope that the future will provide a new voice, and a different identity that takes competing narratives into account.

In the novels, the families have each been cursed with the need to commit suicide. This can be overcome through personal relations and the recognition that there is no single narrative viewpoint. When this family history is read alongside Zionist history the texts critique ideology, highlighting repeated mistakes by successive generations in the process of creating the state. Even if this situation is due to the conditioning of a collective consciousness, rather than an active choice on the part of the participants, the authors call out to the naïveté and blind commitment of Zionists who frame the nation's narratives, and disrupt these traditions through the image of suicide.

Hilu and the Absent Palestinian

By contrast with the two previous works, Alon Hilu's novel *The House of Rajani* appeared at a time of greater openness about the construction of Zionist history within a nationalist framework. Though there has been increasing acceptance for the plurality of Jewish narrative experiences of the creation of the Israeli nation, he addresses a taboo in exploring the Palestinian historical narrative, and looking back to the very earliest pioneering history and a Jewish past. The novel was deemed anti-Zionist by many critics for its portrayal of a Zionist hero as a dubious, corrupt, and vile womanizer, who seduces the mistress of the Rajani estate in order to possess her family's land, as well as for its representation of an Arab connection to the land that suggests a delegitimization of Zionist interests. "The novel . . . has been lavishly praised and condemned in equal measure. Israeli president Shimon Peres described it as 'an extraordinary book' while critics have condemned it as unpatriotic."[31] But as Linda Grant explains in her review of the book in the *Guardian*, its success lies in precisely this search for the nation's roots.

The novel's enormous popularity in Israel attests to a hunger to explore the truth of the mythologized past of Zionist narrative: to know who was there before and how they came to be expelled, long before wars or terrorism.[32]

Tammuz had attempted to find a common ground between Arab and Jew in his novel, which works best in Bella-Yaffa's summer home through her connection with the servant woman and the gardener. Yehoshua goes further in presenting Ivor's narration of Mani's boundary crossing both literally in his work as a spy and figuratively in his increasing adoption of Arab dress and traits. Mani's attempt to create equality between Arab and Jewish notions of nationhood by attempting to inspire an Arab nationalist movement is a comic failure.

Hilu in many ways builds on these earlier novels, showcasing the Arab presence in the novel with a greater degree of equality than his predecessors. Rising above the orientalist discourse of Tammuz, and the instability of Arab representation in Yehoshua, Hilu attempts to create a Palestinian voice in the narrative. In the process he demonstrates a form of early Zionist colonialism, which in many reviews of the novel has led to its public condemnation. The affair between Afifa Rajani and the Russian immigrant Luminsky is an act of miscegenation which may be considered patriarchal and colonialist. But the relationship between Luminsky and Salah, Afifa's son, is more complicated and suggests a real affection through which Jews and Arabs may come together. At the same time however, there is also a reenactment of the Hamlet story, and Luminsky serves as the patriarchal, but dangerous Claudius to the emotionally vulnerable Hamlet. The shared tenderness between Luminsky and Salah complicates both the Hamlet narrative, and the Israeli narrative with its clear "them/us" division. Luminsky's last encounter with the boy Salah is described with sadness and love:

> "Looking upon him I was saddened, for I recalled our first meeting. How great was the distance we have come from then until today! I thought of how he had said to me, in a voice as thin and quiet as a schoolgirl's, 'You are a Jew,' and how his cheeks reddened like a virgin's, and in my mind's eye I leafed through the pages of our shared history like a man reading a book in the

evening, and with each page I turned his character changes, from page to page and chapter to chapter, and a deep sadness filled my chest for this deterioration of relations between us, for the love this boy had for me that was replaced by a taste for vengeance, and for the sweet secrets that became schemes and intrigues." (HR,186)

Salah's response to the same meeting:

The good angel was looking at me, his expression one of sadness and disappointment for all the terrible things I have done to him, and pictures formed in my mind — how he fluttered his wings at me and came to me in my room, how he sat with me on the sandstone cliffs by the sea while our happy future spread out before us from one end of the horizon to the other, how I made a bitter error in accusing him of deceit and terrible acts. (HR, 188)

Both the man and the boy see their final harmony as a son coming to his father for love and protection — thus there is a demonstration that a possibility remains of finding agreed-upon moments in this hostile process of narrativization. The novel's conclusion expands this idea in its description of Luminsky's future which involves the conflicting work of building Palestine for Jews, and attempting to reconcile Jewish and Arab interests.

In Hilu's novel, complicating the Hamlet intertext, it is the Arab child Salah who commits suicide. It is one of the very few suicides by Arab characters (outside the framework of suicide bombings) that exists in Hebrew prose, if not the only example. The book, which was first published in Hebrew with the title *Ahuzat Dajani* (*The House of Dajani*) won the Sapir prize in 2009, and then as part of a series of scandals that plagued the novel's reception, the prize was withdrawn. Following a court case, the author was awarded half the prize money, but not the title; nor was any other novel awarded the prize that year. In a second court case, the family of the little known Haim Margaliot Kalvarisky, a real-life Zionist pioneer of the 1890s, who served as an inspirational figure for the speculator protagonist, accused the author of misrepresenting the Kalvarisky family history and so the book's publication in English saw a change to the title (from Dajani to Rajani) to the prospector's name (from Kalvarisky to Isaac Luminsky) and an additional authorial note at the book's close, which also appears in later Hebrew editions of the book.

The specter of suicide lingers over the entire novel, linked to the boy Salah's madness, a trope we have seen previously in *Mr. Mani* and *Requiem for Na'aman*. Like the first Bella-Yaffa, we are never sure of the boy's relationship to reality and the Hamlet intertext, with the father haunting his son prefiguring the expectation of tragedy:

> "From the day I spoke to my father in his grave, from the day I pricked myself with the blade, from the day I sensed his eyes upon me, observing all my good deeds and bad, I have been hearing dead Father's voice echoing in my head, and he commands me to do things that would cause any heedful ear to ring upon hearing, as in calling me to murder the good angel and then drown Mother and then draw a rope around my own neck and hang myself from it in my room, and I beseech him to leave me in peace, and he commands me again, and in fact I already comprehend that this is not Father but that swindling genie or some other malevolent spirit or thought that contains no truth or life, but this voice is stubborn and evil and doubts sprout on the bedrock of my soul, for perhaps Amina and all my detractors were right and I am in the grip of madness, and I gaze from a gaping hole in the wall to the heavens and lo, the trees have ganged together in groups of two and three and the sky has switched places with the earth and the birds caw viciously, and one raps at my window and says, Go out, Salah! Revenge! . . . but their cackling gibberish disturbs my peace of mind, and I shut the window and wrap a thick blanket around my head and press it to my nose and into my nostrils, and the sweet absence of warm air suffocates my breath until my soul flutters, but the birds, the birds chatter still in their cacophonous chuckle, saying, Salah has lost his mind, Salah is taking his own life, Salah is hanging from a rope and his throat is suffocating and his soul is making its final gasps before disappearing into the dark thickness of death." (HR, 183)

From the beginning of the novel we expect Salah's suicidal death. At first the mystical and fantastical elements of the book frame that death as a passive dissolution in which he is sucked into darkness by magical genies; couched in a complicated relationship between mystical spirits in the wooded landscape or in the silent pools of water. Later this suicide is linked to self-destruction caused by the presence of the "Dark Angel" Luminsky, who attempts to buy the family estate near Jaffa and dupe the family out of their claim to ownership. Salah's madness, and his recurring belief in his own destruction, set the audience in a state of tension awaiting either his mental recovery, or his likely end. His suicide completes the bizarre tragic twist, when wearing his mother's wedding dress and shoes, he walks to the wadi, drowns himself, and is found floating down the river like Ophelia.

The wild ramblings and crazed monologues which bear grains of prophetic truth but remain inaccessible to others because of their lack of clarity (and believability) connect content and form in the text. This particularly manifests in the instability of the novel's narration. Told through the diary extracts of Isaac Luminsky, Salah's musings, and a series of fantastical and esoteric literary texts written by Salah, the narrative voice swiftly loses credibility. Though Salah's visions describe a cast of major Zionist figures including Theodor Herzl, Golda Meir, and Moshe Dayan, and a description of the Azrieli skyscrapers in an overly theatrical expression of the land's destruction, at other times his interactions with spirits and water genies, and his narration of his mother's behavior suggest a mental instability which challenges his role as prophet. Though Luminsky's diary, written in rational and clear language, at first seduces the reader with an illusion of authenticity suggesting Salah's untrustworthiness, we rapidly see Luminsky's self-censorship by comparison with Salah's entries. Soon we realize that the prospector's own version of the truth is confused by his perceptions and position in Palestine, and by his ideological agenda, while Salah's renditions cannot be relied upon because of his confusion between reality and fantasy. This process of narrative construction is further destabilized in the book's frame. The novel's preface sets up the book as "based on the letters and diaries of Isaac Luminsky, agronomist and member of the First Aliya" and presents the text as "undated and unsigned pages in Arabic [that] were found appended to the black-bound diary that proved to be journal entries and short stories written at the same time as Luminsky's (1895–96) by a young man named Salah, scion of the celebrated Rajani family of

Jaffa." This preface acknowledges the work of a publisher, whose translation decisions are the only editorial impact on the text. Yet the book concludes with an "Author's Note" in the English translation that comes after an epilogue describing the final fate of the characters beyond the frame of the diary/journal entries in which the author, in his own voice, explains:

> I wish to emphasize that in contrast to the way it was expressed in the Preface, and also in contrast to the impression that readers may have formed, *The House of Rajani* is absolutely a work of fiction and is not based on any so-called "diaries."
>
> *The House of Rajani* is in no way or form a historical document. It is a work of fiction, and this is how I would ask my readers to treat it.

The addition of the author's name, location (Tel Aviv), and date (2010) offers legitimacy to this final claim that further plays on the way that each diary entry is presented with a date and a location. The postmodern elements and literary awareness that featured in Hagar's conversation in *Mr. Mani* are also evident in Hilu's novel:

> A feeling both puzzling and terrifying at once rose up inside me that the two of us, the good angel and I, I and the good angel, are nothing but fictional characters trapped inside a dreadful book written over any pages, and we change from page to page, from chapter to chapter, as the eyes of others — readers — watch us at all times, and hands turn the pages of our story then lay us down by the bed and talk about us, and what do they think of us? Do they bear us a grudge? Are they angry with us? Do they judge our characters, and are they as unforgiving as we of ourselves? (HR, 188)

This text provides a multilayered postmodernist critique of the process by which historical narrative is constructed, arguing convincingly that there is no empirical and external truth that may be arrived at through careful reading of the past and that all renditions of the past are a story shaped by the author. The entangled claims that plague both Israeli and Palestinian renditions of history are discredited through the novel's undermining of the very act of creating conceptions of the past.

In this text form and content work together to destabilize the process of narrativity. While the speculator is depicted as increasingly deceitful and despicable, stealing the Rajani/Dajani estate, the Arab owners and tenant farmers remain passive. Only Salah, who wishes to stop the "Dark Angel's" advancement, attempts to create an alternative future, and he is depicted as mad. Despite critical reviews of the novel that saw it as anti-Zionist by reaching back to the earliest national narratives and challenging them and their exclusion of the Palestinian voice, this novel functions as more than simply a critique of Zionist history's selection and molding of past events to serve as a motivating force. It also challenges a Palestinian narrative by representing the *effendi* Rajani/Dajani's self-indulgence and absence. His mismanagement of the estate, the superstitious folk ways of the passive tenant farmers who fail to direct their own fate and are eventually evicted from the estate, the ease with which Afifa Rajani is duped, and in Salah's own madness and suicide, Hilu demonstrates the breakdown of any viable Palestinian legacy. Finally the house and land are left barren, uncared for and abandoned.

As with the other novels, history weaves in and out of this personal and fantastical saga, and the drunken destitute poet, struggling with his inspiring poem that would motivate an entire nation, is revealed to be Naftali Hertz Imber, who is credited with writing the words for the national anthem, and whose line "Our hope is not vanished" — turns out to be supplied by Salah in his last letter to Luminsky."[33] The topographic landscape of the estate is broken down through Salah's visions to represent identifiable landmarks in Tel Aviv, while the Muslim cemetery in which his father is buried and in which he attempts to kill Luminsky in a homoerotic and confused battle of wills is depicted as the site of a public park and notorious gay pickup site. Unlike the satire of Tammuz, and the critique of Yehoshua, Hilu never quite avoids the polemical and didactic. Though he deploys spectacular linguistic pyrotechnics re-creating a lost period of Hebrew (this fictional Hebrew is a nuance lost in English translation), he otherwise lacks the prose mastery of the other two more seasoned writers. Still, the book's phenomenal success with sales demonstrates a hunger within Israeli society to move beyond the structured narrative past that has dominated the state since before its establishment.

Conclusion

The characters' suicides in these three novels are the literary trope used to magnify the personal nature of the individual and focus the reader's attention on the disparity between recorded history, which has a national purpose manifested through a linear historical chronicle, and the personal world, which has a fragmented narrative structure. In considering these works, we can see the ways in which "the novel represents a theatre of Zionist struggle and enactment within a family context."[34] The novels are concerned with cycles, those of family and of history, and explore personal memory and family destiny, in contrast to the linear narrative of the collective identity and memory of Zionist history.

The construction of the novels provides a source of protest against the meta-narrative of Israel's history. By relating family stories against a background of national history, the authors demonstrate the conflict between personal and national destiny. The act of storytelling and other expressions of personal communication such as the conversational monologues in Mr. Mani coupled with the historical forewords and afterwords, or the narrative frame in The House of Rajani present the nature of individual identity, but also serve to remind the audience that history is constructed through a consciously organized process. The contrast between public speech-making and private silences in the novels also reflects this national/personal division by representing the difference between publicly espoused ideology and privately held beliefs. The writers show that as the characters come to understand themselves and forge a link with their personal destiny, they can exist within a reformulated version of the Zionist state. Although the novels do not come to accept the dominant Ashkenazi Labor Zionism that they previously rejected, they are able to offer new pluralistic readings for the Jewish presence and the creation of the state, in Israel.

The twin elements of destiny and coincidence that run through the novels highlight the vulnerability of human interactions, showing the difference between constructed national history, which has an obvious and explained unifying narrative, and the fragmented story of a family. The lack of personal communication demonstrates the breakdown of human relations, and in turn, personal identity; but the need to be recognized and distinguished from the collective remains the core motivation of the individual lives in these novels. As these authors show, personal stories contrast with national historical narratives, which ignore individual involvement but provide a meta-framework, justifying the lives and contributions to the collective, even if that collective is itself a fantastical fabrication. By committing suicide, the characters are able to escape their obligations as part of the community and claim an independent, personal, family identity.

The principles of agricultural work and more broadly the rural landscape within these texts envisage the new Jew's connection to the ancestral homeland.

> The pioneer's visual and verbal paean to the Israeli landscape — both the natural landscape and the landscape he domesticated — was also a way of saying that he had severed ties with the Diaspora's landscape and thus with its culture and had put down roots in his new homeland.[35]

Knowledge of the land linked a Jewish history of farming, which had been almost entirely unknown outside the Talmud during the Middle Ages, with the Zionist endeavors to develop and repopulate the untamed geography. The pioneering collectives, farms, kibbutzim, and moshavim not only taught "the love of nature"[36] drawing on European romantic ideals and their manifestation in the writings of A. D. Gordon, they also became incubators for social construction. Camaraderie was sacrosanct within the mainly socialist ideology that dominated these commercial enterprises which meant that these projects also created a network of nepotism known as *protekzia*, the Israeli model of an *old boys'* network, expanding the importance of these institutions in the nation-building enterprise. As a result of writers and poets' odes to the landscape and the very real political capital that the agricultural projects possessed, kibbutzim and moshavim were the paradigmatic models of building the land. However, despite this rhetoric, many new immigrants were more likely to find themselves in cities than in the countryside, and building the first Jewish city in two thousand years would prove as momentous and ideologically significant as any agricultural movement.

CHAPTER 4

Tel Aviv Necropolis

This city doesn't deserve to exist. This is just a
misunderstanding.

—YAAKOV SHABTAI, *Past Continuous*

The founding and growth of Tel Aviv reverberated with the ideology of
Jewish national revival and the quest to build a modern Jewish city different than both the Jewish shtetl in Eastern Europe and the cities of the
Levant. Established in 1909 as a suburb of Jaffa, Tel Aviv was cast as the
first Hebrew city in two thousand years. It was named after the German
Zionist novel *Altneuland* (1902), written by Theodor Herzl, founder of
the World Zionist Organization (1897). Set in a utopian Jewish city, this
bestselling novel was translated into Hebrew by Nahum Sokolov, who
took its title "Tel Aviv" (Hill of Spring) from the book of Ezekiel (3:15).
The significance of naming the city Tel Aviv, like naming the first school
the Herzliya Hebrew Gymnasium, reflected the interconnected relationship between the biblical past, Zionism's political roots, and reality in
the Land of Israel. Paralleling other creation narratives of the Zionist enterprise, Tel Aviv's conceptual focus was embodied in the city's motto "I
will build you and you will be rebuilt," taken from Jeremiah (31:4). The
biblical source of this expression represented the connection between the
exilic past and the national present, as did the city's municipal symbols —
the beacon and the gate — which denoted a symbolic light to the Diaspora

and demonstrated Tel Aviv's position as the doorway to Israel. "In Tel Aviv, the desire for authoritative roots coincided with the somewhat contradictory desire to emphasize the city's newness, modernity, and epistemological distance from the Diaspora."[1] Offering a modern urban dream to complement traditional agricultural ambitions, by accepting an ideology in which the citizens were being built with the city, they were able to reject the negative aspects of their past, accept those facets which reinforced the ideology, and embrace a role as urban pioneers in the new collective.[2]

Although criticism of Tel Aviv, mainly from the Labor-Zionist establishment (which preferred an agricultural ideal), existed from the very beginning of the city's construction, hostile descriptions of the urban landscape were rarer in fiction and poetry. It was not until the 1970s — late by comparison with portrayals of "the city" in Europe — that writers adopted negative urban topoi, widespread in European and American literature, to depict Tel Aviv; imagery representing the urban environment as a place of alienation, decay, disillusionment, and failure, with its attendant sexual, financial, and moral corruption. Finally the city is portrayed as a monster, and a graveyard. Its lone flâneur protagonist is isolated and alone. The city is depicted frequently with dark, forbidding streets, and a seedy underworld dense with corruption and prostitution through which the antihero wanders in horror.[3]

Given the symbolic Zionist ideological construction of the city and the powerful rhetoric in its foundational phase, the adoption of negative imagery and the inversion and rejection of the city's particular signifiers (such as the insinuation that the first Hebrew city is no more than an Arab backwater or a European ghetto) offered Hebrew authors the opportunity to criticize the narrative, and even suggest Tel Aviv had failed. The city becomes a hostile place that embodies the futility of Labor Zionism with its agenda of inclusiveness and communal involvement. The white architecture that had once celebrated the city's innovations and aspirations now stands as a monument to the city's past. The buildings, serving as tombstones, enhance impressions of the city as a necropolis. One hundred years after the first lots were cast Tel Aviv has come to signify, in a modernist tradition of the city, a place of alienation. "The Hebrew City" has become indistinguishable from other metropolises and is represented as a place of corruption, decadence, decay, and death. In this chapter, I consider four literary works that share the centrality of Tel Aviv in the narrative and the suicide of one or more protagonists in the novel: Yaakov Shabtai, *Past Continuous* (1977), *Requiem for Na'aman* (1978), Yehudit Katzir, *Closing the Sea* (1990), and Etgar Keret, *Ha-Kaitanah shel Kneller* [literally, *Kneller's Summer Camp*, 1998; published in English as *Kneller's Happy Campers*, 2009].

Tel Aviv, like the depictions of other modern cities in literature, is "a projection screen for meanings" even when those meanings are "in no way identical to the actual city."[4] Literature representing the city adopts imagery and metaphors that exemplify these projections even while the texts may simultaneously challenge, attack, or even destroy these same meanings. Hannah Wirth-Nesher has suggested that different cities are represented through mediated perspectives. Joyce's Dublin is mediated through language, while Bashevis Singer's Warsaw is mediated through history.[5] Each city's "recognized cultural meanings" as Barbara Mann has termed this conceptual framework, are therefore relative, dependent on associations specific to that locale. For Tel Aviv it was ideology and the historical framework that imbued its creation with political significance.[6] In becoming a city that no longer builds its inhabitants, but instead is now a place of death, the deconstruction of Tel Aviv's myths serves as a literary device to critique its origins. The act of suicide in this context serves as a metaphor for the ideological failures of the founding generations.

Tel Aviv: The First Hebrew City

> Tel Aviv did not just happen to appear. It was imagined and realized through conscious decisions and actions undertaken with specific purposes.
>
> — TROEN, *Imagining Zion*

The name Tel Aviv not only reflected the city's ideological roots, it also reflected the Jewish renaissance taking place in Palestine. "Tel" is an archaeological mound that reveals layers of civilization, while "Spring" was seen as fitting with its reference to the renewal of Jewish life in Palestine; the decision to name the city after Herzl's novel in 1910 demonstrated the commitment to Zionism that the urban pioneers felt. "In choosing this name the founders of Tel Aviv expressed their hope that it would become an ideal, modern city in the ancient homeland" . . .

"Their moral, aesthetic, and political ideas were expressed in the innovative physical design with which they attempted to shape that city."[7] The first landmarks were the water tower, signifying new life (both a practical and symbolic marker) and the Herzeliya Gymnasium whose namesake connected the educational and ideological leanings of the new community with the Zionist movement. Thus from its very inception, land, ideology and the literary imagination were intimately interconnected.[8]

"As the 'first Hebrew city,' Tel Aviv was portrayed by writers, painters, photographers, and city planners as new, clean, and modern — everything the crowded neighborhoods of Jaffa were not — a city sprung from the sands."[9] This depiction is evident in the novel *Requiem for Na'aman* discussed in the previous chapter. The novel traces the lives of this family from the first Zionist immigrants to Palestine who are involved in the building of Tel Aviv, to the flourishing urban metropolis that it has become during the 1960s and early 1970s. Tammuz captures the dreamlike importance of Tel Aviv in the early years of the twentieth century with his description of Aminadav and Sarah. Having left the agricultural settlement of his father, preferring not to work the land, Aminadav chooses the only acceptable alternative. He moves to Tel Aviv in 1915 and opens a factory that makes bricks, and specifically *levanim*, the white bricks used for the Bauhaus-style architecture that still dominates the city today. Aminadav is linked figuratively and literally to the ideology of building the new Israel that Tel Aviv represented. Tammuz, like other Israeli novelists, was working within an inheritance of what Mann has shown to be "a powerful set of vividly imagined tropes, anecdotes, and images concerning the city."[10] By the novel's close, the decadence and corruption that has imbued every aspect of life within the city signifies its total failure within the Labor-Zionist mythology that governed Israel until the late 1970s.

Nostalgia for the Lost City of Tel Aviv

Yaakov Shabtai's *Past Continuous* takes up where Tammuz's novel leaves off. Set in Tel Aviv during the 1970s, it describes three discontented middle-aged friends (Goldman, Israel, and Caesar) and the founding generation of their parents. The novel opens with the death of Goldman's father, and the promise that Goldman will commit suicide exactly nine months later. As a result, all the events in the novel are presented in this framework of death.

Lev Hakak has argued that writers like Shabtai became preoccupied with a search for the lost past and disillusionment with the realities of their present. As a result, their literature came to represent isolation and the breakdown of collectivity.

> Following the establishment of the State, the writers who comprised the literary generation of the War of Independence yearned for the pre-State days in which the values of the labor movement prevailed. The contrast between past and present, the disappointment with what followed the breakdown of their social dreams, produced a satiric-ironic attitude toward Israeli reality. These writers focused instead on the individual and on his desire for independence.[11]

In a form of escapism, *Past Continuous* reflected the nostalgic attitude that had started in the 1930s in the longing for the "small and intimate neighborhood where everyone knew everyone else" that continued to develop during the 1940s and 1950s.[12] Maoz Azaryahu identifies a series of these expressions, such as Natan Alterman's 1938 protest against the relocation of Beit Ha'am, and the repeated refrain of longing for the disappearance of the *holot* (sands) articulated by important public figures such as the writer Moshe Shamir, and in 'BaHolot' (In the Sands) a popular song of the period. This evocative longing culminated in Nahum Gutman's 1959 collection of stories and drawings of personal memories produced for the fiftieth anniversary of the city that was a "nostalgia-laden testimony" to the city's foundational phase.[13] By constructing "a monolithic and naive panoramic picture with sand dunes, white buildings, blue sea, and sky," Shabtai reinforced a myth echoing the "messianic and utopian spirit that ha[d] pervaded the entire Zionist project."[14] Thus Shabtai tapped into both the reality of the 1970s and the idealized attitude toward Tel Aviv's early years.

Shabtai's immortalization of Tel Aviv juxtaposes the sense of the decaying city of the 1970s with a nostalgia-laden perception of Tel Aviv's foundational era during the protagonist Goldman's youth. Through Goldman, Shabtai presents the longing for a childhood landscape that has now been vanquished: "The empty lots and gardens and parks and little woods and virgin fields . . . had now disappeared and given way to streets lined with apartment complexes and offices and commercial and industrial areas" (PC, 75). This depiction corresponds to the "nostalgic sentimentality [that] was prevalent mainly among old-time residents, for whom the disappearing cityscapes were associated with the geography of childhood."[15] The novel's popularity and canonical status derive from Shabtai's encapsulation of the labor-oriented elite's fears in a period when the decline of the political and cultural hegemony of the Labor movement became increasingly manifest.

The novel's nostalgic longing represented this particular moment in Tel Aviv history and contrasted sharply with the city's previous political narrative that celebrated urban development. In 1951 a monument to commemorate Tel Aviv's founders "told the story of Tel Aviv as one of the transformation of a sandy wilderness into a blossoming, modern city."[16] Shabtai's novel, by contrast, represents the city in anthropomorphic descriptions as a "crazy creature" expanding over the "vineyards and the melon patches" which distresses the character Baruch Chaim. Unable to keep up "with all the new houses and roads and factories," Baruch Chaim represents a challenge to Tel Aviv's "build and be built" mythology. Shabtai inverts this well-established narrative in Past Continuous, suggesting that the building of Tel Aviv had a destructive effect on the local landscape. Moreover, the story documents a sense of estrangement from the city: "His pride was mixed with a feeling of distress because the city was slipping away from him and making him feel like a stranger" (PC, 183). This ambivalence toward the city's formation also integrates the traditional topos of alienation within the urban landscape. As Goldman witnesses the process of deterioration and destruction in the city, he conflates the annihilation of the old landscape with the influx of a new population: "The town, which in the course of a few years had been filled with tens of thousands of new people, who in Goldman's eyes were invading outsiders, turned him into a stranger in his own city" (PC, 183). Georg Simmel observed the alienating effect of the thronging metropolis, where strangers lived side by side.[17] However, for Goldman the strangers were newcomers and invaders: his alienation evinced a feeling that he was no longer familiar with "his city." By portraying a space filled with strangers as well as longing for the sands of the nostalgic past, Shabtai contests the success of building something new and wholesome in Tel Aviv, a city that would be "something clean, beautiful and healthy." It seemed wrong — "anti-Zionist" — to exchange the conditions of a European ghetto for a Middle Eastern one.[18]

Shabtai's novel confronts this vision of a modern city through Grandma Clara's despair. After having dragged Grandpa David from the Diaspora because of her involvement with groups promoting a "Love of Zion," she is soon disheartened to discover the discrepancy between her dreams and the reality:

> Among the square white houses and glaring wastes of sand which got into her shoes, and sometimes even into her food, in the harsh light of the sun, in the dusty, fly-filled heat, she felt alien and deceived, and many years had to pass for this feeling to fade a little and lose its sharpness, but in the meantime she expressed her disappointment in a stream of Yiddish and Polish and Russian curses and a flood of abuse and angry, indignant complaints. (PC, 135)

In this dystopian representation of the city under construction, Tel Aviv was an exhausting, ugly, and chaotic place. The sand in Grandma Clara's shoes, the symbol of the desert and the Orient, indicates that the city had not become the European metropolis that it was intended to be. Simultaneously, the use of Yiddish, Polish, and Russian curses signifies Tel Aviv's failure to escape the burdens of European ghetto life. For Goldman, the sands' reappearance is both nostalgic and a challenge to the narrative of its banishment in the emergent metropolis. Instead, the city is being consumed by the natural landscape which cannot be held at bay.

Tel Aviv — The Monster City

Baruch Chaim's depictions of the city's intrusion into nature and Grandma Clara's observation of the sands' encroachment on the city highlight the constant battle between the city and the hostile locale. Ultimately Tel Aviv becomes a ravenous force consuming everything in its path, leaving destruction in its wake. This widespread depiction of the city as a destructive monster is a trope commonly found in modernist art and literature. Examples include Baudelaire's images of the city as a whore in *Les fleurs du mal,* the Moloch Machine in Fritz Lang's 1927 landmark modernist film *Metropolis,* and the tension of John Huston's 1950 film noir classic *The Asphalt Jungle.*[19] The "symbolic speech of the city as 'moloch,' 'whore,' 'labyrinth,' or 'asphalt jungle,'" according to Klaus Scherpe, "tries to master the complexity of the modern metropolis in an atavistic manner, by reducing it to elementary formulas."[20] This effect is achieved by describing the city as a terrifying creature; as Raymond Williams has shown, the city becomes "a destructive animal, a monster, utterly beyond the individual human scale."[21]

Yehudit Katzir's 1990 novella *Closing the Sea* about Ilana, a schoolteacher from Haifa who visits Tel Aviv for the day, develops this primordial imagery in her bestial representations of the Dizengoff Center in Tel Aviv. Ilana's emotional crisis and subsequent suicide occur following her visit to Tel Aviv and the failure of her plans to see a childhood friend and experience the promised delights of the city. Katzir belongs to a generation of authors emerging in the late 1980s and early 1990s, including Etgar Keret and Gadi Taub, who described Israel in tropes reminiscent of American literature.[22] Nicknamed the "thin language" generation for their representation of contemporary life in Israel using the vernacular, they wrote Americanized Hebrew literature which, according to Miri Kubovy, included "an increasing number of American themes, characters, landscapes, and experiences . . . usually [presented] in contrast to Israeli reality."[23] Katzir denotes aspects of American consumerism in her depiction of Tel Aviv's Dizengoff Center (Israel's first mall) and its manifestation as a "great white beast," stressing Tel Aviv's savage nature (CS, 125).[24] Eventually, Ilana's awe and praise for the American-style shopping mall turns to dread as she becomes alarmed and confused by the chaos:

> She didn't know which side of the beast she was on now, the front legs or the hind legs, but her own legs hurt, and her stomach was cramped and her head was spinning and her eyes needed to be shut. (CS, 126)

Ilana's hysterical breakdown is triggered by the city's dynamism and her visceral response to the shopping center's monstrosity. Katzir's use of the Dizengoff Center engages with Israelis' nuanced perceptions of

Tel Aviv's success in the 1980s and 1990s. At first, Ilana celebrates the center's external appearance; once inside, however, Ilana's experience is one of terror and horror. She buys an expensive and inappropriate dress from a macabre shop assistant, and then in a moment of hysteria is unable to find the shop again when she decides to return the dress. Finally she finds the shop but cannot return the item. A series of ghoulish scenes reinforce the mall's sinister nature. In the bathroom stall Ilana finds graffiti describing a lurid sexual act, with her name and a telephone number attached. She feels assaulted and violated by this message on the wall. There is no respite from the horrors of the beast. Instead of a relaxing café, she is consigned to the neon-lit food court, and a drink that fails to quench her thirst. Concurrently, she listens to widows as they discuss their husbands' lives and deaths in grisly detail. Through this image of the Dizengoff Center that engenders panic-stricken terror in Ilana, Katzir suggests Tel Aviv's corruption is evidenced in its materialistic consumerism and disregard for human welfare.

Katzir's contrast between the external image of the shopping mall and the horrors found within echo Grandma Clara's disappointment in Shabtai's novel, that Tel Aviv has failed to escape the Levant and to fulfill the promises of its founders to build a modern European city. Clara's contact with the flies and sand disgusts her; a sensory relationship evident in both novels. Tel Aviv's squalid and visceral reality assaults Ilana's senses of smell, touch, sight, hearing, and taste from her very first moments in the city:

> The bus reached the Central Bus Station and opened its doors with a hiss of relief. Ilana got out, and the hot heavy air enveloped her in a sticky embrace, with the smells of urine and nutshells and frying oil and the shouts of fruit vendors and people selling cassettes, and noises too ornate, like the Oriental sweets she had never learned to like. At the base of the dirty green columns sat blind old men or amputees. (CS, 118)

The city is dirty and the air suffocating. The violent smells and the shouts of vendors over a background noise of *Mizrahi* music, represented by the selling of cassettes, indicate the Levantine character of the city. The image of the amputees sitting against the pillars evokes European shtetl life and Arab cities, radically challenging the heroic, healthy Sabra image. This picture challenges the Tel Aviv mythology in early posters, photographs, and Gutman's drawings of cool boulevards on which elegantly attired men and women promenade.[25] Instead, the city now resembles the early twentieth-century Jaffa that Tel Aviv had tried to escape.

Buildings and Death: Physical Decay

Central to Shabtai's novel, *Past Continuous*, is the city's decay. In describing the urban landscape, he suggests the buildings are homages to European design that had once "attempted to imitate the architectural beauties and splendors of Europe, in the style of Paris or Vienna or Berlin, or even of castles and palaces." Instead, the city's putrefaction is seen in the buildings' collapse: "All these buildings no longer had any future because they were old and ill adapted to modern tastes and lifestyles" (*PC*, 269). The narrative of Tel Aviv as "the white city" with new, modern buildings contrasts with the decay of the city—through the image of death. Death takes two forms; that of the city and that of individuals. In the first, there is the detailed representation of the city's cemeteries. Shabtai's novel and Amos Gitai's 1995 film adaptation *Devarim* open with the surreal hunt through the city's graveyards to find Goldman's father's funeral. Unable to meet up with the mourners at the cemetery, Israel and Caesar's return to Goldman's apartment metaphorically extends these sites of death to include the whole city. The juxtaposition of the tombstones against the city's high-rise buildings in Gitai's film symbolizes "the feeling that nothing has really been achieved."[26] The search through the cemeteries and among the tombstones parallels Goldman's own aimless wandering through the city. Goldman roves among the white Bauhaus buildings of Tel Aviv lamenting the loss of his childhood world—a place of Zionist commitment to building a new society, of hope and innocence. In this flânerie, the city becomes a figurative cemetery: "This is already not my city, and she will never be. This is just rubbish . . . this city doesn't deserve to exist. This is just a misunderstanding. . . . This is just nothingness. This is a graveyard" (*PC*, 375).

Writing about Tel Aviv has used the suicide of individuals (along with other forms of death) to convey disillusionment with the city. Katzir's main protagonist Ilana dies after a day in Tel Aviv, and at least twenty-four characters die in Shabtai's novel. Death saturates the text, as illustrated by Zipporah, Goldman's aunt. She visits the graves of the many characters who die in the course of the narrative: "Until in the end the dead enmeshed her life in so dense a web that one day, in an hour of repose, she said humorously to Uncle Lazar, that with so many dead people and so many visits to graveyards it sometimes seemed to her that she herself was already dead" (PC, 376). In stark contrast to the optimistic, future-oriented "build and be built" ideal, both the city and the individual are doomed.

The images of Tel Aviv as a necropolis are even more menacing in literature of the 1990s. In *Closing the Sea* Katzir even suggests that the city is killing its inhabitants by sucking the life out of them.

> [Ilana] tried to admire the fountain that spins and plays music . . . but her eyes were drawn instead to the old people sitting on the hard cement benches around it. The sun hung over them in the steamy air like a round lemon drop sucking whatever sap they still had left. (CS, 126)

Etgar Keret extends this image in his fantastical novella *Kneller's Happy Campers*. This darker, sinister view depicts the city as an endless nightmare in which all of the characters are already dead, having committed suicide — and are now living in Tel Aviv, a symbolic hell. The whole city has become an inescapable place of death.

Just as Katzir describes the Dizengoff Center as admirable because it is "just like in America," so too, in Keret's depiction of Tel Aviv, the city has lost its distinct character as a Hebrew or Jewish city (CS, 126). Keret's Tel Aviv unites specific local indicators with aspects of a universal metropolis. He compares the city to Frankfurt, thereby denying the distinctly Hebrew aspect of Tel Aviv which early Zionist ideology had celebrated as its essential feature. Haim, the main protagonist in Keret's novel, works in a pizza parlor that is part of a chain. Haim's German roommate also works at this afterlife pizzeria. His roommate's statement that the area reminds him of his home merely compounds the effect; Tel Aviv seems just like Frankfurt. The definitive criticism of Tel Aviv comes when Haim remarks that Frankfurt too must be "a hole" (KSK, 48).

Haim and his friend Ari conclude that now that they are dead, Tel

Aviv is like any other city, a metropolitan hereafter: "This place is just like where I came from, only a bit worse" (*KSK*, 72). Keret's novella was written two decades after Shabtai's novel, and opens with a description reminiscent of Shabtai's notorious opening sentences observed by Caesar about the death of Goldman and his father: "Goldman's father died on the first of April, whereas Goldman himself committed suicide on the first of January" (*PC*, 3). Keret's poignant: "Two days after I committed suicide" displaces the external narrator with the protagonist's voice, underscoring the absence of any other survivors left to tell the tale. Keret expands upon the image constructed by Shabtai of Tel Aviv as a cemetery (*KSK*, 47). In this dystopia the city is no longer just a symbolic graveyard, the last resting place of ideological dreams; it is the place after death. Tel Aviv becomes the figurative punishment meted out to people who have taken their own lives. In this allegory of Tel Aviv, Keret is suggesting that the "Hebrew City" has become a place of the living dead.

In what appears to be a return to early tensions between urban and agricultural Zionists, the city with its overtures of death forms a contrast to the idyllic country, which offers salvation. This is equally true in the writing of Shabtai, Katzir, and Keret. For Katzir's heroine Ilana, spying the Mediterranean Sea visible during the bus journey between Tel Aviv and Haifa, offers safety and salvation. On her outward and return journeys, she searches for a glimpse of the waves which would calm her fears and offer deliverance from the terrors of the destructive city. However, this salvation never materializes; the pastoral ideal is just that, an ideal. The title of the novel, *Sogrim et ha-Yam* (*Closing the Sea*), reflects the inaccessibility of this psychological landscape. The sea, with its redemptive powers, is closed to Ilana. It cannot prevent her further despair as she returns to Haifa nor stop her from committing suicide moments later.

In Keret's novel, the countryside is a place of escape and freedom. Kneller's summer camp, from which the novel draws its title, is located in the rural landscape. This is a place of miracles where anything is possible. It appears to be an escape from the city and its endless world of suicide. However, this too proves to be an illusion. The countryside is a mysterious place with sudden dark occurrences such as the disappearance of a dog, or Haim's endless wandering in a dark wood with no path. Haim eventually finds a strange house with naked women, wild rock music, and a man who appears to be a Messiah whose elusive behavior and strange pronouncements finally culminate in his death. This fantastical act which is offered as an act of suicide in a kind of performance by the rock star–style Messiah, in a place in which everyone has already killed themselves, establishes the countryside as a place of wild and uncontrolled extremes, whose gothic overtones establish it as even more terrifying than the city. The unknown countryside is no more redemptive than the urban home he fled. At least within Keret's imaginary Tel Aviv, the surreal makes sense.

In Shabtai's *Past Continuous* the intricate minutiae of the country and the processes of cultivating the land for food are described through Goldman's recollection of childhood experiences spent with his Aunt Zipporah and Uncle Joel on their farm. In his mind, this was a redemptive period: "Goldman would feel so proud and happy that he wanted to burst" (PC, 300). In this rural haven, Goldman's activities nourished his soul. This description parallels the ideological working of the land that had been the Zionist idyll. For Goldman "these summer holidays in the country, so full of freedom and adventure, which always merged in his mind with the visit he had paid to Avinoam, remained engraved in Goldman's memory as the best days of his life" (PC, 302). Other characters in the novel also find the countryside the source of freedom. Caesar escapes the oppressive forces of the city in order to escape his obligations:

> He really didn't want to see anyone, and he went on driving aimlessly until he emerged from the city and started speeding along the highway, which stretched between the uncultivated fields and the low loam hills and the settlements and eucalyptus groves and cultivated fields lying serenely in the warm, pleasant evening twilight, and he abandoned himself to the pleasure of speeding through the open countryside. (PC, 239)

Within the city, Caesar is tense, he hungers for isolation, and roams like a caged energy, whose violence lies dormant waiting to erupt at any moment. It is only with the expansive nature of the rustic landscape that he can find true pleasure and relaxation. As in all of these representations of the countryside, Tel Aviv is contrasted with the more acceptable version of the rural idyll. "The city becomes the entire universe and the country, if invoked, is a pastoral or romantic convention that exists only in the cultural repertoire of the characters."[27] Nonetheless, this country escape is not real. Shabtai exploits the idyllic depiction of the countryside as a haven from the decadent and destructive city by representing Goldman's actual behavior, rather than his nostalgic recollection of the occasion. When Goldman had returned as an adult to stay on the farm with Avinoam and his family he is quickly bored and frustrated. Goldman leaves after four days instead of remaining for the entire week as he had planned. He is part of the city though he suffers from alienation within it.

Tel Aviv, like other cities, is represented as a place of waste and profligacy, thereby contrasting urban living with the innocent rural idyll. Yet it is not possible for the characters to escape from the oppressive forces of the city which continue to influence their lives and lead to their psychological breakdowns. The city becomes the site of suicide because it is the last place left. In using the countryside as a point of contrast, suicide comes to represent not just disillusionment with city life, but in a wider sense, disillusionment with the broader Zionist project of building, development and connection to the land.

Tel Aviv as a Place of Corruption

The city's physical decay is also a metaphor for the decay of human beings through moral, sexual, and financial corruption. Hence this symbolism represents the city's ideological failure as a positive force. Even in the early years, literary depictions of Tel Aviv contested the city's claims to foster personal and architectural Zionist development in contradistinction to agricultural Zionism's success. In *Tmol Shilshom* (*Only Yesterday*, 1945) S. Y. Agnon illustrates the disillusionment of second aliyah members who perceived urban Zionism to be a betrayal of Zionist ideology. Agnon's antihero Yizhak Kumer is incapable of working the land because he lacks the skills of the Arab laborers. Offered the opportunity to find alternative work in the city or flee to Jerusalem, Yizhak abandons secular Socialist Zionism and returns to a religious world. Similarly in *Requiem for Na'aman*, Elyakum's attack at his brother's wedding on the petit bourgeois nature of Tel Aviv, as opposed to agriculturally redemptive Zionism, encompasses much of the early criticism of Tel Aviv (*RN*, 62). But it would be incorrect to suggest that Tel Aviv lacked Socialist Labor Zionism influences.

The architect Ze'ev Rechter's introduction of Engel House, an apartment building on Rothschild Boulevard with communal spaces for social interaction created beneath the building by the raised columns, and on the roof with a terrace, became "a defining mark of Tel Aviv's central neighborhoods."[28] Furthermore, the *meonot ovdim* (workers' housing) was a focused attempt to "implement a collective or communal ideal in the construction of residential neighborhoods."[29] As Ilan S. Troen discusses in his work on the creation of Tel Aviv, the architect Arieh Sharon persuaded future residents of an early workers' housing estate to scale down the proportions of their dwellings to blend with Tel Aviv's "still low-profile and relatively modest skyline."[30] In these central Tel Aviv neighborhoods this Bauhaus style was influenced by an immigrant wave of Viennese architects who designed buildings to "encourage a sense of community that would foster working-class solidarity and nurture the kind of individuals who would grow into and participate in proletarian societies."[31] Nevertheless, within forty years of this construction period, Shabtai attacked the city for failing to realize its socialist ideological ambitions.

Moral Decay

Paralleling the ideology behind building Tel Aviv Shabtai relates the story of Goldman's father and his friend Leviathan in *Past Continuous*. Horrified by Tel Aviv's development, the two men attempt to found a new urban-collective city. They spend two years drawing up the charter, "which embraced all aspects of individual, family and social life; took into account all the rights and obligations of the members and all the problems and deviations which might confront them" (PC, 55). In marked contrast to the earlier construction of Tel Aviv, the pioneers do not sell their possessions, leave their jobs, or abandon their former lives when they move to the collective. The lack of commitment to the project results in its ultimate failure. This allegory contends that Goldman's generation abandoned the Zionist project (and for Shabtai this meant a Socialist Zionist framework) which resulted in Tel Aviv's failure. A second allegorical representation of Tel Aviv is found after Goldman's suicide in a manuscript that he appeared to be translating about Prevlova, a fantastical world. Consequently, Goldman's death is also associated with this story within a story, an allegory of the city as a malevolent place. Prevlova's inhabitants are rootless hordes, challenging Tel Aviv's symbolism as the Jewish homeland and the end to Diasporic wanderings. The bodies in this imaginary land live for a single day, but expand to hideous proportions, fed by the decadence of the city, finally dying and rotting. "The creatures that remain floating on the surface of the water are boiled by the midday sun and serve as nourishment for the approaching hordes of nomads" (PC, 383). Decay is not just the state of the landscape, but the condition of the individual. As a comment on Tel Aviv, Shabtai suggests through this story that each successive generation leaves nothing of substance or meaning. Goldman's suicide is an expression of this ideological failure.

The Tel Aviv Flâneur

Goldman appears always as "a man walking, as if alone, in its streets."[32] This depiction is part of a literary tradition that uses objects and urban tropes to indicate the "separated subjectivity of the observer."[33] Goldman exemplifies a pattern of isolation evident in other characters in the novel and he, like Baruch Chaim, experiences a sense of alienation in the expanding city. Other examples of this fragmented urban identity are evident in sexual and familial relationships. There is no loyalty between spouses, and parents and children are hostile to one another. Husbands and wives do not communicate; Uncle Lazar leaves his wife and disappears until she believes he is dead and so she remarries only to have him return. Goldman lives in silence with his mother and Israel makes love to his friend's girlfriend. The breakdown of personal relations makes interior spaces, such as homes, offices, restaurants, and studios socially oppressive environments. Just as there is nowhere to escape to in the streets, there is no sanctuary within the buildings. The beauty of Tel Aviv lies in the nostalgic past of the city, a place to which Goldman cannot return.

Shabtai casts Goldman as the traditional European flâneur (the stroller) in the vein of Baudelaire's nineteenth-century poetic conceptions of a man walking the city to experience it. Like Edgar Allan Poe's 1840 story "The Man of the Crowd," this figure becomes an urban scientist wandering through the city analyzing the landscape as he promenades without purpose, resisting incorporation into the milieu, forever standing on the edge of a crowd, isolated and alone. This characterization of the city reflected the new dynamic complications of modern life. Social and economic changes brought by industrialization changed the face of the city. Though at first these representations were neutral they eventually came to depict a dark forbidding space, where an underworld with its seedy corruption and prostitution take center stage. In adopting these images for Tel Aviv it was possible for authors to represent the Hebrew city as an ideological failure. Suicide as the fate of characters living in Tel Aviv meant the death of the dream that had once existed, in ideology if not in reality.

Goldman's endless flânerie (the stroll) that forms the spine of Shabtai's novel denotes the isolation of the protagonist, symbolizing imminent death. The psychological breakdown of the protagonist is represented through the failure of the social and institutional structures of the city. Simmel has claimed that the stranger, unlike the "wanderer," exists spatially fixed, unable to leave and trapped in a dislocated present.

> He is, so to speak, the potential wanderer: although he has not moved on, he has not quite overcome the freedom of coming and going. He is fixed within a particular spatial group, or within a group whose boundaries are similar to spatial boundaries. But his position in this group is determined, essentially, by the fact that he has not belonged to it from the beginning, that he imports qualities into it, which do not and cannot stem from the group itself.[34]

It is both the individual and the landscape that become fractured in the urban metropolis. In order to achieve the sense of dislocated reality and convey the fragmented narratives that echo the competing voices of the city, writers use the conventions of stream of consciousness or internal monologue writing styles. Williams argues that

> these processes compose a powerful response to what is known, even conventionally, as city experience, but even when they are held at what appear directly aesthetic levels they are profoundly related to underlying models of life and society; quite as clearly,

in the end, as when they explicitly overlap with ideological versions of an essential isolation, alienation, loss of community.[35]

Goldman wanders through the Tel Aviv streets feeling the oppressiveness in the air, which is "hot and motionless, heavy and muggy" (PC, 246). The character's anxiety, due to the impending meeting with his girlfriend Dita, is reflected in the description of the landscape: "there was a kind of tension in everything, in the trees and in the bushes and in the clouds, which spread and thickened" (PC, 246). The external reality mirrors Goldman's emotional state. Wandering through the city in a trance, he begins a dialogue with the streets. He considers Yarkon Street despicable and frightening, and he associates it with prostitution which engenders a feeling of terror and shame. Instead of representing the wholesome new society, Shabtai represents the street as a place of decay.

The street signifies the immorality that at once attracts and repels Goldman. He formulates theoretical arguments to justify his increasingly corrupt conduct; "the only morality acceptable to him as a non-believer [who] did not repudiate prostitution, nor adultery." Instead of religion, which he refers to as conventional morality, he prefers to adopt a humanistic morality based on reason with no social limits. Hence Goldman can justify all behavior as he gropes at random for experiences that become unfulfilling. The only boundaries are those represented by the walls and buildings of the city. "The girls standing with their little handbags on the corners or in the doorways of the gloomy old buildings . . . most of which were in darkness so that they looked as if nobody lived in them and all they contained were broken bits of furniture and dust and cobwebs and evil spirits" (PC, 214). These symbols of corruption, such as the prostitutes, are at once inviting and repellent. Goldman as flâneur is tortured by the ugliness he witnesses in his soul, which is reflected back in the depictions of the city. For Goldman Tel Aviv is abandoned, no one lives in the apartments, the furniture is broken, there are symbols of decay; the dust, cobwebs, and ghosts haunt the buildings. In this version Tel Aviv becomes a ghost town. The evil spirits may be living people, or they may be the ghosts of things past with no distinction between the living and the dead.

Goldman's street echoes his feelings. When he is anxious and worried the street becomes a tense place, and similarly when he is calm he sees the street's beauty, thereby resurrecting the once positive ideological view of the city. Wandering through the streets in a tranquil atmosphere, the internal and external world mirror each other. The city, preparing for the Sabbath, is empty of traffic and people, just as the external world is undisturbed, and so "a great calm descended" on Goldman. The city without its constant thronging milieu can become a heavenly utopia again, and Goldman can feel love for it, "a love which he only rarely, in moments of grace, felt in its pure, undiluted form" (PC, 216).

However, this peaceful, ideologically fulfilling representation is immediately crushed as the calm city hides shadowy mysteries. It is in this mood of calm reflection that the city again comes to haunt Goldman. He suddenly sees Naomi, his dead sister, walking toward him, a reflection of a conversation about her that he had had moments before with Uncle Lazar. The worlds of imagination or memory collide with reality and in doing so these two oppositional views jar. "He stood staring until she walked passed him with her rucksack on her back, looking like an American tourist, and when she had passed he turned his head and gave her one more long look and went on walking down the street, which began to grow dim and dark" (PC, 217). Strangers take on the form of others; there is absolute anonymity in the city, while at the same time the morass of humanity becomes interchangeable, the familiar alien and the unusual familiar. Simmel describes the urban dweller's blasé attitude from overstimulation which he concludes finally leads to a deep reserve, an aversion to contact with others, and the appearance of emotional indifference.[36] Goldman does not even stop for the woman whom he thinks is his sister. He cannot care for anything or anyone. Even though the woman is not his sister, who has been dead for many years, he is not surprised that he believed he saw her.

The city's facelessness and impersonality are evident everywhere. Instead of the communal interaction that the boulevard's construction had promised, Tel Aviv is represented as a place where the characteristic movement is a hurrying, seemingly random passing of men and women.[37] Williams, commenting on Dickensian London, explains that literary representations of cities show "an absence of ordinary connection and development." "These men and women do not so much relate as pass each other and then sometimes collide."[38] These urban citizens inhabiting the modern street excluded from the warm lit interiors that they pass can be witnessed in Shabtai's descriptions of Tel Aviv. In his endless wandering, Goldman is chronicling the demise of his city, physically and ideologically (PC, 268).

Even though it appears that the traditional flâneur is walking anonymously through the city, as Mann has argued, Goldman's flânerie, and that of the other characters in the novel, is fundamentally flawed: because, though they feel themselves estranged from the landscape, the paths they tread are not anonymous and they cannot truly lose themselves, they are fixed by the boundaries of, as Simmel claims, the wanderer who stays. Tel Aviv is caught up between the desire to be a new, modern place and a familiar home. It succeeds at neither. "Goldman's passage through the sand in which he stumbles physically over pieces of the past and tries to describe them, sieve-like, in the net of his present, is an allegory of the narrative's attempt as a whole to remember, to catch the past in the net of the present tense."[39]

The death of the individuals in the novel is paralleled with the death of the city. This ambulation is Goldman's walk toward death, conveyed through the increasing alienation of the inhabitants who had lived there from birth and now find that in the city they have become strangers. Disgust with the Tel Aviv in which the flâneur now finds himself expresses the rejection of the city, as well as the rejection the protagonists feel by the city.

The city's failure exists not only in the decline of the dream but in its inability to ennoble its inhabitants despite the drama and promise of its reputation as the first Hebrew city since the exile. In a city where only individuals exist attempting to survive the anonymous hordes, the need to satisfy personal appetites becomes the only activity of the disempowered. The curse of the city is that though it can feed every caprice, no person can experience everything at every moment. The city dwellers constantly feel excluded, believing that at any time they are missing something else. Hence there is no satisfaction in any pleasure, since any decision closes off other options. Wirth-Nesher explains that cities intensify the human condition of missed opportunities, choices, and inaccessibility. "Every glimpsed interior, every passerby, every figure in a distant window, every row of doors, every map itself is both an invitation and a rebuff."[40] This becomes the final paralyzing terror for the characters of Shabtai's novel, that they may miss something. They grope at random, trying to fulfill their lives.

Ideological Failure

Shabtai uses Goldman's father to represent the old guard who are ideologically motivated and had belonged to the generation of state-building Zionists. The son who is removed from an interest in politics conveys the failure of this former generation. Just as Aminadav and Sarah build Tel Aviv in Tammuz's novel, these men in Shabtai's work have also accepted the national enterprise. Yet there is also satire in Shabtai's depiction. Goldman's father has many books and the shelves are crowded with volumes by "Berl Katznelson and Ben Gurion and Bialik and Brenner and Sholem Aleichem and other old and new books (which Goldman's father had devoted great efforts to acquiring and which he had guarded jealously, although he hardly ever looked inside them)" (PC, 64). Though the great ideological and political actors of Zionism wrote these books, Goldman's father with all his pretensions of ideological edification has not read them, and in essence the ideas remain inaccessible to him. Shabtai is suggesting the ideological failure of Tel Aviv lies not with the decadence of the young, but the dogmas of the previous generation.

Ideological promiscuity is a continual theme in Shabtai's novel, and it appears in several characters' attitudes. For example, Manfred, Goldman's mother's suitor, is ideologically adulterous. He fluctuates between different, contrasting, worldviews, studying philosophy, then literature and poetry, followed by research into historical and religious phenomena (PC, 64). He becomes a skeptic and then a nihilist, works as a builder and a gardener, then as a junior assistant in a research project on bird migration, and then in optics. Zionism is set up as just one more passing fancy. If this particular ideology is a mere temporary aberration, then the permanence ascribed to Tel Aviv is powerfully undermined as another inconsequential and temporary dalliance.

The generation of Goldman's parents, with its changing beliefs seems erratic and hypocritical, even when characterized by sincerity. Shabtai suggests the inaccessibility and failure of their ideas was due to a fundamental impossibility in the system to which they devoted their lives, rather than resulting from a lack of goodwill. The commitment to ideology, though erroneous, provided its believers with moral fiber and courage following their involvement with these movements. The ongoing battle between these older characters, such as Caesar's father and his father's friend is a constant motif in the novel:

> Erwin, who in his youth had been a Zionist and a socialist and who had emigrated to Eretz Yisrael as a pioneer and lived for a number of years as a member of a kibbutz, continued to regard himself as a Zionist and a socialist with political, social and moral principles, although during the course of time these principles had been subjected to an almost imperceptible process of erosion until they were distorted beyond recognition. (PC, 92)

The failure of the Zionist dream in this founding generation leaves the succeeding generation with a sense of disillusionment. Empty of any ideology, this new generation is cruel and unsympathetic. Caesar wanted to be like his father who because of his wit and humor could make platitudes that seemed innocuous become funny and interesting. However, Caesar does not succeed because even though he repeated them, trying to copy his father's tone, his lack of values makes the remarks appear bitter and vicious. Even more than their beliefs, it is the older generation's sincerity which is absent in the younger generation. *Past Continuous* is the story of the loss of the ideological generation, and its replacement with a generation of purposeless individuals. As Yudkin has argued:

> This book can be read partly as a social critique. Here is Israeli society populated by the post-religious Jew, floundering in the enticing, open, unchartered sea of the world, excited but directionless. His capacity to swim in it and navigate it is both limited and inevitably doomed.[41]

The urban dwellers in post-1970 literature fill their lives in a variety of ways, through sexual pleasures, business, and consumerism, but these are shown to be corrupt forces that are inherently destructive. The centrality of the city's sexual corruption extends metaphors of Tel Aviv's decline. Sexual depravity in the novels compromises ideological promises for a new Jewish future with wholesome overtones. The themes of sexual betrayal, prostitution, promiscuity, and loveless marriages in the masculine world of Shabtai's novel become common tropes in representations of Tel Aviv. Similarly, in Closing the Sea Ilana is confronted by images of naked breasts on the magazine covers at the kiosk in the bus station and the sexual suggestions in the Dizengoff Center bathroom. On her return journey from the city a religious man sits next to her in the shared taxi, covers his knees with his coat and, while feeling Ilana's thigh, proceeds to masturbate. The licentiousness and pornography that characterize Ilana's experience accord with Williams's view of the city as a place of waste and profligacy represented through promiscuity, prostitution, and pornography.[42] These themes, evident in Shabtai's novel, pervade all of the relationships the three young male characters have, in which images of bizarre, sordid, or depraved pornography and sex destroy every meaningful connection the men might explore. The inventory of sexual depravity the novel cites symbolizes the betrayal of Tel Aviv's Zionist ideals in two ways. First, the reality cannot match the expectations of fantasy, and in the search for the erotic fulfillment they dream of, they turn to increasingly extreme sexual acts. Second, the liaisons cannot bear fruit, either emotionally or physically. Rarely do any of the interactions lead to children and when Israel's girlfriend is pregnant he rejects her and the child she bears. Her response is to move to Jerusalem, suggesting that Tel Aviv cannot sustain life.

Prostitution is a universal theme of the urban environment. Richardson, Fielding, and other eighteenth-century British novelists were quick to use this image, and it was not until a century later that prostitution featured in French literature.[43] In English literature, prostitution depicted a changing fate for women (as with Fanny Burney's Evelina) from which they could rise and return to society, or alternatively sink into obscurity and perhaps die. It was not until the late nineteenth century, with the rise of modernism, that the prostitute became a vehicle for representing "male fantasies about female sexuality," a depiction that served "to focus male ambivalence about desire, money, class, and the body."[44] In Tel Aviv fiction, suicide and prostitution are paralleled, becoming dominant images of the city's corruption. Shabtai's use of prostitution reflects the demise of the puritanical and idealistic ethos that characterized the early pioneering phase of the Tel Aviv Zionist narrative.

Goldman's constant pursuit of prostitutes is frequently humiliating. In his first encounter the woman took his money but "all she let him do was embrace her a little and touch her breasts through her dress and kiss her once or twice" (PC, 165). On another occasion, Goldman "once received a beating on account of a prostitute." Goldman's sexual relationship with Paula, the hostess of a nightclub, also suggests prostitution. Many of his sexual acts with Paula are conducted in public among other middle-aged men "who had come to find a little release and a little happiness in the company of the hostesses" (PC, 163). The squalid and transitory nature of the hostesses and their social situation is matched by Goldman's encounter. He dreams that Paula, or some other woman, will provide an act of such sexual debauchery that he will finally fulfill all his desires and his fantasies: "After it was over he was left with nothing but the sense of shame and sin, and a feeling of disappointment, because none of it bore any resemblance to the wild sexual fantasies which he cultivated in his imagination" (PC, 164).

As a child, Goldman saw his neighbor, the prostitute Kaminskaya — whom he lusted after — commit suicide. The sexual promise she represents is unattainable at first because he is too young, and then because she dies. Like the Tel Aviv dream, she is forever out of reach. Goldman's father views prostitutes as moral decay within the society he venerates, by contrast his son is attracted to them rather than repelled indicating a breakdown in moral values between generations. This is further exemplified in the discussion of suicide, which is paralleled with that of prostitution. For Goldman, the very arguments that legitimize prostitution (control over one's own body and fate) are the same as those for suicide.

Yet the naïveté of Goldman's argument is at once evident since he remains insensitive to the dynamics of power and masculinity that differentiate between a woman's choice to become a prostitute and a person's choice to commit suicide. Perhaps this is a weakness in Shabtai's own construction of the self-absorbed masculinity that dominates the novel. In fact the defense of prostitution appears in service of the more important argument about the lack of culpability for suicide. Goldman's pursuit of prostitutes, like his subsequent suicide, reveals his disdain for the morality of the collective. In prostitution, sexual acts no longer have procreative properties. Therefore, the association with suicide indicates the material death of the city and of its ideals. Sexual depravity and the ambiguous moral attitudes toward it prefigure the popular conceptions of Tel Aviv in the 1980s and 1990s as a "sin city," where transgression of moral conventions is rendered positive, signifying the city's success.[45]

The hypersexual nature of Shabtai's text is coupled with the pursuit of financial excess, and together these themes convey a wild decadence that would have seemed abhorrent to the Labor-Zionist founders of the city. Caesar feeds Goldman's sexual fantasies with his own licentious behavior. His attitude to sexual relations is merely an extension of his parents', Zena and Erwin's, coupling of sexual and financial excess. Their overindulgence of all things obscures their hatred for one another. Erwin assumes his wife forgets his adulterous betrayal because of her extravagant purchases. However, her shopping expeditions barely satisfy her, and her new acquisitions often remain packed in their bags. This representation of consumerist decadence characterized Tel Aviv throughout its history, with Dizengoff Street "associated with pleasure, entertainment, fun, and consumption."[46] However, even Tel Aviv acquired new dimensions of debauchery and dissolution with the rise of a nouveau riche middle class in the 1960s and 1970s.

Tammuz's *Requiem for Na'aman* explores the image of hyperconsumption in his depiction of a generation committed to the good life made possible by an emergent affluent class that was not committed to the puritanical, pioneering ethos of an earlier decade. In this novel, the fashionable homes of the upper classes in Tel Aviv have now become monuments to consumerism. In a deeply satirical portrayal of wealth, he ridicules the compulsive acquisitions of this class, and those who could not afford full integration into this status and social connection, and therefore choose their own systems of imitation in order to compete in this hierarchy:

> In all the best houses one could find special clay pots, archaeological, bearing the signature of a Minister of Israel; he who knew the Minister personally received such potsherds as a gift; and he who was not so fortunate paid the full price, in shops in New York, when he was on a graduate trip there. (*RN*, 189)

In describing the archaeological artifacts of Israel, divorced from their religious or social context, which become objects of social rank, Tammuz suggests the dislocation between a genuine interest in the history of the national homeland and its use as a status symbol. The items are purchased in New York, rather than the result of personal excavations, since these people do not work the land and are removed from it physically and ideologically. Yet, his description of this social class still ties consumption to unique aspects of local Canaanite or Palestine archaeology.[47] The items belong to the Land of Israel and hence status is still measured by an ideological connection. However, in Shabtai's novel, even this final link to Zionism is severed. The artifacts mentioned in *Past Continuous* are African masks, or items from Asia, China, and the Far East, demonstrating the disconnection between national ideals and Tel Aviv society.

In Shabtai's novel, financial corruption in the city is also a mark of moral decay, symbolized by Max Spillman. Max lives in an unnecessarily lavish accommodation, "a five-room apartment in one of the expensive new buildings," contrasting the modest socialist housing values employed in Tel Aviv's Bauhaus period (*PC*, 194). Spillman has been convicted for corruption: he diluted petrol with paraffin and tampered with the indicators on the pumps; yet even after being tried, convicted, and fined, he feels no remorse because he believes neither the crime is serious nor that he will be punished for it. Even his customers do not consider his actions to be "an unpardonable sin, but at the very most as an unfortunate slip which should be forgotten as soon as possible and which was no reason for upsetting their relationship with him." Spillman represents Tel Aviv's moral corruption: "Even the devil has run away and left them in the hands of a rabble of animals like Max Spillman and all kinds of mad dogs who called themselves Jews" (*PC*, 235).

Tammuz similarly describes fashionable Tel Aviv society's financial duplicity during the relatively affluent and politically stable 1960s and 1970s, when traditional ideals of selfless service eroded, giving way to cynicism and the pursuit of personal gains through bribes and corruption. The new elite behaved in fraudulent ways by letting their self-interest triumph over moral obligations to the collective.

Tammuz and Shabtai's representations of Tel Aviv anticipate the celebration of sin and hedonism that particularly characterizes the public discourse of Tel Aviv from the late 1980s. Though Tel Aviv's vibrant night-life had informed the city's reputation since the 1930s, by 1989, "The Nonstop City" had become its official slogan.[48] But in Katzir's represen-tation of 1980s Tel Aviv, Ilana's inability to enjoy her time in the city renowned for its good-time atmosphere demonstrates the failure to access the "nonstop city" advertised by its slogan. Ilana's failed attempts to bask in the social and economic luxuries of Tel Aviv due in part to her naïveté and in part to her friend's betrayal are exemplified in the city's oppres-sive heat, which forces her to acknowledge the impossibility of roaming through Tel Aviv in order to reach the seafront as she had dreamed.

Shabtai, Tammuz, Katzir, and Keret are criticizing the founding myths of the Zionist narrative, and particularly the myths involved in the crea-tion of Tel Aviv. These writers are using accepted literary tropes of the city such as decadence and corruption (moral, social, financial, and sexual), alienation of the individual, the breakdown of the family, the facelessness of the city, fragmented interactions with anonymous individuals, and an inability to form meaningful attachments. In so doing, they are locating suicides in a landscape of destruction and despair. The suicides of Gold-man, as well as Kaminskaya, Shalva, and Ariyeleh in Shabtai's novel; of Ilana in Katzir's novel; and of the whole society in Keret's work are more shocking because the founding generation had sought to raise an image of Hebrews as remote as possible from the old image of the Diaspora Jew. "In this opposition of polar extremes, 'Israel' symbolized what was new, healthy and upright, whereas 'Diaspora' stood for the old, sickly, and stooped."[49] Tel Aviv was intended to be an architectural manifestation of this newness. But by Shabtai and Tammuz's generation, it was already possible to represent alienated adults, disappointed in what they believed to be the failure of the Zionist dream. In the following generation, Katzir and Keret indicate not just the failure of that dream, but the annihilation and corruption of the society that remains. Tammuz and Shabtai are writ-ing against a tradition in which Israel still holds center stage. The failure of Tel Aviv is seen as the failure of ideological Socialist Zionism. Katzir's and Keret's Tel Aviv is the depiction of a society where there is no Zion. Tel Aviv has lost its unique character as a Jewish city, leaving it open to function as a symbolic trope for the rejection of the universal concepts of the city as a hostile environment, a place of alienation and death.

Destruction of "Tel Avivness," Creation of "a City"

The protagonist of Keret's novella, Haim, believes that life is meaningless and pointless, that "nothing matters" (*KSK*, 51). He eventually learns to find significance in his life, and rejects the passivity of his role among the living dead, finally abandoning his pessimistic outlook at the story's close. Having overcome his infatuation with Ergah the woman for whom he first killed himself, partly out of despair for her unrequited love, and partly to make her suffer guilt, he becomes romantically interested in Lihah. He often thinks of this new woman, whose real presence and shared emotional connection demonstrate a bond he never shared with Ergah. In turn, this real relationship highlights the ways in which he 'dreamed' but did not 'think' of Ergah. With Lihah: "I don't dream about her at all, but I think about her a lot" (*KSK*, 51). As with the other novels considered here, the longing for a female fantasy is paralleled with the dreams the early pioneers had for Tel Aviv, a dream which can never be realized in its pure, ideal but impractical form. By contrast, in embracing the real city, which includes both the urban space to which Haim returns, and the symbolic female who returns his love, Haim is transformed. By choosing 'life' rather than a fictional 'dream', a connection suggested by the meaning of his name Haim (life) he is able to reclaim his position within a new society. In the closing lines he remarks that Lihah has advised him to make a conscious effort to do things differently, and to try and live life by the less imaginary principles that she suggests, like "doing things just slightly wrong so that you know you are living" (*KSK*, 51), perhaps a recognition that it is no longer necessary to live in the shadow of an ideology that cannot be realized in its perfect form, but should be embraced in its real, if alternative guise.

Keret's novel is heir to a literary tradition that rejects the ideological tenets which first formed Tel Aviv. From the beginning of the twentieth century, the city had been imagined in literary terms that were later conceived of in physical ways. Expressed in various ideological manifestations throughout the century, fiction continued to question Tel Aviv's ability to fulfill the founders' visions. Even as the city abandons its heritage as "the first Hebrew city" by becoming a city like any other in Keret's novella, the sense of Tel Aviv's ultimate success is reinforced. For, as the writers examined here have shown, by using images of the flâneur, sexual decadence, and corruption in the city, Tel Aviv's universal aspects as a metropolis are celebrated. Although earlier visions of socialism had collapsed, the nature of Tel Aviv as an international city just like any other, a burgeoning metropolis that fulfilled the "build and be built" philosophy underlying its construction and growth is manifested in the city's very existence. Nevertheless, even at the dawn of the twenty-first century, Keret does not entirely abandon the special nature of the city either; he also highlights those aspects unique to the city's geographical locus. The sea, the streets, and even the characters reflect a modern Israeliness. The juxtaposition of celebrating and criticizing these local regional markers characterizes cities like Tel Aviv that stand in the shadows of the great metropolises such as Paris, London, or New York: "The underlying idea being that a sense of provincialism and a thirst for recognition are often two sides of the same coin."[50] Keret's protagonist Haim is a synonym for the city, for in just surviving Haim and Tel Aviv fulfill their purpose, while Haim is also a symbol of the Tel Aviv inhabitant whose life is on the one hand modern and urban, and on the other constrained by the particular situation in Israel.

In the Zionist imagination Tel Aviv represented family and social cohesiveness, as well as the ideals of high European culture, while a Jewish socialist flavor was to permeate every sphere. However, these novels depict the social and familial fragmentation of Tel Aviv. From Europe, only ideas of the ghetto remain, while Tel Aviv becomes more like the Arab world it was meant to reject. The sand, the symbol of the desert, once the foundation for the build and be built philosophy, now encroaches over the roads and streets, eroding the ideological past. Consumerism, decadence, and corruption have destroyed the last of the socialist ideals. Jewishness no longer has a place in the secularized city. As I have illustrated here, representations of suicide framed within these depictions of this city indicate tension with these early ideas. Suicide comes to mean an expression of hopelessness and abandonment, demonstrating that the metaphoric use of suicide in these works indicates the ideological failure of Tel Aviv. Suicide to some extent is used to criticize the construction of ideological expectations, but in the main, its role is merely to highlight the disparity between the construction of ideological dreams and the Tel Aviv reality.

But in its conclusion Keret's novel argues that neither Haim nor Tel

Aviv are the living dead. Instead, both appear to do things "just slightly wrong" and in doing so demonstrate their existence. The city more than deserves to exist — it does exist! It is this literary vision of the city that balances recognizable universal urban topoi and specific local identity symbols. Motifs of decay and death dominate depictions of Tel Aviv, thereby highlighting the disparity between the early urban pioneers' dream and the modern reality, yet — as the literary imagery shows — Tel Aviv as a modern metropolis signifies the city's ultimate success, and the suicides which have dominated its literary depiction release it from its ideological burden.

CHAPTER 5

Nothing Left to Live For:
Women's Suicide

Women's bodies (or more precisely, women's wombs) are
understood to be a national resource.
—SUSAN SERED, *What Makes Women Sick*

In Judaism, the choice for a woman appears to be between marriage with
children, and death. Though Christianity offered women the alternative
option of a cloistered life, marriage to God rather than marriage to a man,
historical Judaism did not offer women this alternative.[1] "In Judaism,
even more than in Christianity, women were defined by their social role
of motherhood . . . in the eyes of the Law, and society, their major obligation was to procreate rather than create."[2] Modern Zionist ideology trans-
ferred this religious obligation for God to an obligation toward the state,
and its attendant expectation of procreation as a weapon in the battle for
demographic superiority in Israel. Ben Gurion's call for women to fulfill their national duty was manifested within the state through "several
powerful institutions, each with its own distinct ideological and organizational structure, [which] encourage[s] women in the national mission
of motherhood."[3] A woman who fails to execute her maternal duty has
failed the national enterprise.

These national expectations about motherhood are so pervasive that
they represent the social norm. This archetypal maternal image becomes a
focal point in depictions of women's suicide in modern Israeli literature. In

fiction in which women commit suicide there is an underlying assumption within the text that women who fail to procreate successfully fall outside the expectations and values of mainstream society. This chapter explores the profound influence that social ideology has had on women in Israel, and the ways in which this expectation of fertility has transmogrified to create the trope of women's suicide in literature. In contrast to the previous chapters, where suicide has functioned as a challenge to the nation's narratives, within the frame of women's lives suicide becomes an image that reinforces the ideology of national expectations. Examining a small selection of examples, many of which appear in the novels dealt with elsewhere in this book (or by the same authors) and focusing in detail on Yehudit Katzir's novella *Closing the Sea*, I point to a phenomenon which, though marginal (as is the depiction of women in general), appears pervasive.[4]

Until recently female characters were rarely found at the center of novels as the major protagonist. Their marginal roles as wives, mothers, or girlfriends, according to Esther Fuchs, derive from the "myopic political vision which focuses exclusively on male-produced workers and on male subjects as national symbols."[5] The Israeli film industry has been dominated by men and male-oriented concerns "addressing women's issues only insofar as they seem relevant to nationalist rhetoric."[6] Similarly, in fiction women play a subsidiary role in the Zionist narrative, which is conceived in the main around procreation and child rearing. While expectations about motherhood can be traced to biblical and traditional Jewish sources, many of today's myths and ideals about reproduction and women's obligation emerged in the early formative Zionist period. Yael S. Feldman explains that

> the liberatory impulse of Zionism has never "overcome" the traditional Jewish valorization of motherhood. Diaries, letters, and other documents from the early decades of this century bear witness to this conflict, "the curious combination of female liberation and the return of women to their traditional roles as wives and mothers."[7]

Examining birth and childhood manuals between the 1920s and 1950s, Sachlav Stoler-Liss has shown that "a coherent ideological picture emerges that placed motherhood and proper child rearing at the very heart of the

Zionist effort to shape a 'new society' and a 'new Jew.'"[8] Furthermore, the massive loss of Jewish life after the Holocaust and the military struggles for independence made fertility a national priority in Israel.[9] Women's duty has been partly framed in terms of replacing "the six million Jews who died in the Holocaust and [the need] to produce the next generation of soldiers and citizens of the Jewish State."[10] As mothers, women are recruited to "produce the next generation of fighters and instill in them loyalty to the nation and a willingness to sacrifice their own lives."[11] Women experience pressure to "serve as reproductive vehicles for the nation's need for 'cannon fodder.'"[12] Childbirth is considered "women's national service" and is "paralleled to military conscription for men."[13] This is often phrased in terms of the demographic struggle to maintain a Jewish majority within Israel.[14] Women are encouraged to believe that their wombs bear a responsibility toward the population. "Fertility is a major concern of Israeli society," and there is considerable stigma attached to infertility in all sectors of Israeli society.[15] In a society where bearing children confers status on women, and legal and medical measures have been put into place to propagate this national project, research shows that the vast majority of women conform to nationalist expectations.

> Historically, both Palestinian and Israeli women accepted their roles as wives, mothers, and widows of soldiers, and to a large extent, even as they fought for gender equality within their societies, they accepted the nationalist paradigm and their roles in it.[16]

These obligations are not restricted to any one social group, and research on family planning in Israel has shown that couples are encouraged to start breeding early and have as large a family as possible. This trend has been described as a "perspective that assumes that woman's main purpose is to bear and raise children."[17] The overwhelming preponderance of evidence demonstrates clearly that "women in Israel have little worth if they are not mothers."[18]

As Pnina Lahav has noted, the ideal image of motherhood has pervaded Israeli society and, after conducting three surveys in the Hebrew University's department of sociology, she concluded, "for the students, the ideal wife was the homemaker, possessing the traditional feminine characteristics and satisfying herself within the framework of home and family."[19] She speculates that this is due to the influence of religious Judaism in certain political and social spheres in which women in Israel are still discriminated against today. "In the rabbinical tribunals all judges are men. It has long been an established tenet of Judaism that the woman's place is in the home and her education is a waste of time if not a cause of her corruption."[20] Not only do women continue to be judged through the lens of a patriarchal society, but these sociological surveys also demonstrate that any attempt a woman makes to liberate herself, for example through education, is seen not only as a negative choice, but one that will lead to a woman's eventual corruption.[21]

During the history of the State of Israel, legal and medical measures have been in place to encourage women to bear children.[22] Simultaneously these measures socially devalued those women who did not bear children. As Daphna Birenbaum-Carmeli concludes from her extensive research, Israel's reproductive policy is probably more proactive than even that of pro-natalist European countries.

For an affordable sum, women (including singles and lesbians) are able to have donor insemination as part of the public health service. Israel was the first country to enable women without fallopian tubes to become pregnant and give birth. In 1996 Israel's high court ruled that "discrimination against unmarried women, whether gay or heterosexual, regarding access to artificial insemination or IVF is unlawful, as it restricts their reproductive freedom and rights to parenthood." Israeli religious authorities and courts have endorsed these procreative technologies, and have extended their rulings to include more controversial issues, such as embryo transfer after divorce, and post-mortem sperm aspiration. In 1996 the Embryo Carrying Agreement Law was passed, making Israel the first country in the world to legalize surrogate mother agreements. These rulings were "justified in terms of compassion towards individual women perceived as suffering the agony of childlessness." They assumed that motherhood was women's primary goal, and where it was not, sought to make it so:

> By state laws, women's familial responsibilities are prioritized over their paid work, and large families are privileged over smaller ones. Obstetric and procreative medicines are highly developed and accessible, whereas family planning services and abortion facilities are less adequate.[23]

Though legal, contraception and abortion are discouraged in Israel, but many of the bureaucratic challenges to abortion disappear if the fetus has birth defects. Abortion is permitted if the health of the mother is at risk so that she is unable to "respond to the needs of the child, [as a result of which] there is a large danger that the child will not develop emotionally into a healthy person." Alongside these medical considerations, state laws prioritize women's familial responsibilities over their paid work, "and large families are privileged over smaller ones." Given the social pressures these factors create, women who do not bear children are devalued in terms of their standing.

Motherhood and Gender Discrimination

Birenbaum-Carmeli traces the attitude toward motherhood to the pre-state period, arguing that although women had been more integrated into "traditionally male occupations," a situation that was partly feasible "thanks to subsidized childcare facilities and an enhancing ideology," these accomplishments were gradually eroded with "the improvement of the local economy and the replacing of socialist ideologies by a more conservative outlook." In fact, as a result of these changes women returned to "occupy traditional female niches."[24]

> The primacy of motherhood has an impact on public attitudes toward gender discrimination in employment as well. There is widespread ambivalence about women engaging in high-commitment careers at a possible cost to family life. In studies of work values, women attribute greater importance to convenient working hours and to the ability to integrate home and work and less importance to opportunities for advancement than do men. Religious men and women put even greater value on woman's roles as housekeeper and mother and significantly less value on her role as worker outside the home than do secular Israelis.[25]

Research in the field of women's employment in Israel at the start of the twenty-first century demonstrates that women continue to serve in mostly conventional female roles in the army, such as welfare and low-rank administration, and in health and social services, areas that usually have lower pay.[26] In general, women are paid less per hour and per month even when they occupy the same position as men.[27] In 2013, national elections saw a bump in the percentage of female members in the Israeli Knesset (Parliament), up from 13 percent; currently they make up 23 percent, the largest percentage of women on record. However, apart from the occasional exception, women rarely hold the highest offices in government, and religious law is still a male-dominated sphere. As Birenbaum-Carmeli concludes:

> Israeli women of all religious affiliations are subjected to man-made agendas as they are largely excluded from policymaking processes. They have significantly less control over sources of power and have their needs and interests regularly represented by men. The state's reproductive policy . . . is thus primarily a male product, of which women and families are the main objects.[28]

Women in Israel are still encouraged to make home their priority, and reproductive policy in Israel, usually designed and promoted by men, has encouraged women to bear children, thereby confining women to the domestic sphere. It is clear that national policies have encouraged procreation and provided women with positive conditions in which to bear children by providing legal, financial, and medical resources, and in so doing, the state has constructed childbirth and child rearing as positive experiences. In this respect, the state has enhanced women's reproductive autonomy. Yet the glorification of motherhood in turn delegitimizes alternative lifestyles that do not include children. Birenbaum-Carmeli sees "women's readiness to endure long years of fertility treatments" as an "indication of the preeminence of this construction."[29] Medical insurance in Israel covers in vitro fertilization at unprecedented rates, with citizens receiving up to seven rounds of treatment, or up to the birth of two live children. "Treatment in Israeli public clinics is free, and there are no waiting lists."[30] Mother and child clinics offer cheap, high-quality care, but "the main focus continues to be on childbearing."[31] In contrast, contraceptives are not part of the basic basket of health care services, though under some packages they may be subsidized.[32] While such provisions enable those women who wish to do so to have a greater chance of conceiving and bearing children, these policies also shape women's desires.

Israel's reproductive policy undermines women's autonomy at the deeper level of promoting an ideology that positions motherhood at the heart of women's lives. Thus, rather than influencing women's reproductive decisions directly, the state shapes such social climate and material conditions that guide women towards favoring increased fertility. . . . One needs to bear in mind that this policy is implemented within the broad religious contexts of Judaism and Islam, both of which contribute to the pressure on women towards childbearing.[33]

Consequently, a situation has been created in Israel where having children affords women social status, and in turn, makes women who do not bear children social outcasts and deviants:

Public tributes to maternity are among the more poetic expressions of Israeli concern with national survival, population growth, and women's bodies — three themes that have become intertwined in Israeli discourse.[34]

A set of tropes have evolved in Israeli literature, whereby women who commit suicide do so as a result of failing to fulfill maternal expectations. Though elsewhere I have shown that suicide in Hebrew literature has, for the most part, sought to attack national narratives and Zionist ideology since the 1960s, this chapter will demonstrate that as with the early years of ideology when the image of suicide represented commitment and self-sacrifice for the cause, this image can also support ideological objectives and reinforce the Zionist status quo. In a society where "if you're not a mother, you don't exist" the suicide of childless women due to their barrenness or the failure to raise healthy and ideologically sound offspring demonstrates continued support for the mythic tradition of childbearing.[35]

Some Examples of Women's Suicide in Israeli Literature

Given the propensity of Hebrew literature to neglect women characters (at least until very recently), the majority of the examples that exist for women's suicide are for minor characters within the plot. Their deaths are often narrated in a few short lines and their barrenness and suicide alongside their very marginality underlines their dissociation from the national project. I have drawn on examples by authors whose novels have been considered elsewhere in this book in order to illustrate that these selfsame authors who use suicide as a trope for male characters in order to challenge national narratives, use suicide for female characters as a way of reinforcing them. Where possible I examine the suicide of female characters within the same novels in which the suicide of male characters has been explored (Kenaz, Shabtai, Tammuz), though where no such depictions exist, or when they are especially marginal, I have used other books from these authors' oeuvre (Yehoshua, Kenaz). A pattern about ways of representing women's suicide, and the reasons for their suicide emerges in these representations that I will explore more fully in an extended discussion of Katzir's novel.

In A. B. Yehoshua's novel about the end of the first Christian millennium, *Masa 'el sof ha-elef* (*Journey to the End of the Millennium*, 1997), Ben Attar searches for his nephew Abulafia, who has taken a new wife and is living in Europe, refusing to return home to the Near East. Abulafia's "beautiful young [first] wife" receives little mention in the plot, except to inform the reader that she "had drowned herself because of the bewitched, feeble-witted child she had brought into the world, doubling and redoubling by her scandalous death the shame she had brought upon her husband, so that he had been compelled to banish himself."[36] This first description of Abulafia's wife, who remains nameless, only gives a hint of the way in which the woman dies, instead presenting the dishonor the woman brings upon her family. She is shamed for failing to produce an heir, or at least a beautiful child, and instead giving birth to a "monster" (a female child who is disabled) and then by parading her deformed child publicly.[37] It is only some pages later that we are told that she committed suicide: "When at high tide the sea gave up his wife's body, with her hands and feet tied with the colored ribbons she had used to adorn her daughter's clothing, all knew at once that she had taken her own life."[38] The woman was seated on a rock, which she had "clamber[ed] up," before leaping to her death, conjuring up images of both jumping, in this case from the high rock, and of drowning, as she is washed up from the sea. Her decision to commit suicide is inextricably linked to her failure as a mother. Ben Attar refuses to have the child in his own home after Abulafia leaves, and the child is left with a woman hired specifically to take care of her. Finally, her mother, her father, and her uncle have abandoned the child, and though she is the catalyst that causes her father to leave home, the child, like her mother, remains marginal to the plot.

In *Infiltration*, Alon commits suicide after being betrayed by his ideology and his commanding officer, as discussed in chapter 2. In the same novel, the only example of a female's attempted suicide occurs offstage in response to becoming pregnant and being abandoned by Avner. While the first example of suicide demonstrates an opposition to the military hegemony, the second example associates suicide with pregnancy, and the girl's subsequent madness. Her situation is described through a male gaze which characterizes her as unstable and Avner as a rogue. But while Avner is redeemed over the course of the novel, the woman disappears.

> "He's corrupt, rotten. You know what he did? He got one of the girls at school pregnant, and when he found out about it he buggered off, just buggered off and didn't want to have anything more to do with her. She had a breakdown, she went crazy and tried to kill herself and she had to go to a psychologist. He ruined her life." (*I*, 130)

The girl's existence is important only as far as she relates to Avner, and even then, she is voiceless, despite her pregnancy and subsequent suicide attempt. In this discussion she remains nameless, her identity defined by her potential role as a mother and her later failure to fulfill that role. In this example, the thread of madness is particularly emphasized, though it is clear that her insanity is triggered by her abandonment.

Kenaz's most "female" novel, *Ba-Derekh el Ha-Hatulim* (*The Way to the Cats*, 1991), a meditation on aging played out through the central protagonist Yolanda Moscovitz's illness and increasing degeneration, offers suicide as an alternative to the pain and isolation Yolanda experiences. Through the depiction of Yolanda's neighbor Betty Poldy, the only person with whom Yolanda has regular contact after she leaves the hospital, suicide comes to represent an act of insanity. The dignity and attempts at self-sufficiency that indicate Yolanda's recovery are contrasted with Betty's disheveled and increasingly frenetic state. Betty's madness is characterized by hysterical screaming from her balcony. She refuses to dress properly when she leaves the house and wears only her underwear (a petticoat and bra). She is also obsessed with the cats in the alley below the apartment and on one occasion throws the contents of the refrigerator outside for them:

> "Betty sick. She not know what good, what bad," said Mr. Poldy. "Every foods in frigidaire she throw to cats. Only yesterday I go in supermarket. Like dream all the life for Betty, like hallucinate."[39]

Betty's husband is embarrassed by her behavior but cannot stop her, and the couple has no children who, the text implies, might have helped them. Yolanda, though not a friend, is their only acquaintance. In due course Betty commits suicide and is seen lying in the courtyard surrounded by a pool of blood while a neighbor calls out, "she jumped from their balcony." He explains, "I suddenly saw her in the air, falling on to the branches of the tree, breaking them and crash! On to the ground."[40] Echoing similar trends of representing women's suicide the image of her death suggests escape rather than finality.[41]

Shabtai's novel *Past Continuous* explored in the previous chapter for its isolated and suicidal male protagonist disillusioned by the discrepancy between an imagined Tel Aviv and its reality, contains two female suicides: Kaminskaya and Shalva. The prostitute Kaminskaya, like Betty Poldy, jumps from the balcony of her apartment. Marked out and rejected by being a prostitute, Kaminskaya's humiliation is sealed by the litany of her failures: her slovenly abode with its full ashtrays and clothes strewn about the room; her irresponsibility, including leaving a red-hot kettle on the stove; her debauchery (she is a drunken prostitute); and her semiclad state. The symbols of her disgraced status prelude the plummet to her death. By dying in a dressing gown, not properly clothed, she conjures up images of eroticism, wantonness, and sexual corruption. Like Betty Poldy, Kaminskaya's state of undress conveys her dissipation. Thus the women's appearance signifies them as 'fallen' women. The intertwining of suicide, madness, and sexuality in these literary depictions indicates the corruption of women failing to fulfill their duty as wives and mothers.

> Outside the darkness was already complete, but not so black or dense as to obliterate the dark treetops of the poinsettia regia

and the ficus, at the foot of which they had discovered the body of Kaminskaya after she had thrown herself drunkenly from the balcony of her third-floor apartment one summer sometime after the end of the war, and in the apartment full of plants and fine tapestries hanging on the walls, with the lights on in the big room and in the kitchen, they had found ashtrays and glasses full of cigarette butts, empty brandy bottles, newspapers and books and clothes, and a kettle with all its water boiled away standing red hot on the stove. (PC, 75)

By dying "sometime after the end of the war" Kaminskaya has also failed ideologically, since her death is not associated even in a peripheral way with war, but instead occurs at a time of peace when, the text implies, responsible citizens should be contributing to the national enterprise. The 1950s were a period of austerity, yet Kaminskaya's home is filled with luxury in the guise of tapestries, and the many plants signal her distance from agricultural Zionism, with its focus on growing food. The consistent denunciation of Betty Poldy and Kaminskaya represents a trend of marking out unsuitable, marginalized women as irredeemable, whose death indicates their damnation. Yet in leaping from their balconies, the final images of the women elevate their previously debased character, for in flying, rather than plummeting, the women are transformed into angels, borne on the air symbolically liberated from their madness and decay.[42]

Shalva is described, several pages before her suicide is narrated, as the "pretty younger sister Shalva" who in contrast to her sister Yaffa did not have "both feet firmly on the ground" (PC, 128). Within a few days of meeting him, Shalva recklessly married a man she saw playing on the beach and performing somersaults to entertain her. The marriage was over within six months when he suddenly abandoned her and went off to America.

Shalva, cut down with her face still warm and glowing with happiness, shut herself up in her house and imposed a total ban on all her family and friends, especially her father, and all their attempts at conciliation bore no fruit and she deliberately humiliated herself by taking all kinds of stupid and sometimes degrading jobs, and by neglecting herself and giving herself to all kinds of men she hated who left her with a feeling of disgust and degradation, and all this in order to punish the world, and especially her family, for the insult she had suffered and for the terrible blow to her boundless pride. (PC, 75)

Following her abandonment and humiliation Shalva becomes progressively distanced from society. Without children, and isolated from her family, she becomes morally repugnant to herself and others. When she is found dead with a note donating her body to science, "she had taken such good care to conceal and deny all family connections over the years that no one imagined there was anyone to inform when they discovered her suicide" (PC, 233). Shalva is described bathing and washing her hair before dressing in her best clothes and swallowing sleeping tablets (PC, 232–33). This water imagery enhances the sense of Shalva's rejection. Her failure to connect with members of her family, or relate to society at large, is shown through her surviving sisters' "lack of sorrow" (PC, 233). They had not been in contact with her for twenty-five years and it is as though she had ceased to exist long before her actual death. By dedicating her body to science, she is further depersonalized, particularly in a novel in which cemeteries, tombstones, and acts of commemoration play such a central role. It is only by coincidence that anyone comes upon a notice of her death.

The death of Bella-Yaffa in Tammuz's novel *Requiem for Na'aman* which impacts the lives of the remaining characters, as discussed in chapter 3, at first appears to be an anomaly in regard to the descriptions, method, and reasons ascribed to the other examples mentioned here. She is married and has children, unlike the other, childless characters described. After leaving her home, she rides all night, and in the morning she arrives at the foot of a hill and then poisons herself, neither dying submerged in water nor falling from a great height.[43] But Bella-Yaffa's rejection of Zionist ideology, demarcates her as an unbefitting mother, since she fails to inculcate her children into the myths of the state. Her connection to the suicide of the other female characters can be seen in her insanity. In a mad trance, she imagines that she is speaking to her husband and children and describes the reasons for her death. As discussed in chapter 3, Bella-Yaffa's suicide is linked to her love of European open spaces and her discomfort with the local Levantine landscape she is meant to admire (RN, 4).

Having been brought to "the land of my father's dreams," she does not love it as she had loved her home, saying, "I mixed poison in the cup of salvation" (RN, 3). This metaphorical poison is portrayed in the potion that she drinks which leads to her death. In effect, Bella-Yaffa's suicide is the fate of a woman who abandons the collective vision. She has rejected the homeland, on the one hand, and her family's hopes and desires for that homeland, on the other. Increasingly isolated, she is described as "silent," abandoning her husband and the world around her. Although her death is by poison, the gradual breakdown in Bella-Yaffa's identity, her disdain of Zionism, and accordingly her inability to put her womb at the service of the nation, exclude her from the social norm thereby locating her within the Israeli tradition of female suicides.

These few examples demonstrate a pattern in the depiction of female suicide in Israeli literature. The women, having failed to bear children, veer toward madness. Their deaths appear to fit two kinds of models. In the first, a woman who is sexually immoral jumps to her death, while in the second, a woman who is portrayed as sexually innocent dies in a watery grave. Though the death of Bella-Yaffa does seem to be anomalous, when considered in the framework of her abandonment of Zionism, she too embodies many of the traditional aspects of a female suicide's representation. The rest of this chapter considers the ways in which these patterns evolved and the Jewish tradition and European literary heritage that have informed these depictions, analyzing in detail the ways in which Katzir's *Closing the Sea* embodies these well-established literary conventions.

Barrenness and Remembering: Granting Women Identity

The model of mother and homemaker, and the desire to die because a woman finds herself barren, is a female archetype traceable to biblical figures.

> In the Hebrew Bible, childbearing embodies both the fulfillment of a positive *mitzvah* and the showering of prosperity from God. Barrenness, on the other hand, is seen as a curse.[44]

Rachel, the model of motherhood, has trouble conceiving, as do the matriarchs Sarah and Rebecca before her. Other female figures in the later texts such as Hannah in I Samuel, and the mother of Samson in Judges also experience periods of infertility.[45] Their barrenness becomes a trope representing female failure, a situation that, through faith in God, may be overcome. Just as with other biblical imagery and its reuse in contemporary Zionist mythology, the deity is replaced by the state. The Jewish obligation to procreate for religious reasons is reinterpreted as the need to reproduce for ideological ones.

The link between barrenness and death features prominently in the Jewish tradition. Distressed about her infertile state, Rachel calls out to her husband Jacob saying, "Give me children or I die" (Genesis 30:1). Hannah refuses to eat, and when her husband comes to plead with her arguing, "am I not better than ten sons," she still wishes to die (Samuel 1, 1:8). It is clear from the texts that both women are loved by their husbands, but as barren women consider themselves to be devoid of a clear identity.[46] Rachel's cry can be understood to mean that being childless is tantamount to being dead in society or that without children she will physically die. This can be read as both a figurative death and, in the case of Hannah, a literal death. In the texts, childbearing defines these women's identity. This is a position that is reinforced in the later rabbinic literature. Rabbi Yehoshua ben Levi is credited with saying, "A person who is childless is accounted as dead, for it is written, 'Give me children or else I am dead.'"[47]

Rachel, the biblical matriarch, is known by the expression "Rachel our mother," and as such becomes the archetypal representation of motherhood. In Jeremiah, she has a specific lamentation where she refers to the Jewish people as her sons.

> Thus saith the Lord:
> A voice is heard in Ramah
> Lamentation and bitter weeping
> Rachel weeping for her children;
> She refuseth to be comforted for her children
> Because they are not [comforted]. (Jeremiah 31:16)

Drawing on this imagery, the popular Israeli song "Rei Rahel Rei" (1967) written by Shmuel Rozen, a veteran of the Carmel platoon's musical troupe and the Palmach's Hizbatron, evokes the historical connection between Rachel as the mother of the Jewish people, and the Israeli army. Nationalist fervor following the Six-Day War inspired an explosion in music about military victories, and this song addresses the newly gained access to Rachel's tomb, Shechem (Nablus) and Beit Lehem (Bethlehem), calling on Rachel to "transform your voice, Rahel, transform your (voice of) tears" because the Jewish people (the soldiers) have returned and the land has been redeemed. The resonance between the biblical imagery (and later religious texts such as Lamentations, which also reused these earlier ideas) and the contemporary Zionist project demonstrates what Ruth Kartun Blum has described as Hebrew's ongoing palimpsest "in which subliminal layers show through" and is also evident in the use of Samson imagery explored in chapter 1.[48]

Rachel, the biblical matriarch, is accredited in the rabbinic literature with having taught God "mercy" (*rahamim*) — which is etymologically linked to the word "womb" (*rehem*) — since she reminds God to have mercy on "her sons." *Hamu me'ay lo rehem arahemenu naum-Adonai* ("I will have mercy and compassion for him saith the Lord") is taken up in the Israeli postwar song, announcing that all the sons are now present. Hannah cannot bear children, as "God closed her womb" (*Ve-Adonai sagar rahamah*) (I Samuel 1:5) and later this is repeated, "because God closed her womb" (*ki sagar Adonai ba'ad rahamah*) (I Samuel 1:6).[49] The use of *rehem* here means womb, but in this context, it can also be read symbolically as God's lack of mercy in causing barrenness.

When Rachel finally conceives, she is said to have been "remembered" by God. "And God remembered Rachel and he heard her, and God opened her womb" (Genesis 30:22). This becomes a theme throughout the biblical representations of barrenness through which God's remembering ends barrenness.[50] God also remembers Hannah after she supplicates, "remember me and do not forget your bondswoman . . . and God remembered her" (I Samuel 1:11–19). Only when God remembers these women do they bear children, and in turn, as a result of these children the women's function in the text is made apparent. The sons each of these previously barren women births, and the importance these men later have in the Bible, demarcate their responsibility in Jewish history. This is illustrated particularly by the biblical example of Samson's mother, who remains nameless in Samson's story, though his exploits extend for several chapters, her entire identity and description in the text comes from her role as his mother. Zionist ideology has re-evaluated this idea, making childbirth a woman's ideological duty, rather than her religious duty. But it too has drawn on the biblical text and the redemption of the land, which can only be reclaimed by the rightful sons.

In Judaism, women could only choose marriage and childbirth. As Yael Feldman has argued, the option of living a cloistered life, married to God, did not exist in Judaism.[51] The Maid of Ludmir (1815–c. 1892/95) was a Jewish woman who chose to follow a spiritual calling rather than the expected course of matrimony and maternity. In the past, she has been cited as an example to demonstrate the supposedly "liberating" tendencies of Hasidic Judaism. More recently, her story has been portrayed as that of "a deviant, whose ultimate failure serves precisely to reinforce the boundaries which she attempts to cross, not to undermine them."[52]

Increasing Isolation

Women who find themselves in conflict with or outside societal norms are more likely to commit suicide than those who feel a part of the social norm according to sociological research, providing a starting point for analyzing the role that women have in Israeli society. The symbols within the text that reinforce these expectations are clearly identifiable as no alternative model is offered for these suicidal women other than motherhood. In the many short depictions of women who commit suicide, the very simplicity of their representation adds weight to their failure and indicates the inevitability of their death according to these social constructions. Even in the late twentieth century, many of the old ideals about women's place in society continue to be represented in the text's imagery. In the brief examples of women's suicides outlined above, each of the women is shown to be alienated from mainstream society. Betty Poldy and Bella-Yaffa due to their madness (which may in turn have resulted from their desire to escape Israel), Kaminskaya due to her prostitution, Shalva as a result of personal choice stemming from humiliation, and Abulafia's first wife due to the disabled child she bore. Sociological readings of the cause of suicide, based on Durkheimian models, often cite a woman's isolation from society as a major indicator for her later suicide. This isolation can become all consuming, and representations of women's suicide in literature often reflect a trajectory of separation from the collective, which leads to a state of seclusion and loneliness and finally concludes in an act of suicide that is often portrayed as a passive dissolution so that even before her death, a woman is symbolically left without substance.

Female Suicide in European Literature

Nevertheless, despite the link between the biblical and modern texts, though Rachel laments her barrenness, she does not commit suicide. In contrast to the rich historical literature that provides the first accounts of Hebrew male literary suicides, celebrating sacrifice and heroism in narratives about Samson, Saul, and Ahitophel, there are no examples of female suicides in the Bible. Instead, the depictions of women's suicide in modern Hebrew literature can be traced to those models which appear in European and Russian literature. Though this chapter does not pretend to explore European literary suicides, it is pertinent to mention here the two traditional models for female literary suicides in Europe in the medieval and modern periods, and the extent to which these are based on the two traditional female archetypes described in European literature. This acceptance of European models reflects the conventionality of the depictions of female suicide. These patterns are used repeatedly and become literary shorthand for representing the moral character of the female who dies.

Sandra M. Gilbert and Susan Gubar define the two major Christian European female literary archetypes as women who are "fallen," and those who are "angels."[53] These models of womanhood have dominated literary depictions, and in her innocent angelic form woman can be depicted as chaste and virginal. In the literary tradition of suicide, this sexually chaste woman's death is linked to unrequited love; her chastity has not been compromised, and she usually dies in a watery grave. Shakespeare's Ophelia and Tennyson's Lady of Shalott are both examples of this literary convention. According to Irina Paperno, in Russian literature and society, "women who drown themselves are accorded a special place: they join the ranks of *rusalki*, attractive female creatures populating various waters."[54] The mythical *rusalki* are alluring nymphs or sirens, linked to the seasons. They are attractive and desirable in spring and summer, but are described as water-logged corpses, with pallid flesh, lank, dark green hair, red-rimmed glassy eyes, and puffy features in winter. In their seductive form these watery characters resemble the figure in John Keats's "La Belle Dame Sans Merci", a woman who is both alluring and unavailable, a powerful temptress who takes on the guise of an innocent victim in order to lure her prey. The *rusalki* and Keats's poem work within the tradition of depicting innocent virginal women amid water imagery, with water suggesting a prelude to death, and particularly to suicide.

In contrast, the "fallen" woman often has a violent end, usually plummeting to her death from a height. She is a sexually corrupt and corrupting woman whose death transpires following an epiphany about the error of her ways. Her excessive sexuality may lead to other immoral or criminal acts, such as murder. Her suicide is an attempt to erase her former actions and gain redemption. Tosca, Lady Macbeth, and even Anna Karenina, who "falls" under a train after committing adultery, exemplify this trope.[55] Science underpinned the legitimacy of representing fallen women as those most likely to commit suicide. In 1879, the British medical journal *The Lancet*, discussing Guido Morselli's earliest work on suicide, predating the more famous treatise by Émile Durkheim in 1897, acknowledged, "there is an ongoing dialogue which reflected earlier discourse and images of prostitutes and promiscuous women as a high-risk group."[56]

In the nineteenth century in England, women became increasingly associated with jumping off the bridges of London, particularly Hungerford and Waterloo, and this was frequently illustrated in the graphic art of the period.[57] Images of the time show the women suspended in the air, as though they are soaring. This depiction also reinforced the symbolic meaning of the term "fallen woman." Using illustrations from nineteenth-century newspapers, Ron Brown shows that: "alongside the iconography of [. . .] the drowned woman, the falling woman was one of the most enduring and oft-repeated themes in the portrayal of women's suicide."[58] Gilbert and Gubar have suggested that although Catherine in Emily Brontë's *Wuthering Heights* appears to die in childbirth, the symbolism associated with her end and the events leading up to it (the sexual betrayal of her husband with Heathcliff, and of Heathcliff her great love with her husband) imply that her death can be seen as an act of suicide. They explain: "For a 'fallen woman' trapped in the distorting mirrors of patriarchy, the journey into death is the only way out."[59] This image was not simply a mystical response but a socially acceptable, practical solution to the problems associated with being a social outcast.

In nineteenth-century imagery, the depictions of suicidal women flying through the air provided a sense of theatricality to the deaths while simultaneously offering the women as a sacrifice. The images mixed sympathy with sexual desire, "as their saturated clothes allow the artist to highlight or expose the female form. Even in death, 'woman' is destined to be consumed."[60] By depicting the women flying, images romanticized the death, sanitizing the experience. These women, though harlots, become angels, as their dresses fly up like wings. Removed from the sordid aspects of life and from their sexual corruption these women are emblematically released and redeemed. By representing the women in the air, they are not associated with the bloody mess of death. Thus these images depicted the liberation of women escaping from the tyranny of cruel fate.

Frequently, in both types of representation of these female archetypes, the angel and the harlot, "temporary madness [. . .] became represented as a cause of suicide" in nineteenth-century England.[61] According to Brown this attitude implied a kind of sympathy for the suicide as "underneath the criminality and the wrongness of it all was a recognition that personal distress can unhinge the mind."[62] This image when represented in literature is sometimes shown as hereditary insanity, as in the case of Bertha Rochester, and sometimes as a response to unrequited love, as with the Lady of Shalott and the earlier model of Ophelia.[63] This may be a literary response to English societal values, for in the early nineteenth century a suicide could still be buried at a crossroads with a stake through his or her heart and covered in lime. Even after 1823, when a law was passed making it illegal for coroners to bury a person in a public highway, the body still had to be buried within twenty-four hours in a churchyard or public burial place, without Christian rites, and at night between nine and midnight, with all his or her property being turned over to the Crown. However, a judgment of temporary insanity could be returned instead, thereby allowing for normal burial rites and a heritable estate. This verdict was more commonly issued when the suicide was not assumed to have been committed in order to avoid conviction for another crime; so that it became "an aphorism to say that in England you must avoid suicide on pain of being regarded as a criminal if you failed and a lunatic if you succeeded."[64]

Nevertheless, two exceptions seem to have existed legally and symbolically, "cases involving disinterested patriotism in which a person subjects himself to obvious danger or even certain death for the preservation of state secrets," and a woman who commits suicide "in order to preserve her chastity and honor from otherwise inescapable rape threatening her."[65] Again, the woman's preservation of her chastity is seen as primary, and the only other situation that was considered equivalent was the protection of state secrets. In being raped, she would neither qualify to become a virgin married to God, nor a wife and mother, therefore locating herself outside the possible social norms for a woman in the Christian world. In Israeli society, only the woman's duty to procreate exists, and in failing to do so, she no longer performs her role within society. In fiction, this ultimately leads to the protagonist's suicide

Reinterpreting the Christian Tradition in Yiddish Literature

Although Israeli literature draws on images from other cultural histories in order to highlight modern identity, these images are continually read through the Jewish and, its powerful contemporary extension, Israeli tradition. The premium placed on motherhood and childbirth and its inherently Jewish expectation for females is a significant aspect of female suicide in the Yiddish literary canon. While Jewish and later Israeli depictions of women concentrated on motherhood, the Christian tradition centralized excessive sexuality or its inverse, virginity, as the available portrayal of women. Although the expectations for Jewish and Christian women were different, the methods of representation used for the characters' eventual suicides in Yiddish literature were the same as those in European literature. Retaining the methods, drowning or falling, Yiddish literature envisioned the female protagonists through the prism of Jewish ideals and threats to Jewish identity in the modern age. Women who failed to fulfill the cultural norm of mother, the only Jewish model available to women, commit suicide.

A different and curious factor unites most of the literary suicides created by Yiddish authors: it is their failure to marry or, in fewer instances, to remain married once they have forged that bond. Suicide is forbidden, whereas marriage is one of the conventional obligations of Jewish existence. Thus the writers who sympathetically fashion suicidal characters suggest, through them, a hierarchy: the positive significance of marriage outweighs the negative importance of suicide. That is, where the commandment to marry cannot be fulfilled, the prohibition of suicide must be relaxed.[66]

This reaffirms the earlier Jewish position represented in the Bible and traditional texts: that a woman who is unmarried and therefore cannot bear children is subject to a kind of death, whether that be a spiritual or social death, as in the Bible, or literally, as in Yiddish literature.

Among the Yiddish writers describing female suicides in the late nineteenth and early twentieth centuries were Dovid Bergelson, Sholem Aleichem, and Y. L. Peretz. In stories by these men, unmarried women commit suicide. According to the text, they are unmarried because they are unfit to be wives, and therefore they must die. These moral tales concern "the dangers of abandoning traditional Jewish value and practice."[67] Janet Hadda has argued that women in Yiddish literature who are too willful (by conventional standards) to be tolerated commit suicide. Their behavior has an intensity usually directed toward pursuing an independent lifestyle, sometimes involving higher education, a search for knowledge, or unacceptable sexual activities. These women are considered to be unsuitable mothers because of their corrupt sexual mores and their distance from traditional female expectations.

> A woman who is perceived as excessively passionate does not fit the narrow confines of Jewish traditional married life. Thus they are outcasts of their society and where the society is itself considered cut off from other social groups, they become truly isolated.[68]

These women are not necessarily barren in the biblical sense, but through their behavior, they become unsuitable mothers. Barrenness in this literature may be seen as a metaphor for those women who are unable to produce Jewish progeny for reasons other than infertility. In its broadest meaning childlessness becomes a metaphor for the failure to conform to the Jewish ideal: marriage (specifically marriage to a Jewish man) and procreation. Ultimately in the Israeli writings, these barren women are cut off from society; they become increasingly isolated while simultaneously suffering from an erosion of identity, and finally they take their own lives.

Powerlessness

If women are powerless, then suicide was one of the few methods by which a woman could exert control over her person. "But of course, taken together, self-starvation or anorexia nervosa, masochism, and suicide form a complex of psychoneurotic symptoms that is almost classically associated with female feelings of powerlessness and rage."[69] Though Gilbert and Gubar are referring to literature in this example, Simone de Beauvoir makes a similar observation about women who commit suicide in real life. She argues that the wife of Tolstoy feigned suicide "since she had no positive reason to conceal her feelings of revolt, and no effective way of expressing them."[70] Suicide as a form of empowerment offers the powerless a way to escape social expectations. But for this reading to be convincing, other aspects of the text would need to support this idea.

More commonly, women's suicide in fiction, like women's suicide in life reflects a situation of disempowerment. Women attempt suicide more often than men, though they succeed less often, because, as Simone de Beauvoir explains, men have more alternative options before they resort to it.[71]

> [W]omen are more likely to be satisfied with play-acting; they pretend self-destruction more often than they really want it. It is also, in part, because the usual brutal methods are repellent; women almost never use cold steel or firearms. They are much more likely to drown themselves, like Ophelia, attesting the affinity of woman with water where, in the still darkness, it seems that life might find passive dissolution.[72]

De Beauvoir, though talking about life, is illustrating her example with a literary character. Thus, we can see how nineteenth- and early twentieth-century images of women's suicide in life, and the suicide of women in literature, have been equated, paralleled and connected; just as the discussion of Catherine's suicide in *Wuthering Heights* and its connection with late Romantic and early Victorian society, and Irina Paperno's discussion of the *rusalki* imagery in Russia, suggested.

Though literature is undoubtedly affected by the period in which it is written, that is not the only significant influence on the text. European literary trends are insufficient to explain the reasons for suicide in modern Hebrew literature, and only demonstrate the history behind the chosen methods of description for the deaths. As we are reminded by Feldman's landmark study on women in Israeli literature, and by Kartun-Blum's analysis of Yona Wallach's work, the European image of powerlessness and consequent suicide has to be read and reinterpreted through the Jewish ideal notion of motherhood.

> In order to explore her own modern identity, Wallach juxtaposes two idealized types of women from different canonic cultural traditions, the "mystic" in Christianity and the "pious observant" in Judaism. [...] In order to wrestle with the Bible, she avails herself of another tradition and a different notion of femininity. *The ideal for women in the Jewish tradition was to bear children.* The ideal for women in the Christian mystical tradition was marriage with God. By importing Christian myth, Wallach highlights its relevance to her own modern identity.[73]

Betty Poldy's and Kaminskaya's deaths are reminiscent of Brown's analysis of nineteenth-century drawings of women committing suicide by jumping from bridges, while their excessive sexuality is also linked with madness. Shalva's death in the bath and Abulafia's first wife's death in the sea reinforce the image of these women's virginal (and innocent) nature — and their madness echoes the death of Ophelia in *Hamlet* and Edna Pontellier in Kate Chopin's *The Awakening*. The examples of female suicides in Israeli literature, though often the deaths of minor characters within the novels, demonstrate accepted conventions. Sometimes the women's flawed nature can be explained as barrenness, due to biology or circumstances; at other times it is the women's inability to fulfill Zionist expectations — not only to bear children, but to produce ideologically committed progeny — which makes them inadequate mothers. These women are never offered an alternative role and therefore, if they fail as mothers, the only choice Hebrew literature presents for them is suicide.

Closing the Sea — A Novella of Suicide

In her novella *Closing the Sea* (*Sogrim et ha-Yam*, 1988), Yehudit Katzir presents the identity erosion of a thirty-three-year-old woman and her disconnection and isolation from society over the course of one day. Ilana, the protagonist, takes the day off work as a schoolteacher in Haifa, the town in which she grew up, with the intention of meeting her best friend from childhood, Tami, who now lives in Tel Aviv, only an hour's distance away, but whom she has not seen in two years. Despite repeated dreams of visiting the city, and numerous attempts to contact her old friend, only now does Ilana finally succeed in making the trip. She intends to spend the day shopping for something new to wear, eating in a fashionable café, and walking by the sea, before meeting Tami at five o'clock at her apartment. However, as the day progresses, her plans go awry and Ilana becomes increasingly afraid and desperate. The shopping trip proves a failure, and having spent all her money she cannot afford a nice meal, the oppressive heat prevents her from walking around, and she cannot find the sea. After waiting for two hours for Tami who has forgotten the meeting, the visit proves a failure. On her return journey, a stranger in a shared taxi sexually abuses Ilana. Arriving home, Ilana discovers that a schoolteacher she was close to has died and in a mad frenzy she cuts up the expensive dress she had bought in the city. Finally, she commits suicide in the bath.

From the outset of the novella, Ilana is presented as pathetic and vulnerable. Her position as a teacher, which could have represented responsibility and confidence, is weakened due to her fear of the students. At thirty-three her single status is problematic, demonstrated by her abortive relationship with Shmuel (her married university lecturer); the marriage of her twenty-three-year-old cousin, whose wedding she is too embarrassed to attend; and by the symbolic appearance of three widows in the Tel Aviv shopping center, discussing their married lives. Throughout the course of the story, it is progressively apparent that Ilana is unmarried because she has a childlike attitude to life. If she is not an adult, then she cannot enter into adult relationships. While Ilana shelters in a cinema from the oppressive Tel Aviv heat she meets Boris, who makes romantic advances toward her. Despite his kindness and her attraction toward him, she is incapable of responding warmly. Ilana's barrenness is indicated by her lack of children, by her inability to resolve her relationship with her school pupils of whom she is afraid, and by the sterility of other friendships and unions. Tami has forgotten their previous friendship; Ilana's relationship with Shmuel is meaningless to him; shop assistants treat Ilana with disdain; and she rejects the potentially more rewarding relationship that she was offered by Boris. Ilana is single and portrayed as likely to remain so.

Ilana's infantilization is a constant theme throughout the novel. After she lies to the headmaster on the telephone in order to miss a day of work, she crawls into bed to hide, like a child: "she covered her head with a light blanket just as she had used to do on the mornings of holidays during her childhood" (CS, 114). The reader learns that on the previous occasion, on which Ilana had stayed with Tami some years earlier, she had slept on the sofa and, embarrassed by the idea of Tami and Tami's husband sharing a bedroom, she hid under the covers, pulling the blanket over her head so that she would not hear the noises from the other room (CS, 117). Ilana is terrified of displays of sexuality, such as those indicated by Tami's relationship with her husband. Other examples include her alarm at the pornographic magazines she sees at a kiosk, and by a woman in a bikini on a poster at the bus stop. Ilana sees a madman shouting in the street and the experience becomes uncomfortably sexualized as she experiences his madness as a physical attack. "Something inside her was shocked and shaken as though he had touched her and stained her dress" (CS, 125). When Ilana uses the toilet at the Dizengoff Centre, she is traumatized by the sexual proposition written on the toilet wall, both because of the suggestion, which shocks her, and because it is her own name which appears there: "If you want me to lick you call me, and her name was written, Ilana . . . Ilana recoiled" (CS, 129). Although she has had a sexual relationship with Shmuel, who is married and therefore unavailable emotionally to her, the unproductive union (because it gives her neither children nor pleasure) is a failure. In the description of the relationship, Ilana is cast in the role of innocent virgin suffering from unrequited love and never making the transition from child to adult.

At first Ilana revels in her childlike behavior and celebrates what appears to be a still prepubescent body. "Ilana smiled at herself in the mirror and said 'you haven't changed in any way in all these years'" (CS, 115). Her undeveloped adult body fills her with a strange pleasure: "And suddenly she was even satisfied with her gaunt body, with barely discernible breasts, and her matchstick legs" (CS, 115). This childlike figure parallels her emotional development, which also seems hindered. Without passing from childhood to womanhood and, more importantly, without realizing that she should have done so, Ilana remains trapped in a juvenile state. She remembers with delight that her friend Tami "would look at her with envy when they had been girls of twelve" (CS, 116) and Tami had already begun to develop the body of a woman, because even then she already had breasts.

> And Ilana took stolen glances at Tami's breasts that could already be seen clearly in her pink stretchy leotard, like two small plums . . . and at her thighs that had started to become rounder. (CS, 115)

But Ilana does not acknowledge that they are no longer twelve and that the desire for a flat chest, in order to look better in a pink ballet leotard, is no longer pertinent.

Other examples of Tami's increasing sexuality provide a contrast to Ilana's body, and she is revealed to have "raspberry juice" lips (CS, 116). Later Tami's "full round breasts" (CS, 117) are described on the morning of Ilana's visit to Tami's home. Tami is engaged in adult activities, such as preparing breakfast and cooking, and her behavior is contrasted with Ilana's attempt to force Tami to recall their youth together. Ilana continually attempts to relive the past, because she believes that it was a more positive time, but this, too, is an illusion, as her nightmares relating to this period demonstrate. At the end of the text when she admonishes herself, saying "you are not young," she is recognizing that she cannot continue to live in the past. Her realization comes too late, as she has not created a viable adult identity.

Ilana's attempt to wear makeup at the story's beginning is an ambiguous image. She knows that it does not suit her, and that the makeup will not last until the time of the meeting at five o'clock that afternoon (CS, 116). In some sense this is the act of a child dressing up, engaging in pretense. Ilana is trying out the possibility of becoming an adult, shown in a number of symbolic acts such as buying a black dress in Tel Aviv, which is described as an adult color and one she has never worn before. By lying to her boss on the telephone, Ilana is attempting to breach her childlike status for the first time. This is shown allegorically by her taking the day off from school, and although she is a schoolteacher by profession, school represents ties to her childhood and her failure to mature. Leaving the school becomes a metaphor for the move forward into adulthood, but as the day progresses Ilana regresses. Her makeup comes off when, like a little girl, she rinses her face in the washrooms at the Dizengoff Centre. As she returns in her mind to the image of the school and her memories of her early years with Tami she experiences a psychological breakdown between the present and the past, which culminates in her accidental visit to a school in Tel Aviv where she sits in the student's chair. Her panic in the school is part of a cycle of fear that she experiences throughout the day. Ilana conjures up threatening images of the future, which prevent her from enjoying the present, such as when she believes that someone has spotted her on the bus to Tel Aviv and will tell the headmaster (CS, 113). She feels guilt about lying to him and about missing a day of school. Her shock and fear are linked in her description of the school as a "terrible investigative bureau"; she even questions this personal terror, asking, "What are you so frightened of?" (CS, 117). But unable to overcome her terror, she is paralyzed.

School plays an important symbolic role in the story. Ilana never feels fully mature, and her nightmares include traumas she experienced as a child when she failed to remember things in class, and the frightening authority of her teacher Miss Moses. Ilana sees in her memory, not her childhood peers, but her current students. She has never become "Miss," with full control of the class, even though she is the teacher. Her behavior is contrasted with her own teachers, who are always known by this title, and highlights her disparity.[74] Furthermore, her dreams confuse past and present, and since she is both the student and the teacher, she is terrified, and believes that her body will betray her as it had when she was a child. Later, in Tel Aviv she is drawn to a school, much like the one where she has spent her whole life working and studying, indicating her emotional regression.

> Ilana stood at the gate and stared in wonder at this school, that if it were not for the silence resembled exactly her school, the one where she had passed the years of her youth, and where she worked now as a teacher. (CS, 133)

Ironically, Ilana, who has escaped her own school in an attempt to claim a day of freedom, enters this alien school, as it is the only place in Tel Aviv where she feels comfortable. She finds the English classroom, with irregular verbs on the board, exactly like her experience of school as a pupil, and as a teacher. There she reads the story of "Eveline" by James Joyce, which she knows well from English classes with Miss Moses, indicating her childlike need for the familiar. The story tells of a woman who refuses her lover from Buenos Aires and his offer of escape to the Americas (and an adult world), preferring a life with her abusive, violent, alcoholic father, in which she will be forever treated as a child. The story parallels Ilana's own inability to grasp the opportunities of escape offered to her by Boris, and her decision to remain in her adolescent state. Though offered the opportunity to behave as a woman, she opts to return to her childhood fantasies.

In the school, which she embraces as a safe haven, Ilana "went and sat in her usual place, next to the table before last on the right, next to the window"; a student's seat rather than that of the teacher (CS, 134). While there she starts imagining the past, her old math teacher, and later her favorite literature teacher, Rachel Margolis, who has since retired, finally confusing reality and her dream world. Ilana imagines being reprimanded for skipping school and the present and future become intertwined in her mind. In a frightened state she envisions her headmaster asking her for "a note from her parents" (CS, 134) to explain her absence. The last separation between her adulthood and her childhood reality collapses when Ilana tries to find her face in the teachers' photograph in the staffroom; she "searched, without believing, for her face" (CS, 135). Ilana's absence is inevitable since this is not her school, but in her confused mental state, this is incomprehensible to her. Her psychological deterioration continues through the course of the day, so that although the act of putting on makeup at the beginning could have signified the transition from childhood to adulthood, it instead becomes a mocking gesture and a failed disguise. As the makeup and dress are discarded, so is Ilana's persona as an adult.

In contrast, Tami embodies the traditional (and accepted) model of femininity and motherhood; her marriage and pregnancy suggest the ideal that Ilana has failed to fulfill. No other successful female role model, differing from that of wife and mother, is offered in the text, and therefore Ilana's life cannot be read as a thriving alternative. She has failed as a woman; she is not a mother; she is made figuratively infertile by her obsession with childhood, and thus she becomes a warning to other women who would follow in her footsteps. Her suicide comes about after it has become clear that she has no viable future as a woman in Israeli society.

Ilana's Barrenness

Ilana's social breakdown becomes a metaphor for her barrenness. Her emotional disintegration is accelerated as she becomes increasingly alienated from society. Forgotten at her cousin's wedding, discarded by Shmuel and ignored by Tami, there is no longer anyone who will liberate Ilana from her fear, manifested as her inability to live as a mature woman, and to achieve a fulfilling life, something only Rachel Margolis had convinced Ilana might be a possibility. Her failure to build meaningful relationships leads Ilana to become increasingly silent and isolated, and once she realizes Tami will have a child, an impossibility for her, she symbolically ceases to exist.

Like the biblical matriarchs, Ilana's real and metaphysical barrenness show that she has been forgotten, but unlike these archetypes, she is never "remembered." Upon seeing the notice of Rachel Margolis's death, Ilana realizes that the only person who validated her existence has now gone, leaving Ilana's symbolic abandonment complete. Her loneliness and the nonexistence of children, means that there is no redemption that can save her from death.

In the many short depictions of women who commit suicide considered at the beginning of this chapter, the very simplicity of their representation adds weight to their failure and indicates the inevitability of their death according to these social constructions. In the longer depiction of Ilana it is also possible to see, even in the late twentieth century, that many of the old ideals about women's place in society continue to be represented in the text's imagery. The character's psychological breakdown through the course of the narrative provides a rich template for the same arguments about the more summarily treated suicides of other female characters. Ilana's increasing alienation is contrasted continually with Tami's social inclusion. By appearing on stage and screen in Israel and abroad, Tami is connected to a broader social environment.

> Because Tami was in Los Angeles with Yoel her husband and after she returned she went straight to work on a series of advertisements and then started rehearsals for a new play. (CS, 114)

By contrast, Ilana is not even acknowledged by the people with whom she comes into contact. Shop assistants ignore her wishes and force her to purchase goods. The taxi driver does not answer her question and she cannot stop a man in the taxi feeling her thigh (CS, 150). Ilana has begun to disappear metaphorically long before her death, and by the end of the novella her very identity is in question. She is not recognized by others, and has no impact on their behavior. Her shadowy existence, a repeated theme, signals her unimportance throughout the novel. Ilana believes that in the past Tami has been too busy with work to meet; paradoxically, Ilana misses a day of her own employment in order to see her friend, who misses their meeting and has instead spent the day in a café. In Ilana's imagination, unreturned phone calls are explained by Tami's hectic life, but as Katzir shows, Tami immediately returns phone calls to other people. While Ilana has preserved every memory of their past interactions, Tami has forgotten their shared history. By forgetting the meeting, forgetting to return telephone calls, and forgetting the past, Tami challenges the core of Ilana's existence. Her death by drowning indicates the passive dissolution of a woman who is, even before her death, left symbolically without substance.

Silence and Impotence as Preludes to Death

Silence becomes a leitmotif forewarning death as examined in chapter 2 and 3. In *Closing the Sea* Ilana becomes increasingly isolated, demonstrated in the text by silence and her broken interactions with other people. Tami drives Ilana to the central bus station "in silence" and then Ilana remembered the ballet she wanted to tell Tami about, but "didn't say a word." Ilana "whispers goodbye and thank you" to Tami and closes the door behind her in "silence." Ilana attempts to return the evening dress, but the shop assistant "didn't listen to her," and when the cleaner at the school in Tel Aviv accosts the terrified Ilana, she is unable to speak and runs away (CS, 113, 127, 148–49, 135). Between leaving Tami's house and arriving in Haifa, Ilana's process of isolation increases in intensity, signaled by the silence of the taxi driver and the repellent sexual encounter in the vehicle, which she suffers in silence (CS, 150).

Ilana's inability to prevent the "foul-smelling man" from touching her thigh, while simultaneously masturbating, is juxtaposed with the response of a woman in the taxi who successfully prevents a man from smoking a cigarette (CS, 150). Ilana's failure to control her life is a theme that recurs throughout. At the start of the day, she has a piece of the honey cake that her mother gave her "despite her protests" (CS, 116). Though she does not want the cake, she is powerless to exert her will, as with her younger cousin's wedding which her parents force her to attend.

The reader is already aware that Ilana has been trying to get to the shopping center in Tel Aviv for many years but has never managed it before. She wants to see Tami's shows, but she does not even request tickets. "And Ilana wanted to ask, maybe you could invite me some time to see the performance . . . but she didn't ask" (CS, 117). Ilana is never able to insist upon her own preferences, and is instead subject to other people's will. Her powerlessness is reminiscent of the descriptions by Gilbert and Gubar, and de Beauvoir, of women's hopelessness, and correspondingly signifies suicide as her escape from a pitiless situation.

Tami's betrayal of Ilana is another significant step in this identity erosion process. As children, they had imagined their friendship continuing into old age. For Ilana this is a promise of eternal and everlasting friendship, and she is overjoyed, but it is a lie.

And Ilana was suddenly happy, as though she had been promised something wonderful and she smiled at Tami who smeared red lipstick over her face and said importantly "when I am big I will be an actress in the theatre." (CS, 117–18)

Later, when Ilana tries to remind Tami of this incident Tami does not remember it at all. By forgetting Ilana's past, Tami is also challenging Ilana's present. Symbolically Tami's dreams about the future come true, while Ilana's do not. As Ilana is departing, Tami kissed her, but "Ilana flinched a bit" (CS, 124), partly because she is not used to the physical contact, and partly because it is an empty gesture highlighted by Tami's slang English "keep in touch." Ilana realizes that they no longer have any meaningful conversation or communication, and Tami's behavior indicates that she feels no obligation or responsibility toward her former friend.

Just as Shalva in *Past Continuous* dies after she has been symbolically forgotten by her family and society, and the silence evident in the period leading up to Bella-Yaffa's suicide (*Requiem for Na'aman*) can be witnessed in the stages leading up to Ilana's death. Her inability to communicate symbolizes her increasing remoteness and seclusion as she ceases to exist. The actual act of suicide, like those of the virgins in the European Christian literary tradition, reflects this ambivalence with life, and her death in the bath, echoing Shalva's washing before she dies, is not an aggressive final act but a passive dissolution into nothingness. At the end of the text Ilana imagines herself floating away, flying up high, the same imagery used for Betty and Kaminskaya, even though she is in fact in a bath when she dies: "Look, teacher Ilana is flying, teacher Ilana is flying" (CS, 153). At last Ilana attains the status that she has acquired, becoming the "teacher" or "Miss" that was her due as an adult and teacher. But it is only in death that she is liberated. Just as with the other examples of female suicide, Ilana is disconnected from the world around her. She has been so negated by others that in her death she negates herself, but it is in death that she experiences the tranquility she longed for but was unable to achieve in life.

The story analyzes Ilana's realization that being young, which she had glorified in her own mind, has actually prevented her development as a woman. As her celebration of this physical and emotional development is challenged by events in Tel Aviv, her identity is also eroded. Her position as a teacher, her role as Tami's friend, and her conception of herself as young, and therefore on the threshold of life, are destroyed. "You're not young, Ilana, you're not young" (CS, 152) is the expression of Ilana's tragic realization that her imaginary prize of youth is an illusion. Unable to achieve the female ideal of motherhood since her body is that of a child rather than a woman, the collapse of her mental capacities, and her inability to manage adulthood, reveal that Ilana is a failure in terms of Zionist ideology.

In contrast with Ilana, Tami is revealed to be mature, even when still a young girl. She is the embodiment of a sexual, fertile woman. Tami is married, she has traveled abroad, unlike Ilana who has not even taken the short bus journey from Haifa to Tel Aviv in the past two years. Tami is not afraid of life and is active regarding her own destiny. The text implies that as a result, she is able to become a mother. By the end of the story, the reader is aware that Tami is pregnant, and has fulfilled her purpose in the Zionist narrative.

The question remains as to whether these women are killed off in the texts as an ideological warning by the authors, or whether these suicides are presented as a rejection of the expectations of motherhood. Though I am tempted to argue for the latter position, given that the typical use of the suicide trope has been to criticize national ideology, the distasteful way in which these women are presented as squalid prostitutes; as women with no self-respect, because they sleep with loathsome men and wander the streets half-naked; as women who are mad; or as women abandoned by men and by society; it is impossible to claim legitimately that they function in literature as anything but an illustration of the fate of a woman who fails to fulfill her duty.

Since this work set out to investigate the use of suicide in Israeli literature and soon found the use of the image offered writers a way to respond to different national institutions by offering a critique of Israel's founding myths, it seems interesting to note that on first reading, the suicide of women in Hebrew literary texts does not appear as an image of criticism against the state. The deaths of Kaminskaya, Shalva, Betty, Bella-Yaffa, and Ilana indicate a total submersion into and acceptance of the cultural norms. Specifically, since these women cannot bear children, which is their ideological obligation in terms of Zionism and, as I have shown, is also the expectation in Israel, these women accept that they have failed society and have no reason to continue to live. There is no suggestion that they can contribute usefully in some other way. These particular texts do not offer successful female role models as alternatives to the mother, which could have instead been adopted by these barren women.

Given that *Closing the Sea* is written by a female author, it seems that a woman writer may also appear to accept the archetype of motherhood as the only successful state for women. The image of suicide ironically supports and reinforces the institution of motherhood by suggesting a weeding out of the women who do not breed. Yet Katzir's text does, on another level, offer a criticism of other aspects of Zionist ideology. Tami rejects Zionism by moving abroad and working in foreign language productions, foreign films, and even in Israel she performs Russian plays by Chekhov. She has rejected Hebrew culture and Hebrew language, and she is not constrained by the obligations to live in the Jewish homeland, ideas and boundaries considered staple ingredients in the traditional commitment to Zionism. Nevertheless, as with the soldiers who were able to criticize national institutions precisely because they are exemplary models of the finest aspects of the establishment, Tami's critique of Israel is only possible because it functions within the accepted norms for women in Israel. It is possible to criticize many aspects of the national narrative, but myths of motherhood remain sacred and incontestable.

In this chapter, I have considered motherhood as an institution, which is not subject to the same kinds of attacks that have assailed other national narratives in Israeli society. Other symbols of Zionism such as Hebrew culture and an obligation to live in Israel are suggested to be obsolete by these authors, and form ideological resistance, but the presentation of the Jewish, and more specifically the Israeli woman, is still confined to her obligation to give birth to, and rear, healthy children for the state.

Though many images of Israeli society have been shattered and many taboos challenged, such as the need for self-sacrifice by the young male hero for the state, the place of the military as the dominant commemorative body valuing life (and death), and the development of a national narrative with its exclusion of other conflicting personal narratives, it may be that the institution of motherhood remains unassailable. Writers have not yet chosen to scrutinize the implications of this image or challenge its hegemonic status within Israeli culture. I would suggest that perhaps, if the values of Israeli culture were to change, the image of female suicide and its relationship to motherhood might also be transformed. Just as European nineteenth-century society, and the literature that reflected it, offered the additional option of marriage to God allowing for at least one other possibility for women, a transformation in cultural attitudes to women might also inform other meanings for the role of female suicide in fiction.

CHAPTER 6

Suicide in Fiction: Suicide in Life?

Albert Camus has written that there is only one real question posed by the act of suicide: whether life is worth living. In the context of Hebrew literature, the image of suicide poses the question: is life worth living in Israeli society? More accurately, the image challenges the construction of the Israeli national narrative, questioning aspects of the presentation of Israeli myths and the gap between these dreams and the reality.

Suicide in fictional texts can be tragic or heroic, expressing grand emotion — capturing the sensibility of jilted lovers, conveying the dedication of romance, and celebrating devotion to honor. Passion and valor characterize depictions in Western literature. The literary suicide in these narratives generates great sadness or inspires feelings of loyalty on the reader's part. Our feelings are controlled by the portrayal of the death, the character's role within the plot, even our own experiences of the fictional situation. But these kinds of literary suicide can also function as moral lessons, serving to inspire the reader to follow an ideology and suggesting the highest ideals of a society that should be emulated.

In Judeo-Christian societies suicide is generally prohibited, sometimes on legal but always on moral grounds. Cultural traditions within these societies have evolved representations of suicide in popular literature, journalism, religious texts, art, and other mediums which engage with the specific culture's views on suicide, inculcating the expected moral view. But these mediums are also able to engage with the dominant attitude to suicide. As this book has shown, depictions of suicide in literary texts might propose alternative codes that outweigh the prevailing social conventions such as intimating that heroism or excessive emotion can transcend the moral norm. In the Bible, Samson's suicide is an act of sacrifice so that he can protect his people, while King Saul falls on his sword as an expression of his despair at losing a battle. Shakespeare's portrayal of Romeo's and Juliet's suicides conveys the couple's deep love because of which they preferred to die rather than live apart, while Lady Macbeth's suicide is motivated by her guilt and despair. Goethe's Werther commits suicide when he is rejected by his paramour, and Tolstoy's Anna Karenina leaps in front of a train when she feels abandoned. In some cultures and situations suicide represents honor; in others it signifies great tragedy, so to understand a culture's relationship to suicide, or even suicide's role within the text, it becomes necessary to understand the established cultural systems and symbols within which the author is operating. Even within a single society these distinctions can be finely tuned. For example, in late-nineteenth-century Victorian England, suicide in high culture was a romantic, heroic gesture, while in low culture it was a sign of squalor and degradation.[1]

Within a different prevailing moral framework, one that considers suicide merely a banal approach to death, literary depiction in that culture will also reflect social perceptions. For example, in 46 B.C.E. in Utica, Cato the Younger committed a gruesome act of suicide after falling out with Caesar. In that society, suicide was a socially acceptable mode of political protest, and later his death was commemorated and viewed as a victory against Caesar's tyranny. Crucially, the significance of suicide in texts is not only inextricably connected to our ideas about the act of suicide but also to previously established, recognized and accepted beliefs held in society. Consequently, the way we receive depictions of suicide is culturally rooted.

Evidently literary suicide acts on our emotions. But it can do more. The self-sacrifice of a heroic military figure reinforces our perception of his earlier heroism. Portraying the suicide of a prostitute bolsters perceptions of her immoral lifestyle. The suicide of an adulterous woman coming as it does at the end of her betrayal, though tragic, emphasizes a morality code that frowns upon adultery and sexual promiscuity, whereas a woman who commits suicide in order to protect her virginity, or a soldier who is captured and commits suicide rather than betray his comrades, become lauded moral examples influencing our cultural, moral, and even political values.[2] The placement of suicide in the text can generate alternative perceptions — ones which make us explore, or even reject, accepted cultural norms. A soldier who commits suicide because he has been rejected romantically not only challenges the myth of military heroism but contests the celebration of positive notions of self-sacrifice.

In fiction suicide functions as a trope in an author's repertoire, but its meanings (for example, sadness, isolation, heroism) and its role in the text (for example, as opposition to national expectations, or as a warning in a morality tale) only become clear when read in the context of the work, as well as its status within the cultural framework, and after examining attitudes to suicide within the society in which the text is produced. Different values are privileged through the complex interaction between the image of suicide, the narrative in which it appears, and the society that consumes it. A given society's attitude toward texts and narratives will also affect the image's reception. A text's cultural capital is influenced by a multitude of factors, including the relative status and role of high or low culture, established icons and beliefs, and the social acceptability of texts as common currency for communicating ideas (and in the case of Hebrew literature these may be national ideas). Social and historical changes in the periods during which the text was written and in which the text is set affect the ways in which these aspects influence the text, such that attitudes toward similar ideas may have altered due to national or social changes within society, and this, in turn, will affect both the depiction of the suicide and its role in the text.

The model that I have suggested in this book may equally well apply to literatures other than that of Israel. This involves a significant departure from much of the scholarly tradition associated with studying suicide in literary text. Greek tragedy, the Bible, Shakespeare, Victorian melodrama, Russian Realism, French Romanticism, and European modernism all depict images of suicide. Social sciences, particularly sociology and psychology, which offer abstract ways of thinking about suicide, have impacted literary studies, often leading scholars to read fictional characters or even authors as clinical cases.

Current critical scholarship on the image of suicide in literature falls into three categories. These are the author's personal attitude to suicide, the lifelike quality of the literary suicide, and the impact of the literary suicide on the reader (reader response theory). These theories collectively may be considered the *text and life* approach because of the relationship they draw between suicide in the text and suicide in life. Formulating theories grounded in social science to describe a literary character's life often separates the character's death from the text in which it occurs. Representations of suicide exist in tension with the ideology that frames them, and which the text elucidates. The study of suicide in Israeli literature provides a model for examining the allegorical, symbolic potential of suicide and engages with rich interdisciplinary resources that can serve the literary scholar, but only when adapted to consider literary suicide.

Theoretical Approaches

Rather than approaching each critical text as an independent entity and analyzing these scholarly works in isolation, I present the patterns of thought that emerge from these works. First, I want to consider scholarship that examines the relationship between the author and the text, which generally analyses the writer's world. At the most personal level this can be an analysis of the author's own feelings about or experiences of suicide, and the text is read through these expressions and concerns, so that the literature assumes the role of a suicide note.[3]

At the other end of this spectrum is the situation most distant from the author's personal or emotional experience. The author is motivated by a story about a suicide that is told to him or her or one that appears in the newspaper, for example. Intellectual curiosity stimulates the author's interest so that the fiction becomes an attempt to understand the suicidal drive of an individual. Irina Paperno in her analysis of suicide in nineteenth-century Russia presents the case of Dostoevsky's "Krotkaia" ("The Meek One," 1876), a short story inspired by the description of a woman's suicide that had appeared in the press. Dostoevsky was responding to life through literature. Similarly Brown presented the cases of nineteenth-century journalists and sketch artists fascinated with the suicides of young women, which they ghoulishly replicated within the pages of their newspapers.

Second are those theories which evaluate suicide in the novel as though the character is a real-life (sometimes called a clinical) case. Durkheim's sociological theories, which more than a century after they were written remain standard for the classification of suicide, provide a point of reference for literary scholars. His 1897 study on suicide defined four types: altruistic, egoistic, anomic, and fatalistic. Despite extensive research since then, his work has remained a seminal text in the field of suicidology. As David Lester argues, anything that has followed on from this work may be considered an attempt to redefine one aspect, or one premise, of Durkheim's much larger and broader idea.[4] In a literary context we can look to the sociocultural frame in which a character operates such that *anomie* refers to those who commit suicide when they feel outside or unconstrained by cultural norms and therefore isolated. *Fatalism* is where a person chooses suicide over a future or fate that is not considered desirable according to the social norm. *Egoism* is suicide by someone who feels a sense of rejection for a real or imagined slight, and *altruism* is self-sacrifice for the real, or perceived, greater good.

Rather than identifying the sociological likelihood of a character committing suicide, Durkheim's methods should and do provide a set of tools for analyzing suicide in texts. Is a character integrated into society? Does his rejection by that society matter? Within the context of the novel, does the suicide indicate a betrayal of the ideological expectations placed on the individual, who may feel that the only way to serve society is to die in battle? Alternatively, has the suicidal character been placed in an ideologically untenable situation which, feeling divorced from society, he wishes to escape?

Durkheim suggested that different social factors such as wealth, location, identification with the collective, and even religious affiliation may determine the likelihood of committing suicide. It becomes tempting to draw parallels between the deaths of fictional characters in Hebrew literature and the categorizations presented above, and as I have shown, this is a reasonable approach. One may suggest that a female character commits suicide because she feels alienated from society, or suffers because she fails to fulfill the role assigned to her by society, such as a barren woman in a society that only values motherhood as a role for women. Not only would these factors equate with those outlined above, but such a character would also fit into Durkheim's category as a fatalistic suicide, such as the death of Ilana in *Closing the Sea*. Similarly, a man who sacrifices himself for the collective as a soldier and commits an altruistic suicide parallels the Samson model described in chapter 1. The suicides of characters in novels correspond sufficiently with real-life examples for us to identify these suicides as though they were real-life incidences.

Despite providing explanations about the Durkheimian types, their reception, the ways in which the meanings of these terms have evolved, and the ways in which we can understand these classifications today, David Lester warns us that real examples may not easily or neatly fit into these classifications.[5] Furthermore, he highlights Melvin D. Faber's analysis of suicide in Greek tragedy as an example of a critical work that employs scientific categories to evaluate the suicide of figures in classical literature. Yet Lester remains skeptical about using the four Durkheimian types in this way. Perhaps this is the most important argument about the use of Durkheim's categories. While conclusions can be drawn about types of suicide, and patterns of factors can be described — suggesting the statistical likelihood of a person committing suicide — no motives exist that can be used to categorize the causes of suicide in life or in literature. Lester claims that identifying actual cases of people who commit suicide and labeling them according to sociological categorization is a dubious approach. Any analysis of literature using this method is further removed from the social sciences; therefore, it is not relevant to measure specific literary suicides against sociological arguments.

Moreover, in the twentieth century, the study of psychology has also led to its own theories that may be indicators of suicide, such as upbringing, relationship within the family, or ability to manage an emotional crisis. As with the sociological model, psychology has also been adopted by literary theorists, raising targeted questions about suicide in a fictional text that draw on the social science tradition. In the 1960s Edwin Shneidman created a scale to measure a patient's susceptibility to committing suicide for psychological reasons.[6] He suggested that, when faced with unendurable psychological pain, people will sometimes opt for a cessation of consciousness rather than face intolerable emotion and unacceptable anguish. The suicide is the result of frustrated psychological needs and is considered to be the solution to the dilemma or crisis the individual faces. The sense of hopelessness and helplessness is overwhelming, while at the same time, the person has an ambivalence toward actually dying, perhaps hoping to be rescued. Shneidman argues that there is, in most cases, an act of interpersonal communication that relates to the intended final act, though this may be disguised as a cry for other needs such as autonomy. Suicide is seen as an escape route and often results after the person no longer envisages other options, and Shneidman believes that the act is often consistent with other lifelong coping patterns.

Jeffrey Berman's reading of Edna Pontellier's suicide in *The Awakening* (1899) by Kate Chopin explores the psychological signs that she shows during that narrative and the ways in which they accord with Shneidman's scale of suicidal intent. While this example works well, as would such an analysis of Ilana in *Closing the Sea*, this theoretical model could never work for the death of Haim in Etgar Keret's *Kneller's Happy Campers*. The novel opens after the character has already committed suicide and proceeds to show a world in which everyone else is already dead. Though we are given clues as to the methods each person has used — characters show scars from cut wrists, holes from bullet wounds, or are green from drowning — nevertheless we are provided with little or no insight as to why the characters performed these actions and it would be impossible to examine them as clinical cases in the way Berman is able to for *The Awakening*.

Considering Shneidman's findings in a literary framework, means that we can study the character's emotional breakdown over the course of the narrative in order to consider psychological, social, historical, and political issues. However, representing emotional breakdown may not be the only role that suicide has to play in the greater narrative framework; it can be added to the armory of the literary scholar to reveal the relationship between the character, the narrative, and the text.

Third, Berman has proposed, that the suicide of a character or of the author affects the life of the reader. In a more nuanced understanding of the Werther effect (among the first recorded examples of copycat suicide, when a wave of suicides spread through Europe in response to the young hero's death in Goethe's novel), Berman argues that the "reader's identification with a suicidal character may lead to heightened vulnerability." He suggests that reading about suicide can arouse the reader's already present, latent thoughts about suicide. To paraphrase his theory, students should be taught by a responsible teacher trained to understand the effects that suicide in literature can have on the individual. Berman has said in discussing the poetry of Sylvia Plath:

> Suicidal writers do not necessarily write more authentically about suicide than non-suicidal writers, but we read them differently. We scrutinize their writings for clues to their death, and when we find them we cannot avoid attaching psychobiographical signifi-

cance to them. If the writer is highly autobiographical, . . . then we may find ourselves implicated in [his or her] suicidal art. A suicidal poem, no less than an act of suicide, may be a cry for help, and for some readers it is difficult to avoid the urge to intervene.[7]

Berman is suggesting that, for example, teenagers who read Ernest Hemingway or Sylvia Plath in school are more at risk of considering suicide themselves. These students should therefore be educated in an environment where suicide is not taboo and the myths about suicide are exposed responsibly. Perhaps the teacher might even need to be trained as a psychological counselor in some way. Yet, Berman's theory relies on the idea that the suicide of the author or character is a motivating force.

In *Surviving Literary Suicides*, Berman has identified texts whose depiction of suicide awakens emotional responses in the reader. But for Hebrew literature after the 1950s, the act of suicide is usually presented offstage or as a marginal aside in the narrative, even when it is the death of the main protagonist. The death is not climactic and therefore does not produce an emotive response in the reader. It is not designed to be inspiring or to create empathy or anger. Representations of suicide evoke critical responses in Israeli literature, not emotional responses. As this book has shown, Berman's view is entirely antithetical to the way in which Israeli literature operates. The suicides of the characters are usually short or sudden as in "The Way of the Wind" or *Past Continuous*. The suicides occur outside the framework of the novel, as with *Kneller's Happy Campers*, or offstage as with *Hitganvut Yehidim*. The audience is almost never encouraged to identify with the character. The death is usually described as a warning of the excesses in society or the ways of reviewing society's demands.

The Author's Life

The relationship between a writer's thoughts about suicide and the text in which he or she may represent suicide confers the notion that writing about suicide may provide a therapeutic setting in which to explore personal responses to private anxieties. Al Alvarez's moving study about suicide through the ages, *A Savage God*, demonstrates the author's feelings about his friend Sylvia Plath's suicide and reflections on his own suicide attempts. Alvarez claims that literary suicide can be a writer's response to the culture he or she sees; the "more sophisticated and rational a society becomes the further it travels from superstitious fears and the more easily suicide is tolerated."[8] In this framework of study, one which both Alvarez and Berman have explored, when a suicidal writer writes about suicide, new layers of significance are added to the text that may in fact posit questions about the toleration of suicide, while simultaneously giving writers the opportunity to explore their own suicidal fantasies, and offering the reader the chance to do the same.

Writing about suicide may not always be a cathartic experience. Alvarez's study examines a writer's emotional journey as he or she experiments with this image in literary texts showing that "art is a necessary but not always sufficient part of an artist's support system."[9] Acknowledging that this may be true for some authors, but not for others, Berman in his reading of Alvarez's text argues that Sylvia Plath's vulnerability was "heightened by the personal mythology she constructed around suicide. She came to view herself as an escape artist, compelled to commit suicide so that she could be magically reborn."[10] Ultimately, both Alvarez and Berman in different ways conclude that "Plath committed suicide in an attempt 'to get herself out of a desperate corner which her own poetry had boxed herself into.'"[11] In this theory, the author's suicide is presented as an almost inevitable fate. The writing becomes a way of exploring feelings, which may actually advance the author's suicide in some cases whereby "the dredging up of gloomy personal material may heighten 'extremist' writers' vulnerability to suicide and undermine their will to live."[12] For Plath, the process of "reliving" her suicidal feelings through art may have triggered her death, giving credence to Berman's argument that writing about suicide can be dangerous for someone contemplating suicide. However his method of criticism runs the risk of romanticizing the writer's death. Given the numerous examples of suicidal authors, this method may even encourage us to presuppose that a writer writing about suicide is suicidal and that the text represents insight into the author's personal inclinations.

On the occasions when a writer explores his or her attitude to suicide in a text and then goes on to attempt suicide, the text is often perceived as an extended suicide note and is categorized as part of a body of "suicidal communications."[13] Lester explains that, in general, a suicide note is produced when a person feels ambivalence about dying and is crying out for help from others, when the person is not wholly bent on dying and wants to be stopped, and that this may be seen as part of a pattern of increasingly desperate attempts to communicate. Sometimes these letters or other suicidal communications (such as literary works) are written in order to prepare people and to reduce the shock, but as Lester points out this "motive does not seem congruent with the resentment and manipulations which are often characteristic of the suicidal person."[14] When written in advance (not at the moment of death), they sometimes express other emotions; sometimes the suicide has no desire to die but simply wishes to threaten and taunt other people — usually quite successfully, since "most people are severely threatened by statements of suicidal intent, and their feelings of helplessness are very unpleasant."[15] However, as the threats become less effective, or the person is no longer satisfied with the effect achieved, he or she goes on to commit suicide. Suicidal communications may also be no more than statements, reflecting the fact that the individual is preoccupied with thoughts of death. Considering Lester's concerns within a literary framework must lead us to reject the interpretation of works of fiction as suicide notes, since even actual suicide notes cannot reveal the mindset of a suicide.

The popularity of suicide notes in nineteenth-century Russia and their frequent publication in the press speaks to a public with a ghoulish fascination with the subject. Irina Paperno explains that writers' interest in this material was more sophisticated, as these letters, "written as they are in the very context of the suicidal act," offered the intellectual a source for analysis.[16] Fiction writers hoped these letters "would offer a special window into the thinking and the feeling of the act itself" but, according to Paperno, both Edwin Shneidman in his research in psychology and Fyodor Dostoevsky with his amateur examination of suicide notes, were annoyed to find the letters were "filled with the mundane and the trivial."[17] The notes failed to provide the explanations these men were seeking, and: "If the secret of suicide was not known to the subject minutes before death, how then could it be uncovered? If the person committing suicide could not convey, even moments before death, the meaning of this experience, then who could?"[18] We are reminded by these observations that suicide in life is often quite ordinary and not the extraordinary material of fiction.

Moving beyond Berman and Alvarez's ideas that writing about suicide serves an emotional and psychological role, Paperno explains that authors use suicide as a motif in order to explore the act artistically. Dostoevsky was, like many people of his time, fascinated by suicide. Hoping to produce an "artistic vivisection of suicide," he scrutinized the Russian press for suicide notes, newspaper articles, and treatises written on the subject.[19] Yet, according to Paperno, even after exploring the topic thoroughly he concluded that the act of suicide was inaccessible and the artist could not capture it.[20] The Victorian "voyeuristic penetration into the very process of dying" could not provide either meaning or explanation for the act itself.[21] This assumption relies on the belief that the depiction of suicide is artistically achieved, functioning as a vantage point for the soul of the character. In Hebrew literature, there are occasions in which the suicide is barely mentioned. The act occurs offstage, and despite the centrality of the character to the novel, the death may only receive a mention of two or three lines in a novel of several hundred pages. In *Past Continuous*, the suicide of the protagonist, Goldman, is revealed in the middle of his plans to see a fortune teller: "Goldman contacted this palm reader and made an appointment, but a few days before it was to take place he committed suicide and so the meeting never occurred" (*PC*, 370).

Goldman's suicide was not an obvious fate, no personal meaning is ascribed to his death, and it was not triggered by a single event. He certainly had plans for the life that could have been lived had he not died. The following line begins: "At this time, however, he was still enthusiastic about the possibility" in reference to having his palm read — an ironic statement about the future, or the lack of one (*PC*, 371). Similarly, recall the suicide of Ariyeleh, a minor character in the same novel, which was described in the simplest of terms. No reason is given for why he shoots himself in the mouth, and it is the banal aspects of the situation, such as where he was found and what he was wearing — leather suit, floral shirt, and yellow tie — that are emphasized. It is impossible to characterize these examples as acts that provide insight either into the characters' emotional lives or into the manner of their deaths.

Since literature is not life, a text cannot be read solely, or even seriously, in light of the author's suicide. A real death is only determined to be a suicide by a coroner or medical examiner — a method which, by its nature, is fallible.[22] In contrast, in a text the reader makes a judgment based on the information provided by the author. Thus, two things become apparent: (1) the information we may have about an author may not always be correct (motivations, interests, purpose, feelings); and (2) authors make choices about characters which are different from the choices they make about their own lives. A text is produced at a specific point in a writer's life, and writers' feelings change over time. Any literary conclusions about suicide reached by examining the life of the author can be, at times, entirely erroneous. To date, not one of the authors of the Israeli literary texts examined in this volume has committed suicide. Moreover, in the Israeli context most of the characters' suicides are not framed as emotionally driving for the reader, thereby demonstrating that Berman, Alvarez, Paperno, and others do not provide an adequate theoretical framework for considering the place of suicide within the Hebrew literature considered here.

Historical Approaches

A historical approach to the treatment of suicide in literature, such as that adopted by Barbara Gates in her study on the consumption of popular culture and particularly the image of suicide in Victorian society, pays attention to the context in which the text is analyzed. Her examination of *Wuthering Heights* assumes a new historical approach, used to assert the context of the text's production, consumption, and status, while marginalizing the importance of the work's literary construction, and offers a socially conditioned reading of the characters' fates. Gates argues that the presentation of Hindley Earnshaw's death suggests that he should have been legally categorized as a suicide. He died "true to his character, drunk as a Lord" and Heathcliff says about the funeral arrangements, "that fool's body should be buried at the cross-roads, without ceremony of any kind." Gates explains that these comments indicate that if "Hindley did die drunk and debauched . . . in the eighteenth century he would automatically be considered a suicide,"[23] and as a result, his family would have forfeited all their wealth to the Crown. For Gates this is significant because, as she demonstrates, an author is able to indicate suicide without articulating it clearly because social or cultural norms — understood by the readers — allow them to ascertain the meaning encoded in the text. Thus she shows that the culture in which the text was produced has a recognizable set of tropes that enable the reader, the author, and the text to form a silent dialogue based on familiar patterns of meaning. Therefore we can conclude that texts are intimately connected to the culture expected to consume them.

Gates also cites a second example of Cathy's burial at the edge of the churchyard, which is meant to indicate that though she appears to die in childbirth, her death was really a suicide.[24] Again this literary reference indicates the nature of Cathy's death through cultural codes. According to Gates, Heathcliff's specific description of this burial to Nelly "reflects 1823 burial law" on suicide.[25] During 1823 there had been a legal change in the handling of suicides. Before this time, English law stipulated that the bodies were to be buried at a crossroads and covered in lime, but after this date, they were buried at the corner of a churchyard between nine o'clock in the evening and midnight. Though written in 1847, the novel is set in 1803. In the constraints of the novel's time frame Cathy's death as a suicide meant that she should have been buried at a crossroads. Despite the historical inaccuracy, the deaths in *Wuthering Heights* resonated correctly for the audience of the period as readers continued to read the suicide in the earlier images without much confusion, though for contemporary readers the true nature of Cathy's death may be obscured. Nevertheless, during the mid-nineteenth century, as Gates argues, in order to sell novels many authors continued to use the more sensational approach of depicting suicides at crossroads — which accorded with contemporaneous expectations.

Though suicide may have been one of the most discussed social problems of the nineteenth century, as Anthony Giddens observes, yet it is unclear why this is the case.[26] Gates's account of suicide in literature does not explain the reception of suicide in the period, other than to comment on its popularity and sensationalism — and therefore authors' likely commercial success. What did suicide mean in Victorian culture and literature? Did Victorian depictions of suicide undercut the conventional social feelings or responses to suicide, or did they reinforce them? Gates does not ask questions that would connect the texts she analyzes with the society that they reflect and that she conscientiously describes.

Despite these mysteries, we do know that Victorians "openly mourned death and sensationalized murder, but they seem to have deeply feared suicide and to have concealed it wherever possible."[27] Cathy's and Hindley's suicides are obscured in *Wuthering Heights*, with only oblique references to the ways in which they died. Contradicting Gates's argument that suicide was hidden in England, Paperno writes that the custom of publishing suicide notes had been widespread in England since the 1730s, thereby indicating that suicide was not concealed, and was material that interested English society.[28] There appears to be a conflict between representations of suicide in Victorian society as they are explained by Gates and as they are depicted by Paperno. Art offers us a way of resolving this apparent contradiction about the visibility and reception of suicide in nineteenth-century England. In *The Art of Suicide*, Brown makes a distinction between the depiction of suicide in high art and the depiction of suicide in popular culture that corresponds to Bourdieu's idea about the different cultural capital of high and low culture:

> In popular culture and in writing the act of suicide took on meanings of mental instability and of alienation. Also, women's identity was seen as fragmented: feminine deaths either erased identity or reaffirmed it. In high art, those meanings were silenced and a heroic death was depicted.[29]

While suicide in high art and literature is depicted as noble, romantic, and heroic, in low culture suicide carried an assumed link to depravity. Brown says:

> Cheap literature hawked on the streets of London was full of sensational images that performed the dual purpose of warning off the potential suicide and highlighting the importance of keeping one's place, while articles from broadsheets and police gazettes which carried such images verged on the macabre. . . . In these graphic images, social cause and effect were lost in a genre best described as a pornography of violence. On the whole, the writ-

ing is bad, the stories banal, and the graphic illustrations of these "murders most foul" bizarre in the extreme.[30]

Brown reveals that cultural codes are mediated by extreme cultural sensitivity. His analysis takes into account both the medium and the society that produced it. In turn he shows that there has been a growing ambivalence toward the image of suicide within popular culture that distances it from the early images of nobility and heroism.

In examining the society and culture which frame the depiction of suicide, Brown and Gates in part evaluate the "true to life" quality of the portrayal in art and literature. Paperno's method is more sophisticated; she also engages with the discussion of suicide as a product of Russian culture, attempting to explain reasons for the use of the image: "A 'black hole' left upon man's final departure, suicide created a void that asks to be filled."[31] She suggests the reasons for, and the ways in which, suicide is represented in a literary text. She explains that Fyodor Dostoevsky was interested in exploring the mechanics of the mind of a suicide, and that his immediate audience, nineteenth-century Russian society, had a morbid interest in reading about suicide. While she makes a link between the production of the image and the reader, she does not discuss the effects in terms of literary aesthetics.

Paperno's approach is based on a view of Russian culture as exceptionally literary in the nineteenth century. She looks at the complex interaction between life and literature, such as the research and writing of Dostoevsky, and puts it in a larger historical framework. She interprets suicides in Dostoevsky's writings more generally as his response to atheism, but she does not look at the role of suicide within a specific text, or the symbolic or metaphorical meaning that the death has within the narrative. She does, however, examine suicide within a national tradition that assumes a cohesive cultural narrative as a backdrop. It is this process that is central to an understanding of the role suicide plays in Hebrew literature; unlike Dostoevsky, however, the Israeli writers have no duty to observe real life or to understand the mind of a suicide, which frees them to make allegorical use of this powerful image.

As scholars we must be vigilant in remembering that literary suicides are the products of writers' minds and though they may be influenced by life, they are not bound by it. Nevertheless, in rendering a fictional suicide, the writer can portray, by means of the novel or short story structure, social factors and the breakdown in social relationships that led to an individual's death. Through this, writers can communicate the effects of social integration and social regulation in order to criticize those collective systems in that society which may prove detrimental to the individual.

A problem in evaluating suicide through a sociological and psychological framework arises in the assumption these scientific methods make about suicide. There is an inherent bias that suicide is negative, posing "a religious and moral problem for Western culture," long considered "a mortal sin and a crime subject to severe penalty."[32]

In a Judeo-Christian world, both religion and modern society approach suicide as a problem, but other cultures have shown ambivalence and even respect for suicide. The changing attitudes can be seen in classical Greek society. Early Greece frowned upon suicide, believing that life was the gift of the gods. Plato claimed man was the gods' soldier, making suicide tantamount to desertion; Aristotle condemned suicide because he believed it was a betrayal of the fatherland, arguing that every citizen owed allegiance to the state. However, there were certainly other periods during which both Greek and later Roman institutions viewed suicide with toleration. During Nero's reign, Seneca's suicide was considered an appropriate response to his disfavor at court, while Petronius, according to the writings of Tacitus, was also given the option of committing suicide the following year by Nero and his death is represented as a parody of Seneca's. But with the rise of Christianity and its increasing moral power over Byzantium the Judeo-Christian framework that condemned suicide prevailed.[33]

Certainly, there are cultural contexts in which suicide is not considered a sin, but instead has other meaning, such as an act of honor or religious devotion. The ancient Veda books, the religious scriptures of Hinduism, permit suicide on religious grounds. The greatest sacrifice was one's own life. On the other hand, strongly condemning attitudes can be found in the Upanishads. In one of the Upanishads it is said: "Whoever takes his own life will come to the sunless areas covered by impenetrable darkness after death." Hinduism recognized, institutionalized, and accepted *suttee* until recently, believing that the widow's suicide following the death of her husband guaranteed they would both be blessed. Suicide by starvation has also been practiced by certain religious groups in Indian culture; death by these means is known as *sallekhana* and has been executed by ascetics.

Chinese culture and literature historically have been ambivalent about suicide and it was glamorized by popular stories, in which star-crossed lovers — for example, the Butterfly Lovers, and also Pan Yu-Ann and Su Qi in *A Dream of Red Mansions*, one of the so-called four great works of Chinese literature — could be joined together in death. In these stories, death by suicide was the only way that the lovers could unite. A ritual self-disemboweling known as *seppuku*, part of the samurai code of behavior, was in common use in feudal Japan as a way to avoid bringing shame and dishonor upon one's family. These examples from outside of the Western, and particularly European, canon demonstrate the cultural sensitivity required in evaluating suicide in literature.

While this chapter has pointed to different devices that can help us search for the meanings of literary suicide, it also warns against an over-reliance on these frameworks at the expense of close reading. A historical approach will locate the text within the conventions of the society through which it was produced and will identify the images, allusions, and symbolic codes of that society. Sociological theory offers the reader a window through which one may examine the social forces that act on the character and to which the text is responding. Psychological frameworks allow the reader to identify the emotional development of the character that leads to his or her suicide. Used together these tools function along-side textual analysis, which focuses on the interaction between characters, metaphors, the point of climax, and other literary devices. It is this juxtaposition of the internal system of the narrative with the external coded conventions in society that will help to explain the role that suicide has to play in the text. These techniques are not divisible but function as a comprehensive unit enabling the reader to understand the dual aspect of suicide within the text and on broader social and national ideas. This book has considered the ways in which Israeli fiction has explored institutions in Israeli society, and built upon their symbolic meanings. Working with a repertoire of ideas, visions, and coded signs and signifiers writers have used suicide as a way to delve into the mechanics of Israel's national symbols and to examine aspects they deem to have failed. It has shown an internal mode of criticism that operates by using a culture's own understanding of its national beliefs and institutions, and even while critiquing aspects, it can simultaneously work to uphold or reinforce other ideas and values.

The historical, cultural, and social norms that influence the appearance of a text; the representation of society; the use of images, metaphors, motifs, and themes for the depiction of suicide; and the relationship between text and culture will all influence the meaning of suicide in the text. But it is the way these elements are handled, that is, the purpose that suicide plays for shedding light on matters beyond the text, that establishes the meaning of literary suicide. This role will be different from text to text, from society to society, but it will only become clear by assembling the wider information and by seeing the ways in which this information relates to the narrative. Despite all the material available to him, having "considered all the plausible and implausible reasons for suicide and systematically rejected them all," Durkheim understood that the only reason a person commits suicide is "the sudden deterioration of the cement adhering us to a collective, no matter which collective it might be, so that one is left all alone."[34]

"Danny (A Note in Memory)" by Amos Kenan, the *feuilleton* with which I opened this book, clearly illustrates the deterioration of one man's relationship with the collective. The text calls attention to his friendships, his community, and the social structures that formed the basis of his life and tethered him to it. But when Danny is left alone, abandoned by his society, his isolation prompts his death. It is these higher ideas, the place of the personal within the greater narratives of the collective that we must try to understand in our search for the meaning of suicide in literature.

All translations are my own except where otherwise indicated.

Introduction

1. Susan Starr Sered, *What Makes Women Sick? Maternity, Modesty, and Militarism in Israeli Society*, Brandeis Series on Jewish Women (Hanover, N.H.: Brandeis University Press, 2000), 7.

2. Lesley Hazleton, *Israeli Women: The Reality Behind the Myths* (New York: Simon and Schuster, 1977); Sered, *What Makes Women Sick?*, 62; Omi Morgenstern-Leissner, "Hospital Birth, Military Service, and the Ties That Bind Them: The Case of Israel," *Nashim: A Journal of Jewish Women's Studies and Gender Issues* 12 (2006): 203–41, 217.

3. "The Werther effect": copycat suicides linked by method, reason, location, or other factors, named after a spate of suicides by young men emulating the death of Goethe's hero from the eighteenth-century literary success *The Sorrows of Young Werther*.

4. Benedict Anderson, *Imagined Communities: Reflections on the Origins and Spread of Nationalism* (London: Verso, 1991), 4.

5. Motti Regev, "To Have a Culture of Our Own: On Israeliness and Its Variants," *Ethnic and Racial Studies* 23, no. 2 (March 2000): 223–47.

6. Alon Confino, "Collective Memory and Cultural History: Problems of Method," *American Historical Review* 102, no. 5 (1997): 1387.

7. Ibid., 1398.

8. Yael Zerubavel, *Recovered Roots: Collective Memory and the Making of Israeli National Tradition* (Chicago: University of Chicago Press, 1995), xviii.

9. Timothy Brennan, "The National Longing for Form," in *Nation and Narration*, ed. Homi K. Bhabha (1990; reprint, London: Routledge, 2003), 44.

10. Confino, "Collective Memory and Cultural History," 1390.

11. Michael Feige, "Introduction: Rethinking Israeli Memory and Identity," *Israel Studies* 7, no. 2 (2002): v–vi.

12. Nurith Gertz, *Myths in Israeli Culture: Captives of a Dream*, Parkes-Wiener Series on Jewish Studies (London: Vallentine Mitchell, 2000); Zerubavel, *Recovered Roots*.

13. Yael Zerubavel, "The 'Mythological Sabra' and Jewish Past: Trauma, Memory and Contested Identities," *Israel Studies* 7, no. 2 (2002): 115.

14. Feige, "Introduction: Rethinking Israeli Memory and Identity," iv.

15. Ibid., v.

16. Uri Ram, "Postnationalist Pasts: The Case of Israel," *Social Science History* 22, no. 4, special issue: "Memory and the Nation" (Winter 1998): 525.

17. Feige, "Introduction: Rethinking Israeli Memory and Identity," vi.

18. Gershon Shaked, *The Shadows Within: Essays on Modern Jewish Writers* (Philadelphia: Jewish Publication Society, 1987), 165.

19. Simon During, "Literature—Nationalism's Other? The Case for Revision," in *Nation and Narration*, ed. Homi K. Bhabha (1990; reprint, London: Routledge, 2003), 138.

20. Ibid.

21. Ibid., 149.

22. Ruth Benedict, *Patterns of Culture* (Boston: Houghton Mifflin, 1934), 174.

23. Pierre Bourdieu and Randal Johnson, *The Field of Cultural Production: Essays on Art and Literature* (Cambridge, Eng.: Polity, 1993), 9.

24. Ibid., 229.

25. Yerach Gover, *Zionism: The Limits of Moral Discourse in Israeli Hebrew Fiction* (Minneapolis: University of Minnesota Press, 1994), 7.

26. Bourdieu and Johnson, *The Field of Cultural Production*, 19.

27. Ron M. Brown, *The Art of Suicide: Picturing History* (London: Reaktion Books, 2001), 14.

28. Tally Katz-Gerro and Yossi Shavit, "The Stratification of Leisure and Taste: Classes and Lifestyles in Israel," *European Sociological Review* 14, no. 4 (1998): 369–86. Katz-Gerro and Shavit have shown that there is a distinction between high and low culture but they argue that despite the difference in the type of product, there is no social distinction between those who consume each type of product.

29. Bourdieu explains that literary texts not only become part of the world they are describing, but that the cultural theorist also becomes part of this milieu. "The principal function of theoretical culture [is to] provide the means for knowing what one is doing. . . . To speak today on the literary fact is, whether one knows it or not, whether one wishes it or not, to place oneself or to be placed with respect to a space of possibilities that is the product of a long, partly repetitive history or, more precisely, a long struggle among theories and theoreticians, writings and writers, readings and readers." Pierre Bourdieu, "Flaubert and the French Literary Field," in *Principles of a Sociology of Cultural Works: Essays in Art and Literature* (New York: Columbia University Press, 1993), 184. "This is true, however, only in regard to a particular sense of 'features,' namely, that literary texts are . . . 'thickly' implicated in that discourse and cannot be extricated from it, even for the most elementary understanding of their form and content. Indeed, Israeli literature lacks the degree of autonomy—of text, genre, significance, and position—that is attributed to what is usually called 'literature.'" Gover, *Zionism: The Limits of Moral Discourse*, 1.

30. Gover, *Zionism: The Limits of Moral Discourse*, 1.

31. Nancy Ezer, *Sifrut ve-Ideologiah, Mareh Makom* [*Literature and Ideology: Seeing Place*] (Tel Aviv: Papirus, 1992), 7.

32. Midrash Shekol Tov on Bereshit and Shemot by Menahum Ber Shlema ca. 1139, Italy.

33. Hannah and her seven sons, II Macabees 7:2; "Chronicles of Masada" in Flavius Josephus and William Whiston, *The Wars of the Jews*, trans. William Whiston, Everyman's Library 712 (London: J. M. Dent & Sons; E. P. Dutton, 1928), book 7, chap. 9.

34. *Shulchan Aruch* (YD 345:3).

35. Susan L. Einbinder, *Beautiful Death: Jewish Poetry and Martyrdom in Medieval*

France, Jews, Christians, and Muslims from the Ancient to the Modern World (Princeton, N.J.: Princeton University Press, 2002), 23–24.

36. James T. Clemons, *What Does the Bible Say About Suicide?* (Minneapolis: Fortress, 1990), 60.

37. Einbinder, *Beautiful Death*, 17.

38. Ibid., 18.

39. Yael Shemesh, "Hitabdut ba-Mikra Al Reka Tofa'at Ha-Hitabdut Ba-Tarbut Ha-Klallit u-ve-Mekorot Yisrael," *Jewish Studies, an Internet Journal* (2002–3): 1–24.

40. Einbinder, *Beautiful Death*, 18–19.

41. Ibid., 22.

42. Ibid., 22–23.

43. Evel Rabbati 2:1–5.

44. Rashba Respo vol. 2, no. 763.

45. 345:1 Yerach Deah and Maim Yad Evel 1:11; J. M. Tukacinsky, *Gesher ha-Hayyim* vol.1 (1960). Chap. 26 contains a full list of all the laws regarding a suicide.

46. Sem 2:4–5.

47. Émile Durkheim, *Suicide: A Study in Sociology*, trans. George Simpson (London: Routledge, 1989), 155. This low rate of suicide continues to be true today, with Israel having among the lowest suicide rates in the world, though numbers have been boosted since the 1990s with the Russian immigration to Israel. This change in statistics reflects the former Soviet Union's high suicide rate and the Russification of Jews within the Soviet Union. Immigrant Russian males are 1.5 times more likely to commit suicide than their Israeli male counterparts, and immigrant Russian females are 1.2 times more likely to commit suicide than their Israeli female counterparts. Vered Slonim-Nevo and Yana Shagra, "A Comparison of Immigrant and Non-Immigrant Adolescents in Israel," *Child and Adolescent Social Work Journal* 14, no. 4 (1997): 251–62; Division on Violence Prevention, CDC National Center for Injury Prevention and Control, "Rates of Homicide, Suicide, and Firearm-Related Death Among Children — 26 Industrialized Countries," in *Morbidity and Mortality Weekly Report* 46, no. 5 (Feb. 7, 1997): 101–5; Daphna Levinson et al., "Suicide Attempts in Israel: Age by Gender Analysis of a National Emergency Departments Database," *Suicide and Life-Threatening Behavior* 36, no. 1 (2006): 97–102; G. Lubin et al., "Epidemiology of Suicide in Israel: A Nationwide Population Study," *Social Psychiatry and Psychiatric Epidemiology* 36 (2001): 123–27; N. L. Margolin and J. D. Teicher, "Thirteen Adolescent Male Suicide Attemptors," *Journal of the American Academy of Child Psychiatry* 7 (1968): 296–315; Ricardo Nachman et al., "Suicide in Israel: 1985–1997," *Journal of Psychiatry and Neuroscience* 27, no. 6 (2002): 423–28.

48. S. Goren in *Mahanyim* 87 (1964): 7–12; L. I. Rabinowitz in *Sinai* 55 (1964): 329–32.

49. The waves of aliyot (immigrations to Israel) were a successive process, and the number reflects a specific period. Each aliyah had a distinct personality, reflecting the immigration of different ethnic, political, or ideological groups. The second aliyah is characterized by the large immigration of ideologically motivated cultural figures, writers, poets, and artisans from Europe.

50. The treatment of suicide in the literature of European Jewry which was predominantly written in Yiddish is discussed by Janet Hadda, *Passionate Women, Passive Men:*

Suicide in Yiddish Literature, SUNY Series in Modern Jewish Literature and Culture (Albany: State University of New York Press, 1988).

51. Marcus Moseley, *Being for Myself Alone: Origins of Jewish Autobiography* (Stanford, Calif.: Stanford University Press, 2006); David Patterson, *A Phoenix in Fetters: Studies in Nineteenth and Early Twentieth Century Hebrew Fiction* (Lanham, Md.: Rowman and Littlefield, 1988); and Nissan Turov, *Ba'ayot ha-Hitabdut: Mehkar Psychologi-Sociologi [Problems with Suicide: A Psycho-Socio Investigation]* (Haifa: Dvir Press, 1953).

52. Nissan Turov, *Ba'ayot Ha-Hitabdut [Problems of Suicide]* (Haifa: Dvir Press, 1953).

53. Abraham Balaban, *Between God and Beast: An Examination of Amos Oz's Prose* (University Park: Pennsylvania State University Press, 1993), 28; Amos Oz, *A Tale of Love and Darkness* (London: Chatto and Windus, 2004).

54. Michael Stanislawski, *For Whom Do I Toil? Judah Leib Gordon and the Crisis of Russian Jewry* (New York: Oxford University Press, 1988), 65, translation by Stanislawski of Judah Leib Gordon's epic poem *bi-Metzulot Yam* (*In the Depths of the Sea*).

55. Judges 11:29–40.

56. Stanislawski, *For Whom Do I Toil?*, 6.

57. Ibid.

58. Ibid., 73.

59. David Patterson, *A Phoenix in Fetters: Studies in Nineteenth and Early Twentieth Century Hebrew Fiction* (Lanham, Md.: Rowman and Littlefield, 1988), 50.

60. Ibid., 50.

61. Ibid., 29, 37.

62. Arthur Schopenhauer, "On Suicide," in *Parerga and Paralipomena* 2, chap. 13, sect. 160 (1851).

63. Patterson, *A Phoenix in Fetters*, 143, 189.

64. Schopenhauer, "On Suicide."

65. Eric Zakim, *To Build and Be Built: Landscape, Literature, and the Construction of Zionist Identity* (Philadelphia: University of Pennsylvania Press, 2007).

66. Reuven Kahane, "Informal Agencies of Socialization and the Integration of Immigrant Youth into Society: An Example from Israel," *International Migration Review* 20, no. 1 (Spring 1986): 21–39, 32.

67. Gershon Shaked, *Ein Makom Aher: Al Sifrut ve-Hevra [No Other Place: On Literature and Society]* (Tel Aviv: Hakibbutz Hameuchad, 1983), 21.

68. Oz Almog, *The Sabra: The Creation of the New Jew* (Berkeley: University of California Press, 2000), 102.

69. Kartun-Blum insists that the modern writers are mainly expressing their "sense of distance and alienation from [the biblical text]," and that the misreading and rewriting is an act of violence against the text. Ruth Kartun-Blum, *Profane Scriptures: Reflections on the Dialogue with the Bible in Modern Hebrew Poetry* (Cincinnati, Ohio: Hebrew Union College Press, 1999), 3–4.

70. Gover, *Zionism: The Limits of Moral Discourse*, 5.

71. Ibid., 7.

72. Ibid.

73. One of the big issues in sociological and psychological literature is the intention of the subjects compared to their results. Rather than calling cases attempted sui-

cide and committed suicide, they have begun to call those who die completed suicide, thereby implying a continuum since early attempts may lead to later ones. This is not a relevant distinction for literature since, if the character survives the novel, there is no possibility that the character may attempt suicide again outside the pages of the literary work.

74. See Gene and David Lester, *Suicide: The Gamble with Death* (Englewood Cliffs, N.J.: Prentice-Hall, 1971). See p. 20 for a discussion of this issue. Some suicidologists believe that there is a difference between those who attempt but fail and those who attempt and succeed and that they should therefore be evaluated differently.

Chapter 1

1. Zerubavel, "The 'Mythological Sabra,'" 116.

2. Sered, *What Makes Women Sick?*, 5. The idea of the "muscle Jew" has been explored by Daniel Boyarin, *Unheroic Conduct: The Rise of Heterosexuality and the Invention of the Jewish Man* (Berkeley: University of California Press, 1997).

3. Judges 16:30.

4. Einbinder, *Beautiful Death*.

5. David Fishelov, "The Transformation of Biblical Samson, or the Heroic Failure to Escape Myth," in *Myth and Literature*, ed. Lisa Block de Behar (Montevideo, 2003).

6. David Fishelov, *Mahlefot Shimshon: Gilgulei Dmuto Shel Shimshon Hamikrai* [*Samson's Transformations: Changes in the Image of the Biblical Samson*] (Haifa, Tel Aviv, 2000).

7. Einbinder, *Beautiful Death*.

8. Clemons, *What Does the Bible Say About Suicide?*, 21.

9. Almog, *The Sabra: The Creation of the New Jew*; Na'ama Sheffi, "Israeli Education System in Search of a Pantheon of Heroes, 1948–1967," *Israel Studies* 7, no. 2 (2002): 62–83.

10. Yoram Bilu and Eliezer Witztum, "War-Related Loss and Suffering in Israeli Society: An Historical Perspective," *Israel Studies* 5, no. 2 (2000): 3.

11. Ibid.

12. Vladimir Jabotinsky, *Samson the Nazarite: A Novel* (Berlin, 1927).

13. Zerubavel, *Recovered Roots*.

14. In 1924 *Samson* was published in serialized form in Russian, before being published as a novel in Hebrew.

15. David Fishelov, "Gilgulei Shimshon: Min ha-Mikra el Jabotinsky ve-Hollywood" ["Samson's Transformations: From the Bible, to Jabotinsky and to Hollywood"], *Moznayim* 74 (1999): 43 (my translation).

16. Jabotinsky, *Samson the Nazarite*.

17. Ibid., 277.

18. Fishelov, *Gilgulei Shimshon*, 61.

19. "Magash ha-Kesef" ["The Silver Platter"], title of Natan Alterman's poem published in 1947 in response to Chaim Weitzman's quote "No country is given to a people on a silver platter."

20. Bilu and Witztum, "War-Related Loss and Suffering in Israeli Society," 4.

21. Ibid.

22. Ibid.

23. Jabotinsky, *Samson the Nazarite*, 341.

24. Fishelov, *Gilgulei Shimshon*, 64.

25. Esther Fuchs, "The Enemy as Woman: Fictional Women in the Literature of the Palmach," *Israel Studies* 4, no. 1 (1999): 212–33.

26. Ilan Pappe, "Post-Zionist Critique on Israel and the Palestinians: Part I: The Academic Debate," *Journal of Palestine Studies* 26, no. 2 (1997): 29–41; Emmanuel Sivan, "To Remember Is to Forget: Israel's 1948 War," *Journal of Contemporary History* 28, no. 2 (1993): 341–59.

27. Almog, *The Sabra: The Creation of the New Jew*, 15.

28. Ibid., 3.

29. Robert Alter, *The Art of Biblical Narrative* (New York: Basic Books, 1981), 94.

30. Ibid.

31. Ibid.

32. Anadad Eldan, "Shimshon Korea Begadav" ["Samson Rends His Clothes"], in *Levado ba-Zerem ha-Kaved* [*Alone in the Powerful Stream*]: *Poems* (Tel Aviv, 1971).

33. Bilu and Witztum, "War-Related Loss and Suffering in Israeli Society," 5.

34. T. G. Ashplant, Graham Dawson, and Michael Roper, *The Politics of War Memory and Commemoration* (London: Routledge, 2000), 8.

35. By using biblical locations that also appear in modern Israel there is a sense that the struggle is legitimate, since the Bible serves as a title deed for the places. Kartun-Blum and Kadishman, *Profane Scriptures*, ix.

36. See David C. Jacobson, *Modern Midrash: The Retelling of Traditional Jewish Narratives by Twentieth-Century Hebrew Writers* (Albany: State University of New York Press, 1987); and Kartun-Blum, *Profane Scriptures*, on intertextual allusions and biblical rewriting in modern literature.

37. Nathan Zach, *Mivhar* [*Selected Poems*] (Tel Aviv, 1974).

38. King Saul is also considered to have committed suicide, and as it is on the battlefield, we may suggest that this suicide is also linked to militarism.

39. Glenda Abramson, *The Writing of Yehuda Amichai: A Thematic Approach* (New York, 1989), 45.

40. Eldan, "Samson Rends His Clothes."

41. If Samson is the sun and light, then Delilah is the "lilah" — night.

42. Amir Gilboa, *Kehulim ve-Adumim* [*Blues and Reds*] (Tel Aviv, 1963); *Samson the Hero* is a title that Fishelov claims becomes synonymous with Samson just as we talk about Avraham our Father or King David, although it could also be argued that the title is popular because the Hebrew translation of Samson Agonistes is *Samson the Hero*.

43. See Gouri's "Balodam" in Gouri and Chyet, *Words in My Lovesick Blood* (Detroit: Wayne State University Press, 1996).

44. Bilu and Witztum, "War-Related Loss and Suffering in Israeli Society," 23.

45. Published in translation under the title "Where the Jackals Howl" in Amos Oz, *The Howl of the Jackals and Other Stories* (London, 1981).

46. Gershon Shaked, *Gal Hadash ba-siporet ha-Ivrit* [*A New Wave in Hebrew Literature*] (Merhavya, 1970).

47. Moshe Shamir, *Hu Halach ba-Sadot* [*He Walked in the Fields*] (Sifriat Poalim, 1947).

48. Nathan Zach, *Kave Avir: Al ha-Romantikah ba-Siporet ha-Yisreelit ve-Al nosim Aherim: Sihot Miluim* [*Lines of Air: on Romance in Hebrew Fiction, and on Other Subjects: Some Remarks*] (Jerusalem: Keter, 1983).

49. Ronald R. Krebs, "A School for the Nation? How Military Service Does Not Build Nations, and How It Might," *International Security* 28, no. 4 (2004): 85–124, 85.

50. Ibid., 99. Research by Meira Weiss on the attitude of Israelis toward the death of sons in war shows that even at the start of the twenty-first century, this is still considered to be an honorable and worthwhile sacrifice. Though her methodology has recently been called into question, her line of inquiry demonstrates the significant sway that the Israeli military continues to have, and the respect that in general it garners within mainstream Israeli society. Meira Weiss, *The Chosen Body: The Politics of the Body in Israeli Society* (Stanford, Calif.: Stanford University Press, 2002); Meira Weiss, "The 'Chosen Body': A Semiotic Analysis of the Discourse of Israeli Militarism and Collective Identity," *Semiotica* 145, nos. 1/4 (2003): 151–73.

Chapter 2

The chapter title is from Yehoshua Kenaz, *Hitganvut Yehidim*, 7, and the chapter epigraph is from Krebs, "A School for the Nation?," 87.

1. Yaron Ezrahi, *Rubber Bullets: Power and Conscience in Modern Israel* (Berkeley: University of California Press, 1998), 11.

2. Baruch Kimmerling, *The Invention and Decline of Israeliness* (Berkeley: University of California Press, 2001), 220.

3. Ezrahi, *Rubber Bullets*, 80.

4. Originally given the English title *Heart Murmur*, this novel was subsequently published in translation with the title *Infiltration*. *Hitganvut Yehidim* is the final exercise of basic training.

5. Ranen Omer-Sherman, introduction to *Narratives of Dissent: War in Israeli Arts and Culture*, ed. Rachel S. Harris and Ranen Omer-Sherman (Detroit: Wayne State University Press, 2013), 9.

6. Ezrahi, *Rubber Bullets*, chap. 9.

7. Ibid.

8. Yaacov Yadgar, "From the Particularist to the Universalistic: National Narrative in Israel's Mainstream Press, 1967–97," *Nations and Nationalism* 8, no. 1 (2002): 55–72.

9. Ibid., 66.

10. Ibid.

11. Bilu and Witztum, "War-Related Loss and Suffering in Israeli Society," 1–31.

12. No distinction is made by Bilu and Witztum about the kind of mental illness.

13. Bilu and Witztum, "War-Related Loss and Suffering in Israeli Society."

14. Ibid., 16.

15. Don Handelman and Lea Shamgar-Handelman, "The Presence of Absence," in *Grasping Land*, ed. Eyal Ben-Ari and Yoram Bilu (Albany: State University of New York Press, 1997), 87.

16. Concepts of nation building through sacrifice have been presented in Benedict Anderson, *Imagined Communities*; and Ashplant, Dawson, and Roper, *The Politics of War Memory and Commemoration*. For specific references to Israel, Handelman and Shamgar-Handelman examine the relationship between the dead soldier and the landscape; see also Eyal Ben-Ari and Yoram Bilu, eds., *Grasping Land: Space and Place in Contemporary Israeli Discourse and Experience* (Albany: State University of New York Press, 1997). Yael Zerubavel has explored how these ideological beliefs about sacrifice,

something she has called the "cult of the fallen," have been promulgated in Israeli society. See Zerubavel, *Recovered Roots*, xvi.

17. Michael Feige, "New Directions in Memory Research in Israel," *Israel Studies* 7, no. 2 (2000) (my italics).

18. Ibid.

19. Bilu and Witztum, "War-Related Loss and Suffering in Israeli Society," 3.

20. Many of the largest publishing houses were established in kibbutzim and were therefore connected to the Labor-Zionist establishment.

21. Gertz, *Myths in Israeli Culture*, 124.

22. Feige, "New Directions in Memory Research in Israel."

23. Ibid., ix.

24. Liav Sade-Beck, "'We Shall Remember Them All . . .': The Culture of Online Mourning and Commemoration of Fallen Soldiers in Israel," in *Narratives of Dissent: War in Israeli Arts and Culture*, ed. Rachel S. Harris and Ranen Omer-Sherman (Detroit: Wayne State University Press, 2013), 117–34.

25. I will not speculate about the reasons that have been given for soldiers' refusal to fight, whether they are personal (for example, to do with loss of income) or in response to political opinions (they do not agree with the war); suffice to say that the decision by increasing numbers of soldiers not to fight is a trend that indicates a move away from the all-encompassing total commitment to the army seen in the past.

26. Michael Feige, "Rescuing the Person from the Symbol: 'Peace Now' and the Ironies of Modern Myth," *History and Memory* 11, no. 1 (1999): 141–68, 147.

27. Ibid., 147–48.

28. Opening paragraph of the signature letter for the *Yesh Gvul* movement.

29. In December 2004, at the high point of opposition to military activities in Israel, there were only 557 signatories. By February 2006, there were even fewer, at 445. http://www.yeshgvul.org.il/refusal/?id=b4676cc1c8d7a7397d69cce8ede1ac7c. In January 2014, as this book is going to press, a recent examination shows that the letter is no longer available on the website. Moreover, the movement and its site have diversified their offerings. They supply aid to soldiers (and their families) who refuse to serve, and have called an end to violence against prisoners. They also award the "Leibowitz prize" to those who, in their estimation, have promoted the cause of peace. But it appears that the site has now become less a grassroots movement and more a coordinated, left-wing organization. It is worth noting that the site has been silent, with no additional postings since March 2011.

30. "Israel Army Desertions Rise," *Guardian*, November 19, 2002.

31. Adam M. Garfinkle, *Politics and Society in Modern Israel: Myths and Realities*, 2nd ed. (Armonk, N.Y.: M. E. Sharpe, 1999), 114–15.

32. Hannah Naveh, "On Loss and Bereavement in Israeli Existence," *Alpayim* 16 (1998): 85–120; Ruth Malkinson and Eliezer Witztum, eds., "Bereavement and Commemoration: The Double Face of the National Myth," in *Loss and Bereavement in Jewish Society in Israel* (Jerusalem, 1993), 231–58.

33. Handelman and Shamgar-Handelman, "The Presence of Absence," 87.

34. Alex Weingrod, "How Israeli Culture Was Constructed: Memory, History and the Israeli Past," *Israel Studies* 2, no. 1 (1997): 228–37, 230.

35. High Court in Israel, Wikselbaum v. The Minister of Defense, at 195; CA 6024/97.

36. Alan L. Mintz, *Translating Israel: Contemporary Hebrew Literature and Its Reception in America* (Syracuse, N.Y.: Syracuse University Press, 2001), 46.

37. Mark Aronoff, "The Origins of Israeli Political Culture," in *Israeli Democracy Under Stress*, ed. E. Sprinzak and L. Diamond (Boulder, Colo.: Lynne Rienner, 1993), 47–63.

38. Ezrahi, *Rubber Bullets*, 168.

39. Hannah Hertsig, *Ha-Shem ha-Perati: Masot Al Yaakov Shabtai, Yehoshua Kenaz, Yoel Hofman* [*Personal Names: Essays on Yaakov Shabtai, Yehoshua Kenaz, Yoel Hofman*] (Tel Aviv: ha-Kibbutz ha-Meuchad, 1994), 57.

40. Rakefet Sela-Sheffy, "What Makes One an Israeli? Negotiating Identities in Everyday Representations of 'Israeliness,'" *Nations and Nationalism* 10, no. 4 (2004): 487.

41. Hertsig, *Ha-Shem ha-Perati*, 74.

Chapter 3

The first chapter epigraph is from Alex Weingrod, "How Israeli Culture Was Constructed," *Israel Studies* 2, no. 1 (Spring 1997): 228–37, 229.

The second chapter epigraph is from Elie Podeh, "History and Memory in the Israeli Educational System: The Portrayal of the Arab-Israeli Conflict in History Textbooks (1948–2000)," *History and Memory* 12, no. 1 (2000): 65–100, 70.

1. Zerubavel, *Recovered Roots*, xiv.

2. Ibid., 1.

3. Arnold Band, "The Impact of Statehood on the Hebrew Literary Imagination: Haim Hazaz and the Zionist Narrative," in *Divergent Jewish Cultures*, ed. Deborah Dash Moore and Ilan Troen (New Haven, Conn.: Yale University Press, 2001), 256–57.

4. Homi Bhabha, *The Location of Culture* (London: Routledge, 2004), 201.

5. Gertz, *Myths in Israeli Culture*, 1.

6. Zerubavel, *Recovered Roots*, xviii.

7. Ibid.

8. Timothy Brennan, "The National Longing for Form," in Bhabha, *Nations and Narration*, 50.

9. Gertz, *Myths in Israeli Culture*, 2.

10. Benedict Anderson, *Imagined Communities*, 4.

11. Mintz, *Translating Israel*, 46.

12. Lev Hakak, *Equivocal Dreams: Studies in Modern Hebrew Literature* (Hoboken, N.J.: Ktav, 1993), 92.

13. Possibly a reference to Yigael Gluckstein (1917–2000), better known as Tony Cliff, a Marxist and activist. Born in Palestine to Zionist parents, he attempted to forge a movement uniting Arabs and Jews, but abandoned this project and in 1947 moved to Britain, where he was a Marxist writer active in British politics, becoming the de facto leader of the Socialist Workers Party.

14. The letter *Bet* also starts the Bible: "Bereshit bara Elohim et-hashamayim ve-et ha-aretz" (In the beginning God created the heavens and the earth). Her study of all the flora and fauna of the land has only reached the letter often signified for its association with a Jewish identity, perhaps also suggesting that a unifying Jewish past transcends that of the Zionist identity that has replaced it. Though Tammuz had belonged to the Canaanite movement, his travels to Europe led to a rejection of this ideology and an embracing of a Jewish identity which also encompassed its Diasporic past.

15. Menuha Gilboa, *Halomot ha-Zahav ve-Shivronam: Sifrut ve-Ideologyah bi-Yetsirat Binyamin Tammuz* [*Dreams of Gold and Their Fragments: Literature and Ideology in the Works of Benjamin Tammuz*] (Tel Aviv: ha-Kibbutz ha-Meuchad, 1995), 66.

16. Gilboa, *Halomot ha-Zahav*, 66.

17. See Yael Zerubavel, "Changing Name-Death of the Exilic Jew and the Rebirth of a Sabra," *Israel Studies* 7, no. 2 (2000).

18. Ibid., 118.

19. Rachel's family, the Cordoveiros, who were Sephardim and had many Arab friends, publicly eschewed any military response, while funding the Irgun and Lehi, and contributing sons to the Haganah and the British army.

20. Gilboa, *Halomot ha-Zahav*, 13.

21. Ibid., 18.

22. Hakak, *Equivocal Dreams*; Zach, *Kave Avir*.

23. Hakak, *Equivocal Dreams*, 137. Hakak examines Natan Zach's preoccupation with madness, suicide, murder, and alienation in his analysis of the work of Tammuz, Shabtai, Be'er, Oz, Kenaz, and Yehoshua.

24. Mintz, *Translating Israel*, 181.

25. Ibid., 184.

26. Ibid., 181.

27. Ibid., 174.

28. Shaked, *The Shadows Within*, 225.

29. Yudkin, *1948 and After: Aspects of Israeli Fiction*, in *Journal of Semitic Studies*, monograph no. 5 (Manchester: University of Manchester Press, 1984), 157.

30. The text implies that two identical conversations are taking place. One is the conversation in the novel between the two men; the other is going on between the two women in the family, a conversation that the audience is not privy to: "Very well. Let there be two stories, an upstairs and a downstairs one. As for the truth, it can run up and down between them . . ." Yehoshua, *Mr. Mani*, 214.

31. Simon Round interview with Alon Hilu, *Jewish Chronicle*, February 25, 2010.

32. Linda Grant, "*The House of Rajani* by Alon Hilu," *Guardian*, April 9, 2010.

33. Ibid.

34. Yudkin, *1948 and After*, 159.

35. Almog, *The Sabra: The Creation of the New Jew*, 161.

36. Ibid.

Chapter 4

The chapter epigraph is from Yaakov Shabtai, *Zikhron Devarim: Roman* (Tel Aviv: Mifalim universitaiyim le-hotsa'ah la-or, 1977). All translations are from the Dalya Bilu translation, Yaakov Shabtai and Dalya Bilyu, *Past Continuous* (Philadelphia: Jewish Publication Society of America, 1985), 285.

1. Barbara Mann, "Tel Aviv's Rothschild: When a Boulevard Becomes a Monument," *Jewish Social Studies* 7, no. 2 (2001): 35.

2. S. Ilan Troen, *Imagining Zion: Dreams, Designs, and Realities in a Century of Jewish Settlement* (New Haven, Conn.: Yale University Press, 2003).

3. Francis Carco and Ford Madox Ford, *Perversity* (Chicago, 1928); Jean Rhys, *Good Morning, Midnight* (New York, 1939). *Perversity*, translated by Rhys, is the story of a

prostitute and her pimp cavorting in the Paris underworld watched by the girl's voyeuristic brother, and is characteristic of modernist representations of urban sexual depravity.

4. Klaus R. Scherpe and Mitch Cohen, "Modern and Postmodern Transformations of the Metropolitan Narrative," *New German Critique*, no. 55 (Winter 1992): 71. In *Mythography of a City* (Syracuse, N.Y.: Syracuse University Press, 2007) Maoz Azaryahu presents competing images of Tel Aviv as "The White City" or "The Non-Stop City," demonstrating this changing projection for meanings.

5. Hana Wirth-Nesher, *City Codes: Reading the Modern Urban Novel* (Cambridge: Cambridge University Press, 1996).

6. Barbara Mann, "Modernism and the Zionist Uncanny: Reading the Old Cemetery in Tel Aviv," *Representations*, no. 69, special issue: "Grounds for Remembering" (Winter 2000): 63–95.

7. Troen, *Imagining Zion*, 90.

8. Azaryahu, *Tel Aviv: Mythography of a City*.

9. Mark LeVine, "A Nation from the Sands," *National Identities* 1, no. 1 (1999): 15–37.

10. Mann, *A Place in History*, 78.

11. Hakak, *Equivocal Dreams*, 80.

12. Azaryahu, *Tel Aviv: Mythography of a City*, 94–95.

13. Ibid., 99–100.

14. Hanna Soker-Schwager and Dalya Bilu, "A Godless City: Shabtai's Tel Aviv and the Secular Zionist Project," *Prooftexts* 26, nos. 1–2 (2006): 240–81, 241–42.

15. Azaryahu, *Tel Aviv: Mythography of a City*, 100.

16. Ibid., 95.

17. Georg Simmel, "The Metropolis and Mental Life," in *Georg Simmel on Individuality and Social Forms*, ed. Donald Levine (Chicago: University of Chicago Press, 1971). Simmel was working in 1903, but Walter Benjamin's observations on Edgar Allan Poe's "The Man in the Crowd" and Baudelaire's *Fleurs du mal* reveal that writers were already constructing such urban spaces from an earlier period. Commenting on Poe and Baudelaire, Benjamin explores the sinister elements of the city as a place of anonymous thronging masses. The passersby can only be differentiated by their wardrobes. This indistinctness among the crowd is a trope present in much of urban literature. Examples are found in the works of Dickens, Sartre, Defoe, Baudelaire, Camus, and Paul Auster, among others.

18. Troen, *Imagining Zion*, 90.

19. David Harvey, *Paris, Capital of Modernity* (Paris, 2003), 265.

20. Scherpe and Cohen, "Modern and Postmodern Transformations," 74.

21. Raymond Williams, *The Country and the City* (London: Chatto and Windus, 1973), 159.

22. Miri Kubovy, "*Inniut* and *Kooliut*: Trends in Israeli Narrative Literature, 1995–1999," *Israel Studies* 5, no. 1 (2000): 244–65.

23. Ibid., 244.

24. The representation of Tel Aviv's savagery is also evident in Yaakov Shabtai (*HaDod Peretz Mamri* [*Uncle Peretz Takes Off*] [Tel Aviv, 1973]) and in *Past Continuous*. Shabtai viewed the Dizengoff Center's presence as a symbol of the monstrous

and alienating metropole as it annihilated the Nordia neighborhood that had been "home to a substantial part of the Shabtai family." Soker-Schwager and Bilu, "A Godless City," 255.

25. Avraham Soskin's work was featured in a retrospective exhibition at the Tel Aviv Museum of Art (2003); Annarita Lamberti, "Preserving the Recent and Most Recent Memories of Tel Aviv," ESF-LiU Conference "Cities and Media: Cultural Perspectives on Urban Identities in a Mediatized World," Vadstena, Sweden, October 25–29, 2006; Mann, *A Place in History: Modernism, Tel Aviv and the Creation of Jewish Urban Space.*

26. Yael Munk, "False Nostalgia and Cultural Amnesia: The City of Tel Aviv in Israeli Cinema of the 1990s," *Shofar* 24, no. 4 (2006): 130–43, 140.

27. Williams, *The Country and the City*, 143.

28. Mann, *A Place in History*, 164–65.

29. Ibid., 165.

30. Troen, *Imagining Zion*, 107.

31. Ibid.

32. Williams, *The Country and the City*, 233.

33. Ibid., 246.

34. Georg Simmel, "Exkurs über den Fremden" (1908), trans. Kurt Wolff, in *The Sociology of Georg Simmel* (New York: Free Press, 1950), 402–8.

35. Williams, *The Country and the City*, 246.

36. Simmel, "The Metropolis and Mental Life," 1903.

37. Mann, *A Place in History*, chap. 3, "Rothschild Boulevard."

38. Williams, *The Country and the City*, 155.

39. Mann, "Tel Aviv's Rothschild," 33.

40. Wirth-Nesher, *City Codes*, 67.

41. Yudkin, *1948 and After*, 114.

42. Williams, *The Country and the City*, 143.

43. Nils Johan Ringdal, *A World History of Prostitution* (New York, 2004), 280.

44. Charles Bernheimer, "1880: Prostitution in the Novel," in *A New History of French Literature*, ed. Dennis Hollier (Boston, 1994), 780. Honoré de Balzac, Gustave Flaubert, Émile Zola, and Joris Karl Huysmans evoke the allure of the prostitute, creating tension between the desire to possess the female body and the fear of doing so.

45. Azaryahu, *Tel Aviv: Mythography of a City.*

46. Ibid., 106.

47. Michael Feige and Zvi Shiloni, eds., *Kardum Lahfor Bo: Archaelogia ve-leumiut be-Eretz-Yisrael* [*A Pickaxe to Dig With: Archaeology and Nationalism in Eretz-Israel*] (Sede-Boker, 2008).

48. Azaryahu, *Tel Aviv: Mythography of a City.*

49. Shaked, *The Shadows Within*, 169.

50. Maoz Azaryahu, "Tel Aviv: Center, Periphery and the Cultural Geographies of an Aspiring Metropolis," *Social and Cultural Geography*, 9, no. 3 (2008): 303–18, 304.

Chapter 5

The chapter epigraph is from Sered, *What Makes Women Sick?*, 9.

1. Yael S. Feldman, *No Room of Their Own: Gender and Nation in Israeli Women's Fiction* (New York: Columbia University Press, 1999), 107.

2. Ibid., 106–7.

3. Sered, *What Makes Women Sick?*, 8.

4. Ruth Almog's *Mavet ba-Geshem* [*Death in the Rain*] (Keter, 1982) and *Shorshei Avir* [*Roots of Air*] (Keter/haKibbutz ha-Meuchad, 1987) both represent female protagonists whose social breakdown, as well as physical and emotional barrenness, are precursors to their death. These women share similar characteristics to Katzir's protagonist. This chapter, like others in this book, serves not as a catalogue of suicides but rather to explain manifestations of the phenomena in literature, through a thematic link, one which Almog's novels share.

5. Esther Fuchs, *Israeli Mythogynies: Women in Contemporary Hebrew Fiction* (Albany: State University of New York Press, 1987), 4.

6. Ella Shohat, "Making the Silences Speak in Israeli Cinema," in *Israel Women's Studies: A Reader*, ed. Esther Fuchs (New Brunswick, N.J.: Rutgers University Press, 2005), 291.

7. Feldman, *No Room of Their Own*, 107. Feldman cites from David Biale, *Eros and the Jews: From Biblical Israel to Contemporary America* (Berkeley: University of California Press, 1997).

8. Sachlav Stoler-Liss, "'Mothers Birth the Nation': The Social Construction of Zionist Motherhood in Wartime in Israeli Parent's Manuals," *Nashim: A Journal of Jewish Women's Studies and Gender Issues* 6 (Fall 2003): 105–18, 106.

9. Lesley Hazleton, *Israeli Women: The Reality Behind the Myths* (New York: Simon and Schuster, 1977). Izraeli and Tabory suggest that the demographic problem has also affected the mythology of the Jewish woman's role as child giver. Dafna N. Izraeli and Ephraim Tabory, "The Political Context of Feminist Attitudes in Israel," *Gender and Society* 2, no. 4 (1988), 463–81.

10. Sered, *What Makes Women Sick?*, 14.

11. Dorit Naaman, "Unruly Daughters to Mother Nation: Palestinian and Israeli First-Person Films," *Hypatia* 23, no. 2 (June 2008): 19–20.

12. Ibid.

13. Morgenstern-Leissner, "Hospital Birth, Military Service," 203.

14. Lesley Hazleton identified "the cult of fertility" in 1977, and her research has informed much of the field. Hazleton, *Israeli Women*, 63–90.

15. Marilyn P. Safir, "Religion, Tradition and Public Policy Give Family First Priority," in *Calling the Equality Bluff: Women in Israel*, ed. Barbara Swirski and Marilyn P. Safir (New York: Teachers College Press, Columbia University, 1993), 57–65, 58, 59.

16. Naaman, "Unruly Daughters to Mother Nation," 20.

17. Ronit Ir-Shai and Yaffah Berkovits Murciano, "Family Planning: A Halakhic-Gender Perspective," *Nashim: A Journal of Jewish Women's Studies and Gender Issues* 12 (2006): 95–128, 95.

18. Alison Solomon, "Anything for a Baby: Reproductive Technology in Israel," in *Calling the Equality Bluff: Women in Israel*, ed. Barbara Swirski and Marilyn P. Safir (New York: Teachers College Press, Columbia University), 102–7, 103.

19. Pnina Lahav, "The Status of Women in Israel: Myth and Reality," *American Journal of Comparative Law* 22, no. 1 (Winter 1974): 107–29, 110.

20. Ibid., 120.

21. I am not suggesting that women in Israel do not have access to education, but that the stereotype of the mother and homemaker still presents a dominant ideal. Lahav notes that Israeli society continues to produce situations which encourage restrictive

attitudes toward women. Today in Israel the system which judges women in the family courts continues to discriminate against them. "A series of restrictions makes women ineligible for marriage under Jewish law. A married woman who has had a romantic relationship with another man is forbidden to marry the latter once her marriage is dissolved. No similar restriction applies to the husband, who may marry whomever he pleases after divorce. A logical extension of this rule is the Jewish conception of illegitimate children. Children born out of wedlock are not considered illegitimate and are not deprived of any rights. However, children born of a forbidden relationship, such as a child born to a married woman and her lover, are considered bastards and subject to several disqualifications, among them ineligibility to marry a Jew. This restriction applies in all circumstances where the mother had been married to another while bearing the child, even when she had long been separated from her husband due to circumstances beyond her control (war, disappearance) or where she had innocently believed him dead" (Lahav, "The Status of Women in Israel," 121). These courts base their rulings on traditional patriarchal systems where, for example, adultery can only be committed by a married woman and not by a married man. Since only women are forbidden to have lovers, it is only women who can create bastards, children born to adulterous mothers who are ineligible to be married under Jewish law. Therefore no responsibility lies with the man and this is seen as "the woman's 'sin'" (ibid.). In this case it is incumbent upon women to preserve their modesty, again reinforcing the traditional gender stereotype. Moreover, since men can also refuse to grant their wives a divorce — creating a woman who is chained to her husband (*agunah*) and unable to marry another — even if the woman has been abandoned, the children she has with another man would be unable to be married under Jewish law, unless marrying other "bastards."

22. Much has been written about the various birthing treatments that are available to women including in vitro fertilization, post-mortem sperm aspiration, legal surrogacy agreements, and by contrast, the social stigma attached to abortion. Meira Weiss, "The 'Chosen Body': A Semiotic Analysis of the Discourse of Israeli Militarism and Collective Identity," *Semiotica* 145, nos. 1/4 (2003): 151–73; Haim Barkai, *The Evolution of Israel's Social Security System: Structure, Time Pattern and Macroeconomic Impact* (Aldershot, Eng.: Ashgate, 1998); Avraham Doron and Ralph M. Kramer, *The Welfare State in Israel: The Evolution of Social Security Policy and Practice* (Boulder, Colo.: Westview, 1991); Jacqueline Portugese, *Fertility Policy in Israel: The Politics of Religion, Gender, and Nation* (Westport, Conn.: Praeger, 1998); Susan Martha Kahn, *Reproducing Jews: A Cultural Account of Assisted Conception in Israel* (Durham, N.C.: Duke University Press, 2000); Susan Martha Kahn, "Reproducing Jews: The Social Uses and Cultural Meanings of the New Reproductive Technologies in Israel" (Ph.D. diss., Harvard University, 1997); Sered, *What Makes Women Sick?*.

23. Daphna Birenbaum-Carmeli, "Reproductive Policy in Context: Implications on Women's Rights in Israel, 1945–2000," *Policy Studies* 24, nos. 2/3 (2003): 110.

24. Ibid.

25. Ibid.

26. Ibid.

27. Shlomo Swirski et al., "Women in the Labor Market of the Israeli Welfare State," paper presented at the Adva Center, July 2001; Shlomo Swirski, Ami Fraenkel, and Barbara Swirski, "Income Maintenance in Israel: From Welfare to Income Mainte-

nance and from Income Maintenance to Welfare Reform," paper presented at the Adva Center, October 2001.

28. Birenbaum-Carmeli, "Reproductive Policy in Context," 102.

29. Hilla Haelyon, "'Longing for a Child': Perceptions of Motherhood Among Israeli-Jewish Women Undergoing In Vitro Fertilization Treatments," *Nashim: A Journal of Jewish Women's Studies and Gender Issues* 12 (2006): 177–202; Ruth Halperin-Kaddari, *Women in Israel: A State of Their Own* (Philadelphia: University of Pennsylvania Press, 2003); Yael Hashiloni-Dolev, "Between Mothers, Fetuses and Society: Reproductive Genetics in the Israeli-Jewish Context," *Nashim: A Journal of Jewish Women's Studies and Gender Issues* 12 (2006): 129–50; Ir-Shai and Berkovits Murciano, "Family Planning," Morgenstern-Leissner, "Hospital Birth, Military Service," and Carmel Shalev and Sigal Gooldin, "The Uses and Misuses of In Vitro Fertilization in Israel: Some Sociological and Ethical Considerations," all in *Nashim: A Journal of Jewish Women's Studies and Gender Issues* 12 (2006): 151–76. According to Sered, Israel has the highest rate of in vitro fertilization usage in the world and specialists in Israel are "global leaders" (Sered, *What Makes Women Sick?*).

30. Solomon, "Anything for a Baby," 102.

31. Halperin-Kaddari, *Women in Israel*, 72.

32. Sered, *What Makes Women Sick?*, 62.

33. Birenbaum-Carmeli, "Reproductive Policy in Context."

34. Sered, *What Makes Women Sick?*, 23.

35. Kahn, *Reproducing Jews*; Kahn, "Reproducing Jews: The Social Uses and Cultural Meanings of the New Reproductive Technologies in Israel," 107; Meira Weiss, "The Body of the Nation: Terrorism and the Embodiment of Nationalism in Contemporary Israel," *Anthropological Quarterly* 75, no. 1 (2002): 37–62.

36. Abraham B. Yehoshua, *Masa el Tom ha-Elef: Roman bi-Sheloshah Halakim* (Tel Aviv: ha-Kibbutz ha-Meuchad, 1997); A. B. Yehoshua, *A Journey to the End of the Millennium—A Novel of the Middle Ages* (Boston: Mariner Books, 2000), 15.

37. Sandra M. Gilbert and Susan Gubar, *The Madwoman in the Attic: The Woman Writer and the Nineteenth-Century Literary Imagination*, 2nd ed. (New Haven, Conn.: Yale University Press, 2000). Gilbert and Gubar explore the image of female as "monster" alongside the image of female as "angel," arguing that Virginia Woolf has called for a rejection of both extreme images "which male authors have generated," 17.

38. A. B. Yehoshua, *A Journey to the End of the Millennium*, 35.

39. Yehoshua Kenaz, *ba-Derekh el ha-Hatulim* (Tel Aviv: Am Oved, 1991); citations from the English translation, Yehoshua Kenaz, *The Way to the Cats*, trans. Dalya Bilu (South Royalton, Vt.: Steerforth, 1994), 280.

40. Kenaz, *The Way to the Cats*, 293.

41. Brown, *The Art of Suicide*, 152–53.

42. Ibid.

43. Tammuz, *Requiem for Na'aman*, 3. Poison is the more common method of suicide for women in French literature, the field in which the author Benjamin Tammuz was a professor. (See Madame Bovary, the heroine of Gustave Flaubert's eponymous novel who died of arsenic poisoning, or the heroine of Émile Zola's *Thérèse Raquin*, who shared a glass of poison with her husband.) Stephanie O'Hara, "Tracing Poison: Theatre and Society in Seventeenth Century France" (Ph.D. diss., University of North Carolina, 2003).

44. Sara Wiseman-Stein, "Kol Akara: The Voice of the Barren Women," *Women in Judaism: Contemporary Writings* (2003).

45. The mother of Samson is given the name Hatzelponi in Chronicles, though her name does not appear in Judges.

46. The term *akara* (barren) is used to describe Rebecca in Genesis 35:21, Hatzelponi (Samson's mother) in Judges 14:4, and Hannah in I Samuel 1:5. The terms *rehem* (womb) in Job 24:20 and *akara* (barren) in Job 24:21 are used in conjunction with the suffering of women who are righteous.

47. Babylonian Talmud, Nedarim 64b.

48. Kartun-Blum, *Profane Scriptures*, ix.

49. See: "and Hannah had no children" (I Samuel 1:2).

50. When God agrees to save Ephraim, a symbol for the Jewish people in Jeremiah's lamentation, he responds to Rachel's cry saying, "I remember him" (Jeremiah 31:20).

51. Feldman, *No Room of Their Own*, 107.

52. Ibid.

53. Gilbert and Gubar, *The Madwoman in the Attic*.

54. Irina Paperno, *Suicide as a Cultural Institution in Dostoevsky's Russia* (Ithaca, N.Y.: Cornell University Press, 1997), 58.

55. "And at the very moment when the space between the wheels was opposite her, she threw back the red bag and, tucking her head into her shoulders, fell under the [train] car on to her hands." Lev Tolstoi, *Anna Karenina* (Moscow: Khudozhestvennaya Literatura, 1978), 2.285 (in the Russian edition, it is section 7, chap. 31). Translation from the Russian with thanks to Michael Rand.

56. *The Lancet*, 1879, the British medical journal in an article discussing *Il Suicido* (1879) by Guido Morselli, which informed Émile Durkheim's study of suicide. Durkheim, *Suicide: A Study in Sociology*. The reference comes from Brown, *The Art of Suicide*, 188.

57. Brown, *The Art of Suicide*, 152–53. "Common to many of these images is the depiction of the ominous womb-like archway in the background, a format that is repeated throughout the century. Like the proscenium arch of a theatre, or an altar, the arch frames and presents these beautiful female bodies to the spectator."

58. Ibid., 157.

59. Gilbert and Gubar, *The Madwoman in the Attic*, 284.

60. Brown, *The Art of Suicide*, 154.

61. Ibid., 183.

62. Ibid.

63. Bertha Rochester is the first wife in Charlotte Brontë's *Jane Eyre*. The "Lady of Shalott" is a character from Arthurian legend, celebrated in a poem by Alfred Lord Tennyson. Ophelia appears in *Hamlet* by William Shakespeare.

64. Barbara T. Gates, *Victorian Suicide: Mad Crimes and Sad Histories* (Princeton, N.J.: Princeton University Press, 1988), 6. Gates cites the example of Sir James MacKintosh, MP. In Parliament on May 26, 1823, when arguing for the abolition of suicide laws, he sarcastically commented that "verdicts of insanity were almost always found in the cases of persons in the higher situations of life; where self-slayers were humble and defenceless, there *felo-de-se* was usually returned." He was cheered by the House and the law was changed on July 4, 1823, as a result.

65. Paperno, *Suicide as a Cultural Institution in Dostoevsky's Russia*. From Russian

law, article 1945/2023/1454. However, a similar idea is expressed in Gates, *Victorian Suicide*, 4–6.

66. Janet Hadda, *Passionate Women, Passive Men: Suicide in Yiddish Literature* (Albany: State University of New York Press, 1988).

67. Ibid., 15.

68. Ibid., 3.

69. Gilbert and Gubar, *The Madwoman in the Attic*, 284–85.

70. Simone de Beauvoir, *The Second Sex* (New York: Alfred A. Knopf, 1993), 620–21.

71. Beauvoir, *The Second Sex*, 496; Lester, *Suicide: The Gamble with Death*, 39.

72. Beauvoir, *The Second Sex*.

73. Kartun-Blum, *Profane Scriptures*, 69–89, 88. My italics.

74. In Israel, teachers are referred to by their first name but with the honorific prefix "the teacher," such as "the teacher Rachel"; in English this would translate as the use of "Miss." For the purposes of clarity here I have used this form where "the teacher" would be found in the Hebrew text.

Chapter 6

1. The discussion of suicide in literature and culture, particularly that of the Victorian period is ongoing and extensive. See Brown, *The Art of Suicide*, which examines low culture in British art during the nineteenth century, while Barbara Gates in her study of suicide in Victorian England takes a new historical approach toward high culture, arguing that the representations of suicide in literature reflected the complicated discourse on death. Irina Paperno, noting the prolific popularity of all things connected to suicide in nineteenth-century Russia, argues that the Victorian "voyeuristic penetration in to the very process of dying" could not provide either meaning or explanation for the act itself. Paperno, *Suicide as a Cultural Institution in Dostoevsky's Russia*, 153. For other texts exploring a culture's relationship to suicide see Olive Anderson, *Suicide in Victorian and Edwardian England* (Oxford: Clarendon, 1987); Brown, *The Art of Suicide*; M. D. Faber, *Suicide and Greek Tragedy* (New York: Sphinx, 1970); Gates, *Victorian Suicide*; Mary J. Joseph, *Suicide in Henry James's Fiction* (New York: Peter Lang, 1994); Rowland Wymer, *Suicide and Despair in the Jacobean Drama* (Brighton: Harvester, 1986); A. Alvarez, *The Savage God: A Study of Suicide* (London: Bloomsbury, 2002).

2. Uri Ilan, an Israeli soldier, was captured, tortured as a spy, and committed suicide in 1955 in a Syrian prison, leaving a note written in his own blood saying, "I did not betray." His death and heroism were represented as exemplary acts of national pride.

3. Lester, *Suicide from a Sociological Perspective*, 22.

4. Durkheim and Simpson, *Suicide: A Study in Sociology*. Durkheim's thesis, first published in 1897, has been one of the most influential books on the study of suicide. Lester categorizes Durkheim's types into two groups: those which are related to issues of social regulation, which is the extent to which society dictates to the individual, and those which are related to issues of social integration, the degree to which people feel part of the group with which they identify. An *egoistic* suicide will result from a low degree of social integration, where a person feels unaccepted or rejected by society. In addition, the person does not feel protected by religion and does not have strong group

ties, family ties, or political affiliations. In contrast, an *altruistic* suicide is the result of a high degree of social integration. This can be witnessed in the demonstration of strong or even excessive support for the group, such as in the case of soldiers whose responsibility to a nationalist collective outweighs their sense of individuality. This high degree of social integration is also evident in the case of religious groups who commit mass suicide for a cause. Therefore, it follows that when there is a moderate degree of social integration, there will be the lowest number of suicides.

Social regulation refers to the extent to which individuals' lives are ordered by their world. A high degree of social regulation will lead to a *fatalistic* suicide which derives from excessive regulation; this is the suicide committed by people whose futures appear "pitilessly blocked and passions violently choked by oppressive disciplines" (Durkheim and Simpson, *Suicide: A Study in Sociology*, 276), and Durkheim cites the example of a slave who has nothing to live for because he has no hope for a more positive prospect. In contrast, a low degree of social regulation will result in an *anomic* suicide. This occurs when an individual's activity is lacking any kind of regulation and consequently suffers from the lack of social organization. Anomic suicides are committed when a person has an imagination, which is hungry for novelty and which, "ungoverned, gropes at random." In this situation, suicide may become a kind of novelty.

Anomic suicide may be most common in what Durkheim calls the economic world, a society based solely on fluctuating financial markets and business trends. Suicides will be common at the peak of an economic boom or during a sudden economic depression. Durkheim suggests that anomic suicide can also be seen in the "crisis of widowhood." This domestic anomie results when the surviving partner cannot adapt to the new situation. In both cases, an event or process has caused an individual to feel a lack of purpose or sense of identity in relation to his or her world. Unsurprisingly, statistics show that where there is a degree of moderate social regulation, the number of suicides will be lowest.

We may summarize Durkheim's categories by saying that suicides are the result of a lack of interaction among the members of a society, a lack of common conscience, or purposes and goals, and a lack of social regulation. Although in extreme examples, a total integration into a society in which the collective conscience exceeds the role of the individual conscience may also lead to suicide.

5. Later sociologists such as Johnson (1965) argue that the divisions are false and can be reduced to a single category, while Lester counters this argument. For a comprehensive account of these divisions, modifications, and countermodifications by sociologists, see Lester, *Suicide from a Sociological Perspective*.

6. Edwin S. Shneidman and Antoon A. Leenaars, *Lives and Deaths: Selections from the Works of Edwin S. Shneidman* (Philadelphia: Brunner/Mazel, 1999).

7. Berman, *Surviving Literary Suicide*, 4.

8. Alvarez, *The Savage God*, 80.

9. Ibid.

10. Berman, *Surviving Literary Suicide*, 140.

11. Ibid., 140, quoting Alvarez, *The Savage God*, xii.

12. Berman, *Surviving Literary Suicide*, 140, quoting Alvarez, *The Savage God*, 36–37.

13. Berman, *Surviving Literary Suicide*, 121–22. The suicide note according to Lester has become "famed through novels and films." David Lester and C. Reeve, "The

Suicide Notes of Young and Old People," *Psychological Reports* 50, no. 1 (1982). Research indicates that the percentage of people who leave suicide notes is only between 5 and 40 percent. Shneidman and Farberow (1961), researching the cases of suicide notes in Los Angeles County, concluded that 35 percent of men and 39 percent of women left notes, of which 30 percent left more than one, but in an attempted suicide only 2 percent of males and 1 percent of females left notes. However, reporting of notes is not accurate because if no note is found with the body then there is less chance of a coroner calling the death a suicide. This may be important to the survivors of the victim (family, friends, heirs) for insurance, legal, or religious reasons. Norman L. Farberow and Edwin S. Shneidman, *The Cry for Help* (New York: McGraw-Hill, 1961); Edwin S. Shneidman and American Association of Suicidology, *On the Nature of Suicide* (San Francisco: Jossey-Bass, 1973).

14. Lester, *Suicide: The Gamble with Death*, 73.

15. Ibid., 75.

16. Paperno, *Suicide as a Cultural Institution in Dostoevsky's Russia*, 114.

17. Ibid. Paperno citing Edwin Shneidman.

18. Ibid.

19. Ibid., 151.

20. Ibid., 183.

21. Ibid., 153.

22. Following on from Douglas's suggestion that the recording of results among authorities may be to blame for the statistics, rather than the statistics themselves, several surveys were run to see if coroners presented with the same cases in different countries showed varying classification tendencies. T. Brugha and D. Walsh, "Suicide Past and Present — the Temporal Constancy of Under-Reporting," *British Journal of Psychiatry* 132 (1978): 177–79. Brooke concludes that Danish coroners are more likely to rule a case of suicide than English coroners; Eileen M. Brooke, *Suicide and Attempted Suicide* (Geneva: World Health Organization, 1974), but Lester disagrees; David Lester, "A Critical Mass Theory of National Suicide Rates," *Suicide and Life Threatening Behaviour* 18 (1988): 279–84, arguing that there are other factors involved with coroners' decisions rather than simply national bias. N. L. Farberow, D. R. MacKinnon, and F. L. Nelson, "Suicide: Who's Counting?," *Public Health Reports* 92, no. 3 (1977): 223–32. After studying 202 counties in western states in North America they found that the suicide rates varied with coroner variables as well as sociodemographic variables. For example, suicide rates were higher if the coroner was a pathologist and lower if the coroner was a lawyer.

P. Sainsbury and B. Barraclough, "Differences Between Suicide Rates," *Nature* 220, no. 173 (1968): 1252. Sainsbury and Barraclough investigated the effects that the coroner had on reported suicides to see if this was a significant factor in the amount of recorded suicides in an area. They carried out this study by looking at English counties in 1950–52 and 1960–62. Thirty-nine boroughs had the same coroner in both of the periods investigated while nineteen had changes in the coroner. The conclusion was that after measuring the correlation in all of the different rates, there was no significant difference. A later survey in 1976 which measured open verdicts against suicidal and accidental verdicts also showed no significant results; however, they did observe that certification practices differed. B. Barraclough, B. M. Holding, and P. Fayers, "Influence of Coroner's Officers and Pathologists on Suicide Verdicts," *British Journal of*

Psychiatry 128 (1978): 471–74; B. M. Barraclough and D. M. Shepherd, "Impact of a Suicide Inquest," *Lancet* 2, no. 8093 (1978): 795. As Lester has explained in reference to Sainsbury and Barraclough's "Differences Between Suicide Rates," "Although reported suicide rates were probably underestimates of the true suicide rates, absolutely accurate rates were not needed, since reporting errors seemed to have little systematic bias. Research in the last twenty years has not indicated that we should modify their conclusions." David Lester, *Suicide from a Sociological Perspective* (Springfield, Ill.: Charles C. Thomas, 1989), 17.

23. Gates, *Victorian Suicide*, 12.

24. Ibid., 11–12.

25. Ibid., 12.

26. Anthony Giddens, *The Sociology of Suicide: A Selection of Readings* (London: Cass, 1971), 37.

27. Gates, *Victorian Suicide*, xvii.

28. Paperno, *Suicide as a Cultural Institution in Dostoevsky's Russia*, 105–7.

29. Brown, *The Art of Suicide*, 138.

30. Ibid., 159.

31. Paperno, *Suicide as a Cultural Institution in Dostoevsky's Russia*, 2.

32. Clemons, *What Does the Bible Say About Suicide?*, 7.

33. Nils Retterstøl, "Suicide in a Cultural History Perspective, Part 1," *Norwegian Journal of Suicidology* 2 (1998): 2.

34. Chukovsky, quoted by Paperno, in *Suicide as a Cultural Institution in Dostoevsky's Russia*, 103. The original citation is from Chukovskii, "Samoubiitsy (Ocherki sovremennoi slovenosti)," *Rech'*, no. 352 (December 23, 1912).

Primary Sources

Hilu, Alon. *Ahuzat Dajani*. Yediot Sefarim, 2008.

——. *The House of Rajani*. Translated by Evan Fallenberg. London: Harvill-Secker Random House, 2010.

Katzir, Yehudit. *Closing the Sea*. San Diego: Harcourt, 1992.

——. *Sogrim et ha-Yam*. Sifre Siman Keri'ah. Tel Aviv: ha-Kibbutz ha-Meuchad, 1990.

Kenan, Amos. "Dani (Tziun lezikro)" ["Danny (A Note in Memory)"]. In Amos Kenan, *Sefer ha-Satirot 1948–1984 and Vice Versa*. Jerusalem: Keter, 1984.

Kenaz, Yehoshua. *Hitganvut Yehidim*. Tel Aviv: Am Oved, 1986.

——. *Infiltration*. Translated by Dalya Bilu. New York: Random House, 2003.

Keret, Etgar. *The Bus Driver Who Wanted to Be God and Other Stories*. New York: Thomas Dunne Books / St. Martin's Press Short Stories, 2003.

——. *Ha-Kaitanah shel Kneller*. Tel Aviv: Zemorah Keter, 1998.

——. *Kneller's Happy Campers*. London: Chatto and Windus, 2009.

Oz, Amos. *Artsot ha-Tan: Sipurim*. Tel Aviv: Agudat ha-Sofrim be-Yisrael Leyad Hotsa'at "Masadah," 1965.

——. *Where the Jackals Howl, and Other Stories*. London: Chatto and Windus, 1981.

Shabtai, Yaakov. *Past Continuous*. Philadelphia: Jewish Publication Society of America, 1985.

——. *Zikhron Devarim: Roman*. Tel Aviv: Mifalim universitaiyim le-hotsa'ah la-or, 1977.

Tammuz, Benjamin. *Rekviem le-Na'aman: Kronikah Shel Neumim Mishpahtiyim, 1895–1974: Roman*. Tel Aviv: Zemorah Bitan Modan, 1978.

——. *Requiem for Na'aman*. New York: New American Library, 1982.

Yehoshua, Abraham B. *Mar Mani: Roman Sihot*. Tel Aviv: ha-Kibbutz ha-Meuchad, 1990.

——. *Mr. Mani*. New York: Doubleday, 1992.

Secondary Sources

Almog, Oz. *The Sabra: The Creation of the New Jew*. Berkeley: University of California Press, 2000.

Alter, Robert. *The Art of Biblical Narrative*. New York: Basic Books, 1981.

Alvarez, A. *The Savage God: A Study of Suicide*. London: Bloomsbury, 2002.

Anderson, Benedict. *Imagined Communities: Reflections on the Origin and Spread of Nationalism*. Rev. ed. London: Verso, 1991.

Anderson, Olive. *Suicide in Victorian and Edwardian England*. Oxford: Clarendon, 1987.

Aronoff, Mark. "The Origins of Israeli Political Culture." In *Israeli Democracy Under Stress*, edited by E. Sprinzak and L. Diamond, 47–63. Boulder, Colo.: Lynne Rienner, 1993.

Ashplant, T. G., Graham Dawson, and Michael Roper. *The Politics of War Memory and Commemoration*. Routledge Studies in Memory and Narrative 7. London: Routledge, 2000.

Atkinson, J. Maxwell. *Discovering Suicide: Studies in the Social Organization of Sudden Death*. Pittsburgh: University of Pittsburgh Press, 1978.

Atkinson, M. W., N. Kessel, and J. B. Dalgaard. "The Comparability of Suicide Rates." *British Journal of Psychiatry* 127 (1975): 247–56.

Azaryahu, Maoz. *Tel Aviv: Mythography of a City*. Syracuse, N.Y.: Syracuse University Press, 2007.

Azaryahu, Maoz, and S. Ilan Troen, eds. *Tel-Aviv, the First Century: Visions, Designs, Actualities*. Bloomington: Indiana University Press, 2011.

Balaban, Abraham. *Amir Gilboa: Mivhar Ma'amre Bikoret Al Yetsirato* [*Amir Gilboa: A Selection of Critical Articles on His Work*]. Tel Aviv: Am Oved, 1972.

———. *Ben El Le-Hayah: Iyun Bi-Yetsirato Shel Amos Oz* [*Between To and Was: A Study on the Works of Amos Oz*]. Tel Aviv: Am Oved, 1986.

———. *Between God and Beast: An Examination of Amos Oz's Prose*. University Park: Pennsylvania State University Press, 1993.

———. *El Ha-Lashon U-Mimenah: Lashon U-Metsiut Bi-Yetsirat Amos Oz* [*To the Language and Back: Language and Reality in Amos Oz's Works*]. Tel Aviv: Am Oved, 1988.

———. *Mar Molkho: Ha-Kivun Ha-Negdi: Iyun Ba-Romanim Mar Mani U-Molkho Me-'Et A. B. Yehoshua, Sidrat Masah, Mehkar, Iyun*. Tel Aviv: ha-Kibbutz ha-Meuchad, 1992.

Band, Arnold. "The Impact of Statehood on the Hebrew Literary Imagination: Haim Hazaz and the Zionist Narrative." In *Divergent Jewish Cultures*, edited by Deborah Dash Moore and S. Ilan Troen. New Haven, Conn.: Yale University Press, 2001.

Barak, Yoram, and Dov Aizenberg. "Patterns of Antidepressants Prescribing and Suicide in Israel." Poster Presentation, 2nd International Conference on Brain and Behaviour, Thessaloniki, Greece. *Annals of General Psychiatry* 5, suppl. 1 (2006): S307.

Barkai, Haim. *The Evolution of Israel's Social Security System: Structure, Time Pattern and Macroeconomic Impact*. Aldershot, Eng.: Ashgate, 1998.

Barr, B. M. "Differences Between National Suicide Rates." *British Journal of Psychiatry* 122 (1973): 85–96.

Barraclough, B., B. M. Holding, and P. Fayers. "Influence of Coroner's Officers and Pathologists on Suicide Verdicts." *British Journal of Psychiatry* 128 (1976): 471–74.

Barraclough, B. M., and D. M. Shepherd. "Impact of a Suicide Inquest." *Lancet* 2, no. 8093 (1978): 795.

Baruch, Miri. *Ha-Romantikan Ha-Mar: Iyun Be-Shirav Shel Natan Zakh* [*Bitter Romance: A Study on the Poetry of Natan Zach*]. Tel Aviv: Alef, 1979.

Beauvoir, Simone de. *The Second Sex*. Translated by H. M. Parshley. New York: Alfred A. Knopf, 1993.

Ben-Ari, Eyal, and Yoram Bilu, eds. *Grasping Land: Space and Place in Contemporary Israeli Discourse and Experience.* SUNY Series in Anthropology and Judaic Studies. Albany: State University of New York Press, 1997.

Ben-Dov, Nitza, ed. *Ba-Kivun Ha-Negdi: Kovets Mehkarim Al Mar Mani Le-A. B. Yehoshua* [*In the Opposite Direction: A Collection of Articles from Mr. Mani to A. B. Yehoshua*]. Tel Aviv: ha-Kibbutz ha-Meuchad, 1995.

Ben-Zadok, Efraim. "National Planning—the Critical Neglected Link: One Hundred Years of Jewish Settlement in Israel." *International Journal of Middle East Studies* 17, no. 3 (August 1985): 329–45.

Benedict, Ruth. *Patterns of Culture.* Boston: Houghton Mifflin, 1934.

Berman, Jeffrey. *Surviving Literary Suicide.* Amherst: University of Massachusetts Press, 1999.

Bhabha, Homi K. *The Location of Culture.* Routledge Classics. London: Routledge, 2004.

——. *Nation and Narration.* London: Routledge, 1990.

Biale, David. *Eros and the Jews: From Biblical Israel to Contemporary America.* Berkeley: University of California Press, 1997.

Bilu, Yoram, and Eliezer Witztum. "War-Related Loss and Suffering in Israeli Society: An Historical Perspective." *Israel Studies* 5, no. 2 (2000): 1–31.

Birenbaum-Carmeli, Daphna. "Reproductive Policy in Context: Implications on Women's Rights in Israel, 1945–2000." *Policy Studies* 24, nos. 2/3 (2003): 102–13.

Bloom, Harold. *The Anxiety of Influence: A Theory of Poetry.* New York: Oxford University Press, 1973.

——. *A Map of Misreading.* New York: Oxford University Press, 1975.

Bourdieu, Pierre. "Flaubert and the French Literary Field." In *Principles of a Sociology of Cultural Works: Essays in Art and Literature.* New York: Columbia University Press, 1993.

Bourdieu, Pierre, and Randal Johnson. *The Field of Cultural Production: Essays on Art and Literature.* Cambridge, Eng.: Polity, 1993.

Boyarin, Daniel. *Unheroic Conduct: The Rise of Heterosexuality and the Invention of the Jewish Man.* Berkeley: University of California Press, 1997.

Brennan, Timothy. "The National Longing for Form." In *Nation and Narration,* edited by Homi K. Bhabha, 44–70. 1990; reprint, London: Routledge, 2003.

Brooke, Eileen M. *Suicide and Attempted Suicide.* Geneva: World Health Organization, 1974.

Brown, Ron M. *The Art of Suicide (Picturing History).* London: Reaktion Books, 2001.

Brugha, T., and D. Walsh. "Suicide Past and Present—the Temporal Constancy of Under-Reporting." *British Journal of Psychiatry* 132 (1978): 177–79.

Brym, Robert J., and Bader Araj. "Suicide Bombing as a Strategy and Interaction: The Case of the Second Intifada." *Social Forces* 84, no. 4 (2006): 1969–86.

Buber, Martin *A Land of Two Peoples: Martin Buber on Jews and Arabs.* Edited by Paul Mendes-Flohr. Chicago: University of Chicago Press, 2005.

Camus, Albert. *The Myth of Sisyphus.* Harmondsworth, Eng.: Penguin, 1975.

Carco, Francis, and Ford Madox Ford. *Perversity.* Chicago: P. Covici, 1928.

Cavan, Ruth Shonle. *Suicide.* University of Chicago Sociological Series. New York: Russell and Russell, 1965.

CDC National Center for Injury Prevention and Control. "Rates of Homicide, Suicide, and Firearm-Related Death Among Children — 26 Industrialized Countries." In *Morbidity and Mortality Weekly Report* 46, no. 5 (February 7, 1997): 101–5.

Clemons, James T. *What Does the Bible Say About Suicide?* Minneapolis: Fortress, 1990.

Cohen-Almagor, Raphael. "Cultural Pluralism and the Israeli Nation-Building Ideology." *International Journal of Middle East Studies* 27, no. 4 (November 1995): 461–84.

Confino, Alon. "Collective Memory and Cultural History: Problems of Method." *American Historical Review* 102, no. 5 (1997): 1386–403.

Cook, David, and Olivia Allison. *Understanding and Addressing Suicide Attacks: The Faith and Politics of Martyrdom Operations.* Westport, Conn.: Praeger Security International, 2007.

Deats, Sara Munson, and Lagretta Tallent Lenker. *Youth Suicide Prevention: Lessons from Literature.* New York: Plenum, 1989.

Dohrenwend, B. P. "Egoism, Altruism, Anomie and Fatalism." *American Sociological Review* 24 (1959): 468–73.

Doron, Avraham, and Ralph M. Kramer. *The Welfare State in Israel: The Evolution of Social Security Policy and Practice.* Westview Special Studies on the Middle East. Boulder, Colo.: Westview, 1991.

Douglas, Jack D. *The Social Meanings of Suicide.* Princeton, N.J.: Princeton University Press, 1967.

Droge, Arthur J., and James D. Tabor. *A Noble Death: Suicide and Martyrdom Among Christians and Jews in Antiquity.* San Francisco: HarperSanFrancisco, 1992.

During, Simon. "Literature — Nationalism's Other? The Case for Revision." In *Nation and Narration,* edited by Homi K. Bhabha, 138–53. 1990; reprint, London: Routledge, 2003.

Durkheim, Émile. *Suicide: A Study in Sociology.* Translated by George Simpson. 1899; reprint, London: Routledge, 1989.

Eglin, Peter. *Suicide, Teaching Papers in Sociology* 7. York: Longman Resources Unit, 1985.

Einbinder, Susan L. *Beautiful Death: Jewish Poetry and Martyrdom in Medieval France (Jews, Christians, and Muslims from the Ancient to the Modern World).* Princeton, N.J.: Princeton University Press, 2002.

Ezer, Nancy. *Sifrut Ve-Ideologyah, Mareh Makom.* Tel Aviv: Papirus, 1992.

Ezrahi, Yaron. *Rubber Bullets: Power and Conscience in Modern Israel.* Berkeley: University of California Press, 1998.

Faber, M. D. *Suicide and Greek Tragedy.* New York: Sphinx, 1970.

Farberow, Norman L. *Suicide in Different Cultures.* Baltimore: University Park Press, 1975.

Farberow, N. L., D. R. MacKinnon, and F. L. Nelson. "Suicide: Who's Counting?" *Public Health Reports* 92, no. 3 (1977): 223–32.

Farberow, N. L., and T. L. McEvoy. "Suicide Among Patients with Diagnoses of Anxiety Reaction or Depressive Reaction in General Medical and Surgical Hospitals." *Journal of Abnormal Psychology* 71, no. 4 (1966): 287–99.

Farberow, Norman L., and Edwin S. Shneidman. *The Cry for Help.* New York: McGraw-Hill, 1961.

Feige, Michael. "Introduction: Rethinking Israeli Memory and Identity." *Israel Studies* 7, no. 2 (2002): v–xiv.

——. "New Directions in Memory Research in Israel." *Israel Studies* 7, no. 2 (2000): ix.

——. "Rescuing the Person from the Symbol: 'Peace Now' and the Ironies of Modern Myth." *History and Memory* 11, no. 1 (1999): 141–68.

Feldhay-Brenner, Rachel *Inextricably Bonded: Israeli Arab and Jewish Writers Re-Visioning Culture.* Madison: University of Wisconsin Press, 2010.

Feldman, Yael S. "The Jacob Complex and Zionist Masculinism in the Work of A. B. Yehoshua." In *Gendering the Jewish Past*, edited by Marc Lee Raphael. Williamsburg, Va.: Department of Religion, College of William and Mary, 2002.

——. *Modernism and Cultural Transfer: Gabriel Preil and the Tradition of Jewish Literary Bilingualism.* Monographs of the Hebrew Union College, no. 10. Cincinnati, Ohio: Hebrew Union College Press, 1986.

——. *No Room of Their Own: Gender and Nation in Israeli Women's Fiction, Gender, and Culture.* New York: Columbia University Press, 1999.

Fishelov, David. *Mahlefot Shimshon: Gilgule Demuto Shel Shimshon Ha-Mikrai.* Haifa: Hotsaat sefarim shel Universitat Hefah; Zemorah-bitan, 2000.

——. "Samson's Transformations: From the Bible, to Jabotinsky and to Hollywood." *Moznayim* 74 (1999): 43–46.

——. "The Transformation of Biblical Samson or the Heroic Failure to Escape Myth." In *Myth and Literature*, edited by Lisa Block de Behar, 47–58. Montevideo, 2003.

Freud, Sigmund. "Fragment of an Analysis of a Case of Hysteria." *Standard Edition* 7 (1905): 1–122.

Frye, Northrop. *The Secular Scripture: A Study of the Structure of Romance.* Charles Eliot Norton Lectures, 1974–1975. Cambridge, Mass.: Harvard University Press, 1976.

Fuchs, Esther. *Israeli Mythogynies: Women in Contemporary Hebrew Fiction.* SUNY Series in Modern Jewish Literature and Culture. Albany: State University of New York Press, 1987.

Garfinkle, Adam M. *Politics and Society in Modern Israel: Myths and Realities.* 2nd ed. Armonk, N.Y.: M. E. Sharpe, 1999.

Gates, Barbara T. *Victorian Suicide: Mad Crimes and Sad Histories.* Princeton, N.J.: Princeton University Press, 1988.

Gertz, Nurith. *Myths in Israeli Culture: Captives of a Dream.* Parkes-Wiener Series on Jewish Studies. London: Vallentine Mitchell, 2000.

Gibbs, J. P., and W. T. Martin. "On Assessing the Theory of Status Integration and Suicide." *American Sociological Review* 31, no. 4 (1966): 533–41.

Giddens, Anthony. *The Sociology of Suicide: A Selection of Readings.* London: Cass, 1971.

Gilbert, Sandra M., and Susan Gubar. *The Madwoman in the Attic: The Woman Writer and the Nineteenth-Century Literary Imagination.* 2nd ed. New Haven, Conn.: Yale University Press, 2000.

Gilboa, Menuha. *Halomot ha-Zahav ve-Shivronam: Sifrut ve-Ideologyah bi-Yetsirat Binyamin Tammuz* [Dreams of Gold and Their Fragments: Literature and Ideology in the Works of Benjamin Tammuz]. Tel Aviv: ha-Kibbutz ha-Meuchad, 1995.

Ginsburg, G. P. "Public Conceptions and Attitudes About Suicide." *Journal of Health and Social Behavior* 12, no. 3 (1971): 200–207.

Gover, Yerach. "Were You There, or Was It a Dream? Ideological Impositions on Israeli Literature." *Journal of Palestine Studies* 16, no. 1 (Autumn 1986): 56–80.

——. *Zionism: The Limits of Moral Discourse in Israeli Hebrew Fiction*. Minneapolis: University of Minnesota Press, 1994.

Hadda, Janet. *Passionate Women, Passive Men: Suicide in Yiddish Literature*. SUNY Series in Modern Jewish Literature and Culture. Albany: State University of New York Press, 1988.

Haelyon, Hilla. "'Longing for a Child': Perceptions of Motherhood Among Israeli-Jewish Women Undergoing In Vitro Fertilization Treatments." *Nashim: A Journal of Jewish Women's Studies and Gender Issues* 12 (2006): 177–202.

Hakak, Lev. *Equivocal Dreams: Studies in Modern Hebrew Literature*. Hoboken, N.J.: Ktav, 1993.

Halevi-Zwick, Judith., ed. *Yehudah Amichai: Mivhar Ma'amre Bikoret Al Yetsirato* [*Yehudah Amichai: A Collection of Critical Essays on His Work*]. Tel Aviv: ha-Kibbutz ha-Meuchad, 1988.

Halperin-Kaddari, Ruth. *Women in Israel: A State of Their Own*. Philadelphia: University of Pennsylvania Press, 2003.

Handelman, Don, and Lea Shamgar-Handelman. "The Presence of Absence." In *Grasping Land*, edited by Eyal Ben-Ari and Yoram Bilu. Albany: State University of New York Press, 1997.

Hankoff, L. D. "The Armed Forces." In *Suicide*, edited by L. D. Hankoff and Bernice Einsidler. Littleton, Mass.: PSG, 1979.

Hankoff, L. D., and Bernice Einsidler. *Suicide: Theory and Clinical Aspects*. Littleton, Mass.: PSG, 1979.

Hare, Cyril. *Suicide Excepted*. London: Hogarth, 1986.

Harris, Rachel S., and Ranen Omer-Sherman, eds. *Narratives of Dissent: War in Israeli Arts and Culture*. Detroit: Wayne State University Press, 2013.

Hashiloni-Dolev, Yael. "Between Mothers, Foetuses and Society: Reproductive Genetics in the Israeli-Jewish Context." *Nashim: A Journal of Jewish Women's Studies and Gender Issues* 12 (2006): 129–50.

Hazleton, Lesley. *Israeli Women: The Reality Behind the Myths*. New York: Simon and Schuster, 1977.

Helman, Anat. *Young Tel Aviv: A Tale of Two Cities* Boston: Brandeis University Press, 2010.

Henry, Andrew Fred, and James F. Short. *Suicide and Homicide: Some Economic, Sociological and Psychological Aspects of Aggression*. New York: Collier-Macmillan, 1964.

Hertsig, Hanah. *Ha-Shem ha-Perati: Masot Al Yaakov Shabtai, Yehoshua Kenaz, Yoel Hofman* [*Personal Names: Essays on Yaakov Shabtai, Yehoshua Kenaz, Yoel Hofman*]. Tel Aviv: ha-Kibbutz ha-Meuchad, 1994.

Hutton, Patrick. "Recent Scholarship on Memory and History." *History Teacher* 33, no. 4 (August 2000): 533–48.

Ir-Shai, Ronit, and Yaffah Berkovits Murciano. "Family Planning: A Halakhic-Gender

Perspective." *Nashim: A Journal of Jewish Women's Studies and Gender Issues* 12 (2006): 95–128.

Izraeli, Dafna N., and Ephraim Tabory. "The Political Context of Feminist Attitudes in Israel." *Gender and Society* 2, no. 4 (1988): 463–81.

Jabotinsky, Vladimir. *Samson Nazore'i: Roman.* Berlin: Slovo, 1927.

Jacobson, David C. *Modern Midrash: The Retelling of Traditional Jewish Narratives by Twentieth-Century Hebrew Writers.* SUNY Series in Modern Jewish Literature and Culture. Albany: State University of New York Press, 1987.

Johnson, B. D. "Durkheim's One Cause of Suicide." *American Sociological Review* 30 (1965): 875–86.

Joseph, Mary J. *Suicide in Henry James's Fiction.* American University Studies, Series 24, American Literature, vol. 50. New York: Peter Lang, 1994.

Josephus, Flavius, and William Whiston. *The Wars of the Jews.* Translated by William Whiston. Everyman's Library 712. London: J. M. Dent and Sons; E. P. Dutton, 1928.

Kahn, Susan Martha. *Reproducing Jews: A Cultural Account of Assisted Conception in Israel (Body, Commodity, Text).* Durham, N.C.: Duke University Press, 2000.

———. "Reproducing Jews: The Social Uses and Cultural Meanings of the New Reproductive Technologies in Israel." Ph.D. diss., Harvard University, 1997.

Kalderon, Nisim, and Perek Kodem: *Al Natan Zakh be-Reshit Shenot ha-Shishim [On Natan Zach in the Early 1960s].* Tel Aviv: ha-Kibbutz ha-Meuchad, 1985.

Kartun-Blum, Ruth, with drawings by Menashe Kadishman. *Profane Scriptures: Reflections on the Dialogue with the Bible in Modern Hebrew Poetry.* Cincinnati, Ohio: Hebrew Union College Press, 1999.

Katz-Gerro, Tally, and Yossi Shavit. "The Stratification of Leisure and Taste: Classes and Lifestyles in Israel." *European Sociological Review* 14, no. 4 (1998): 369–86.

Kellerman, Aharon. "Settlement Myth and Settlement Activity: Interrelationships in the Zionist Land of Israel." *Transactions of the Institute of British Geographers,* new series, 21, no. 2 (1996): 363–78.

Kimmerling, Baruch. *The Invention and Decline of Israeliness.* Berkeley: University of California Press, 2001.

Kirch, M. R., and D. Lester. "Suicide from the Golden Gate Bridge: Do They Cluster over Time?" *Psychology Report* 59, no. 3 (1986): 1314.

Krebs, Ronald R. "A School for the Nation? How Military Service Does Not Build Nations, and How It Might." *International Security* 28, no. 4 (2004): 85–124.

Krouse, F. Michael. *Milton's Samson and the Christian Tradition.* Hamden, Conn.: Archon Books, 1963.

Lahav, Pnina. "The Status of Women in Israel: Myth and Reality." *American Journal of Comparative Law* 22, no. 1 (Winter 1974): 107–29.

Leenaars, Antoon A., John T. Maltsberger, and Robert A. Neimeyer. *Treatment of Suicidal People.* Series in Death Education, Aging, and Health Care. Washington, D.C.: Taylor and Francis, 1994.

Leenaars, Antoon A., and Susanne Wenckstern. *Suicide Prevention in Schools.* Series in Death Education, Aging, and Health Care. New York: Hemisphere, 1991.

Leonard, Calista V. *Understanding and Preventing Suicide.* Springfield, Ill.: Thomas, 1967.

Lester, David. "Anomie and the Suicidal Individual." *Psychology Report* 26, no. 2 (1970): 532.

———. "A Critical Mass Theory of National Suicide Rates." *Suicide and Life Threatening Behaviour* 18 (1988): 279–84.

———, ed. *Émile Durkheim: "Le Suicide," One Hundred Years Later*. Philadelphia: Charles Press, 1994.

———. "Henry and Short on Suicide: A Critique." *Journal of Psychology* 70, no. 2 (1968): 179–86.

———. "Sibling Position and Suicidal Behavior." *Journal of Individual Psychology* 22, no. 2 (1966): 204–7.

———. *Suicide from a Sociological Perspective*. Springfield, Ill.: Charles C. Thomas, 1989.

Lester, David, and N. Heim. "Sex Differences in Suicide Notes." *Perceptual and Motor Skills* 75, no. 2 (1992): 582.

Lester, David, and C. Reeve. "The Suicide Notes of Young and Old People." *Psychological Reports* 50, no. 1 (1982): 334.

Lester, Gene, and David Lester. *Suicide: The Gamble with Death*. Englewood Cliffs, N.J.: Prentice-Hall, 1971.

LeVine, Mark. "Conquest Through Town Planning: The Case of Tel Aviv, 1921–1948." *Journal of Palestine Studies* 27, no. 4 (Summer 1998): 36–52.

———. "A Nation from the Sands." *National Identities* 1, no. 1 (1999): 15–37.

Levinson, Daphna, Ziona Haklai, Nechama Stein, and Ethel-Sherry Gordon. "Suicide Attempts in Israel: Age by Gender Analysis of a National Emergency Departments Database." *Suicide and Life-Threatening Behavior* 36, no. 1 (2006): 97–102.

Levy, Nili. *Me-Rehov ha-Even el ha-Hatulim: Iyunim ba-Siporet shel Yehoshua Kenaz* [*From the Street of Stones, to the Cats: A Study in the Fiction of Yehoshuaz Kenaz*]. Tel Aviv: ha-Kibbutz ha-Meuchad, 1997.

Lieberman, Lisa. *Leaving You: The Cultural History of Suicide*. Chicago: Ivan R. Dee, 2003.

Loraux, Nicole. *Tragic Ways of Killing a Woman*. Cambridge, Mass.: Harvard University Press, 1987.

Lubin, G., S. Glasser, V. Boyko, and V. Barell. "Epidemiology of Suicide in Israel: A Nationwide Population Study." *Social Psychiatry and Psychiatric Epidemiology* 36 (2001): 123–27.

Malkinson, Ruth, and Eliezer Witztum, eds. "Bereavement and Commemoration: The Double Face of the National Myth." In *Loss and Bereavement in Jewish Society in Israel*, 231–58. Jerusalem, 1993.

Mann, Barbara. "Modernism and the Zionist Uncanny: Reading the Old Cemetery in Tel Aviv." *Representations*, no. 69, special issue: "Grounds for Remembering" (Winter 2000): 63–95.

———. *A Place in History: Modernism, Tel Aviv and the Creation of Jewish Urban Space*. Stanford, Calif.: Stanford University Press, 2006.

———. "Tel Aviv's Rothschild: When a Boulevard Becomes a Monument." *Jewish Social Studies* 7, no. 2 (2001): 1–38.

Margolin, N. L., and J. D. Teicher. "Thirteen Adolescent Male Suicide Attemptors." *Journal of the American Academy of Child Psychiatry* 7 (1968): 296–315.

Milton, John, and Ann Phillips. *Samson Agonistes*. London: University Tutorial, 1974.

Mintz, Alan L. *Translating Israel: Contemporary Hebrew Literature and Its Reception in America*. Judaic Traditions in Literature, Music, and Art. Syracuse, N.Y.: Syracuse University Press, 2001.

Morgenstern-Leissner, Omi. "Hospital Birth, Military Service, and the Ties That Bind Them: The Case of Israel." *Nashim: A Journal of Jewish Women's Studies and Gender Issues* 12 (2006): 203–41.

Naaman, Dorit. "Unruly Daughters to Mother Nation: Palestinian and Israeli First-Person Films." *Hypatia* 23, no. 2 (June 2008): 17–32.

Nachman, Ricardo, Ornit Yanai, Leib Goldin, Marnina Swartz, Yoram Barak, and Jehuda Hiss. "Suicide in Israel: 1985–1997." *Journal of Psychiatry and Neuroscience* 27, no. 6 (2002): 423–28.

Naveh, Hannah. "On Loss and Bereavement in Israeli Existence" [in Hebrew]. *Alpayim* 16 (1998): 85–120.

Nora, Pierre. "Between Memory and History: Les Lieux de Memoire." *Representations*, no. 26, special issue, "Memory and Counter-Memory" (Spring 1989): 7–24.

O'Hara, Stephanie. "Tracing Poison: Theatre and Society in Seventeenth Century France." Ph.D. diss., University of North Carolina, 2003.

Oz, Amos. *Sippur al Ahavah ve-Hoshekh*. Jerusalem: Keter, 2000.

——— . *A Tale of Love and Darkness*. London: Chatto and Windus, 2004.

Paperno, Irina. *Suicide as a Cultural Institution in Dostoevsky's Russia*. Ithaca, N.Y.: Cornell University Press, 1997.

Pappe, Ilan. "Post-Zionist Critique on Israel and the Palestinians: Part I: The Academic Debate." *Journal of Palestine Studies* 26, no. 2 (Winter 1997): 29–41.

Patterson, David. *A Phoenix in Fetters: Studies in Nineteenth and Early Twentieth Century Hebrew Fiction*. Md.: Rowman and Littlefield, 1988.

Peele, J. E. "Suicidal Behaviour, Assertiveness and Socialisation Principles." *Social Forces* 43 (1965): 510–18.

Pescosolido, B. A., and R. Mendelsohn. "Social Causation or Social Construction." *American Sociological Review*, no. 51 (1986): 80–101.

Phillips, D. P. "The Impact of Fictional Television Stories on U.S. Adult Fatalities." *American Journal of Sociology* 87 (1982): 1340–59.

——— . "The Influence of Suggestion on Suicide." *American Psychological Review* 39 (1974): 340–54.

Podeh, Elie. "History and Memory in the Israeli Educational System: The Portrayal of the Arab-Israeli Conflict in History Textbooks (1948–2000)." *History and Memory* 12, no. 1 (2000): 65–100.

Pope, Whitney. *Durkheim's "Suicide": A Classic Analyzed*. Chicago: University of Chicago Press, 1976.

Porterfield, A. L. "Suicide and Crime in Folk and Secular Society." *American Journal of Sociology* 57 (1952): 331–38.

Portugese, Jacqueline. *Fertility Policy in Israel: The Politics of Religion, Gender, and Nation*. Westport, Conn.: Praeger, 1998.

Powell, E. H. "Occupation Status and Suicide." *American Journal of Sociology* 23 (1958): 131–39.

Ram, Uri. "Postnationalist Pasts: The Case of Israel." *Social Science History* 22, no. 4, special issue: "Memory and the Nation" (Winter 1998): 513–45.

Regev, Motti. "To Have a Culture of Our Own: On Israeliness and Its Variants." *Ethnic and Racial Studies* 23, no. 2 (March 2000): 223–47.

Retterstøl, Nils. "Suicide in a Cultural History Perspective, Part 1." *Norwegian Journal of Suicidology* 2 (1998).

Rhys, Jean. *Good Morning, Midnight.* New York: Harper, 1939.

Robins, E., S. Gassner, J. Kayes, R. H. Wilkinson, and G. E. Murphy. "The Communication of Suicidal Intent." *American Journal of Psychiatry* 115 (1959): 724–33.

Rudnytsky, Peter L., and Ellen Handler Spitz. *Freud and Forbidden Knowledge.* New York: New York University Press, 1994.

Sadan-Loebenstein, Nilli. *A. B. Yehoshua: Monograpfyah, Poetikah U-Vikoret* [A. B. Yehoshua: Monograph on Poetics and Criticism]. Tel Aviv: Sifriyat poalim, 1981.

Sade-Beck, Liav. "'We Shall Remember Them All . . .': The Culture of Online Mourning and Commemoration of Fallen Soldiers in Israel." In *Narratives of Dissent: War in Israeli Arts and Culture*, edited by Rachel S. Harris and Ranen Omer-Sherman. Detroit: Wayne State University Press, 2013.

Safir, Marilyn P. "Religion, Tradition and Public Policy Give Family First Priority." In *Calling the Equality Bluff: Women in Israel*, edited by Barbara Swirski and Marilyn P. Safir, 57–65. New York: Teachers College Press, 1993.

Sainsbury, P., and B. Barraclough. "Differences Between Suicide Rates." *Nature* 220, no. 173 (1968): 1252.

Sandler, Shmuel. "Territoriality and Nation-State Formation: The Yishuv and the Making of the State of Israel." *Nations and Nationalism* 3, no. 4 (1997): 667–88.

Scherpe, Klaus R., and Mitch Cohen. "Modern and Postmodern Transformations of the Metropolitan Narrative." *New German Critique*, no. 55 (Winter 1992): 71–85.

Schlör, Joachim. *Tel Aviv: From Dream to City.* London: Reaktion, 1999.

Schopenhauer, Arthur. "On Suicide." In *Parerga and Paralipomena* 2, chap. 13, sect. 160. 1851.

Schwartz, Barry. "The Social Context of Commemoration: A Study in Collective Memory." *Social Forces* 61, no. 2 (December 1982): 374–402.

Seh-Lavan, Yosef. *A. B. Yehoshua:, Hearot ve-Hanhayot le-Limud ve-li-Keriah* [A. B. Yehoshua: Thoughts and Hypotheses for Learning and Reading]. Tel Aviv: Or-am, 1978.

———. *Hayim Gouri: Hearot ve-Hanhayot le-Limud ve-li-Keriah* [Haim Gouri: Thoughts and Hypotheses for Learning and Reading]. Tel Aviv: Or-am, 1977.

———. *Yehudah Amichai: Hearot ve-Hanhayot le-Limud ve-li-Keriah* [Yehuda Amichai: Thoughts and Hypotheses for Learning and Reading]. Tel Aviv: Or-am, 1977.

Sela-Sheffy, Rakefet. "What Makes One an Israeli? Negotiating Identities in Everyday Representations of 'Israeliness.'" *Nations and Nationalism* 10, no. 4 (2004): 479–97.

Sered, Susan Starr. *What Makes Women Sick? Maternity, Modesty, and Militarism in Israeli Society.* Brandeis Series on Jewish Women. Hanover, N.H.: Brandeis University Press, 2000.

Shabtai, Edna. "Tel Aviv Ba-Prozah Shel Shabtai" ["Tel Aviv in Shabtai's Prose"]. *Moznayim* 65 (September 1988): 54–78.

Shaked, Gershon. *Gal Hadash ba-Siporet ha-Ivrit* [A New Wave in Hebrew Fiction]. Merhavyah: Sifriyat poalim, 1970.

————. *The Shadows Within: Essays on Modern Jewish Writers.* Philadelphia: Jewish Publication Society, 1987.

Shalev, Carmel. "Halakha and Patriarchal Motherhood: An Anatomy of the Israeli Surrogacy Law." *Israel Law Review* 32, no. 1 (1998): 51–80.

————. "Women in Israel: Fighting Tradition." In *Women's Rights, Human Rights,* edited by J. Peters and A. Wolper, 89–95. New York: Routledge, 1995.

Shalev, Carmel, and L. Boaz. "Public Funding for IVF in Israel — Ethical Aspects." Unpublished ms., 1999.

Shalev, Carmel, and Sigal Gooldin. "The Uses and Misuses of In Vitro Fertilization in Israel: Some Sociological and Ethical Considerations." *Nashim: A Journal of Jewish Women's Studies and Gender Issues* 12 (2006): 151–76.

Shamir, Moshe. *Hu Halakh ba-Sadot.* Merhavya, 1947.

Sheffi, Na'aman. "Israeli Education System in Search of a Pantheon of Heroes, 1948–1967." *Israel Studies* 7, no. 2 (Summer 2002): 62–83.

Shemesh, Yael. "Hitabdut ba-Mikra al Reka Tofa'at ha-Hitabdut ba-Tarbut ha-Klallit u-ve-Mekorot Yisrael." *JSIJ* [*Jewish Studies, an Internet Journal*] (2002–3): 1–24.

Shneidman, Edwin S., and American Association of Suicidology. *On the Nature of Suicide.* Jossey-Bass Behavioral Science Series. San Francisco: Jossey-Bass, 1973.

Shneidman, Edwin S., and Antoon A. Leenaars. *Lives and Deaths: Selections from the Works of Edwin S. Shneidman.* Series in Death, Dying, and Bereavement. Philadelphia: Brunner/Mazel, 1999.

Shneidman, N. N. *Dostoevsky and Suicide.* Oakville, Ont.: Mosaic, 1984.

Shohat, Ella. "Making the Silences Speak in Israeli Cinema." In *Israel Women's Studies: A Reader,* edited by Esther Fuchs. Rutgers University Press, 2005.

Simmel, Georg. "The Metropolis and Mental Life." In *Simmel: On Individuality and Social Forms,* edited by Donald Levine. Chicago: University of Chicago Press, 1971.

Sivan, Emmanuel. "To Remember Is to Forget: Israel's 1948 War." *Journal of Contemporary History* 28, no. 2 (April 1993): 341–59.

Slonim-Nevo, Vered, and Yana Shraga. "Attitudes and Behavior: A Comparison of Immigrant and Non-Immigrant Adolescents in Israel." *Child and Adolescent Social Work Journal* 14, no. 4 (1997): 251–62.

Soker-Shvayger, Chana. "Hatanakh hu lo tokhnit partselatsyah al ertsyisrael: Hahevrati vehapoliti bezikhron dvarim." *Teoryah uvikoret* 8 (Summer 1996): 181–97.

Solomon, Alison. "Anything for a Baby: Reproductive Technology in Israel." In *Calling the Equality Bluff: Women in Israel,* edited by Barbara Swirski and Marilyn P. Safir, 102–7. New York: Teachers College Press.

Stack, S. "Suicide." *Social Forces* 57 (1978): 644–53.

Stanislawski, Michael. *For Whom Do I Toil? Judah Leib Gordon and the Crisis of Russian Jewry.* New York: Oxford University Press, 1988.

Sternberg, Meir. *The Poetics of Biblical Narrative: Ideological Literature and the Drama of Reading.* Bloomington: Indiana University Press, 1985.

Stoler-Liss, Sachlav. "'Mothers Birth the Nation': The Social Construction of Zionist Motherhood in Wartime in Israeli Parent's Manuals." *Nashim: A Journal of Jewish Women's Studies and Gender Issues* 6 (Fall 2003): 105–18.

Swirski, Shlomo, Ami Fraenkel, and Barbara Swirski. "Income Maintenance in Israel:

From Welfare to Income Maintenance and from Income Maintenance to Welfare Reform." Paper presented at the Adva Center, October 2001.

Swirski, Shlomo, Etti Konor, Barbara Swirski, and Yaron Yecheskel. "Women in the Labor Market of the Israeli Welfare State." Paper presented at the Adva Center, July 2001.

Taylor, Steve. *Durkheim and the Study of Suicide: Contemporary Social Theory.* London: Macmillan, 1982.

Travis, Robert. "Halbwachs and Durkheim: A Test of Two Theories of Suicide." *British Journal of Sociology* 41, no. 2 (June 1990): 225–43.

Troen, S. Ilan. *Imagining Zion: Dreams, Designs, and Realities in a Century of Jewish Settlement.* New Haven, Conn.: Yale University Press, 2003.

Turov, Nissan. *Ba'ayot ha-Hitabdut: Mehkar Psychologi-Sociologi.* Tel Aviv, 1953.

Underwood, Michael. *A Clear Case of Suicide.* New York: St. Martin's, 1980.

Weingrod, Alex. "Changing Israeli Landscapes: Buildings and the Uses of the Past." *Cultural Anthropology* 8, no. 3 (August 1993): 370–87.

———. "How Israeli Culture Was Constructed: Memory, History and the Israeli Past." *Israel Studies* 2, no. 1 (1997): 228–37.

Weiss, Meira. "The Body of the Nation: Terrorism and the Embodiment of Nationalism in Contemporary Israel." *Anthropological Quarterly* 75, no. 1 (2002): 37–62.

———. *The Chosen Body: The Politics of the Body in Israeli Society.* Stanford, Calif.: Stanford University Press, 2002.

———. "The 'Chosen Body': A Semiotic Analysis of the Discourse of Israeli Militarism and Collective Identity." *Semiotica* 145, nos. 1/4 (2003): 151–73.

Williams, Raymond. *The Country and the City.* London: Chatto and Windus, 1973.

Wirth-Nesher, Hana. *City Codes: Reading the Modern Urban Novel.* Cambridge: Cambridge University Press, 1996.

Wiseman-Stein, Sara. "Kol Akara: The Voice of the Barren Women." In *Women in Judaism: Contemporary Writings* (2003). http://www.utoronto.ca/wjudaism /contemporary/contemp_index1.html.

Wolman, Benjamin. "Some Problems of Psychic Hygiene and Military Psychiatry" [in Hebrew]. *Harefuah* 35 (1948): 39–41.

Woolf, Virginia, and Leonard Woolf. *The Death of the Moth, and Other Essays.* London: Hogarth, 1942.

Wymer, Rowland. *Suicide and Despair in the Jacobean Drama.* Brighton: Harvester, 1986.

Yadgar, Yaacov. "From the Particularist to the Universalistic: National Narrative in Israel's Mainstream Press, 1967–97." *Nations and Nationalism* 8, no. 1 (2002): 55–72.

Yehoshua, Abraham B. *Masa el Tom ha-Elef: Roman bi-Sheloshah Halakim [Journey to the End of the Millennium].* Tel Aviv: ha-Kibbutz ha-Meuchad, 1997.

Yudkin, Leon I. *1948 and After: Aspects of Israeli Fiction.* In *Journal of Semitic Studies,* monograph no. 5. Manchester: University of Manchester Press, 1984.

———. *Beyond Sequence: Current Israeli Fiction and Its Context.* Northwood: Science Reviews, 1992.

Zach, Nathan. *Kave Avir: Al ha-Romantikah ba-Siporet ha-Yisreelit ve-al Nosim Aherim: Sihot Miluim [Lines of Air: On Romance in Hebrew Fiction, and on Other Subjects: Some Remarks].* Jerusalem: Keter, 1983.

———. *Mivhar [Selected Poems]*. Tel Aviv, 1974.

Zakim, Eric. *To Build and Be Built: Landscape, Literature, and the Construction of Zionist Identity*. Philadelphia: University of Pennsylvania Press, 2007.

Zemon Davies, Natalie, and Randolph Starn. "Introduction to Special Issue: Memory and Counter-Memory." *Representations* 26 (Spring 1989): 1–6.

Zerubavel, Yael. "Changing Name-Death of the Exilic Jew and the Rebirth of a Sabra." *Israel Studies* 7, no. 2 (2000): 115–44.

———. "The Death of Memory and the Memory of Death: Masada and the Holocaust as Historical Metaphors." *Representations* 45 (Winter 1994): 72–100.

———. "The 'Mythological Sabra' and Jewish Past: Trauma, Memory and Contested Identities." *Israel Studies* 7, no. 2 (2002): 115–44.

———. *Recovered Roots: Collective Memory and the Making of Israeli National Tradition*. Chicago: University of Chicago Press, 1995.

Zillboorg, Gregory. "Differential Diagnostic Types of Suicide." *Archives of Neurology and Psychiatry* 35 (1936): 271.

INDEX

Gubar, Susan, 190, 194, 203
Gutman, Nahum, 147, 152

Hadda, Janet, 193, 229n50
Haganah, 34, 43, 100, 111, 113, 119–20
Haifa, 150, 154, 196, 203, 230–31, 251
Ha-Kaitanah shel Kneller (*Kneller's Happy Campers*) (Etgar Keret), 145, 153–55, 170–72, 215
Hakak, Lev, 147
Hameiri, Avigdor, 31
Hannah, 21, 186–87
Hebrew culture, 3, 19
Hebrewism and Hebrew language, 8, 20, 26, 31–32, 44, 78, 93, 116, 135–36, 139, 143, 153, 169, 187, 189
Hebrew literature, ix, 12, 14, 18–19, 27–28, 30, 32, 35, 37–38, 47, 59, 64, 67, 112, 179, 209, 211, 213, 216, 219–20, 223; modern, 8, 10, 19, 26, 67, 189, 195. *See also* Israeli literature
Hebrew texts, 7, 243
hegemony, 16, 57, 97, 119
Hemingway, Ernest, 12, 216
heroism, 11, 15, 32, 40–42, 45, 47–48, 55, 57, 63, 67, 76, 81, 83, 85, 93, 95, 97, 121, 189, 210–11, 223; myth of, 57, 69
Hertsig, Hannah, 80, 89
Herzl, Theodor, 8, 98, 124, 137, 143–45
hillul hashem, 21, 31; and conversion to Christianity, 22. *See also* martyrdom
Hilu, Alon, 9–11, 98, 133–35, 138–39
historical novels, 97, 124
history, 10, 13–15, 17, 20, 95, 97, 99, 103, 112, 115, 122, 125, 127, 130–32, 139–40, 145, 167–68, 176, 195; recorded, 103, 124, 126, 140
Holocaust, 32, 37, 66, 108, 175; and Adolf Hitler, 119; making fertility a priority in Israel, 175
home, concept of, 31, 40, 82, 100–101, 110, 112, 123, 127, 153, 158, 162, 167, 175–78, 180–81, 184–85, 196
homeland, Jewish national, 6, 8, 13–14, 28, 78, 96, 168, 185
honor, 24–25, 28, 43, 46, 48, 66, 105, 192, 209–10, 224
House of Rajani, The (Alon Hilu), 98, 133–41
Hezbollah, 75
Husseini, Haj Amin-al-, 119
Huston, John, 150

idealists, 105–7
ideals, 8, 10–11, 36, 45, 56, 62, 94, 121, 167, 171, 174
identity, 7, 11, 13, 16, 34–35, 71, 79–81, 87–88, 91–92, 95, 109, 128, 133, 181, 188, 194, 205; individual, 115–16, 140; modern, 192, 195; women's, 186, 222
ideology, 6–7, 15, 17–18, 20, 33, 35, 60, 82, 85, 87, 91, 107–8, 111, 121, 127, 131, 143–46, 157, 159, 163–64, 170, 174, 179, 181, 209, 212; ideological dreams, 110–12, 154, 171; ideological failure, 145, 158–59, 163; ideological failure of Tel Aviv, 163, 171; ideological framework, 76, 104–5, 118
IDF. *See* Israel Defense Forces (IDF)
Ilan, Uri, 84–6, 243n2
independence, 6, 11, 34, 45, 47–48, 52, 62, 69, 108, 175; poetry of, 11, 47–57. *See also* War of Independence (1948)
infertility, 12, 179. *See also* fertility and family planning
Infiltration (*Hitganvut Yehidim*) (Yehoshua Kenaz), 32, 66–94, 216
insanity, 98, 110–11, 115, 121, 136, 139, 181–85, 188, 195, 197
institutions, 5–6, 9, 13, 17, 29, 31, 66, 70, 74, 85, 92–94, 104–6, 141, 173, 206, 225
Intifada (second), 74
Irgun Tvai Leumi (Etzel, or ITZL), 43, 119
Israel Defense Forces (IDF), 6, 9, 11, 25, 48, 59, 63, 65–69, 71–77, 79, 81, 83, 85–87, 89, 91, 93–94, 187; in Israeli society, 11, 66
Israeli culture, 20, 106, 207
Israeli identity, 8, 10, 16, 36
Israeli literature, 5, 8, 10–12, 20, 36, 38, 47, 99, 173, 179, 185, 192, 195, 205, 212, 216; and the Arab, 10; and identity formation, 11. *See also* Hebrew literature
Israeli military, 67–68; desertions, 74. *See also* Israel Defense Forces (IDF)
Israeli myths, 48, 73, 77, 209
"Israeliness," 80, 85, 93, 120, 171
Israeli society, 5, 7, 11–13, 15, 18–20, 29, 33–34, 36–37, 40, 46, 57–58, 63–64, 67–68, 70, 73, 75–80, 84, 93–94, 96–97, 100, 139, 164, 175, 188, 192, 201, 206, 209, 225; wealthy post-1967, 115
Israeli soldiers, 48, 73, 75; televising of humiliated captured soldiers during the Yom Kippur War, 9, 58. *See also* soldiers; Israel Defense Forces

Jabotinsky, Ze'ev (Vladimir), 8, 43, 45–46, 231, 251, 253
Jaffa, 10, 12, 102, 152
Jane Eyre (Charlotte Brontë), 191
Jephthah's daughter, 27–28
Jerusalem, 7, 25, 31, 58, 104, 113, 122, 127, 129, 156, 165
Jewish Brigade, 35
Jewish history, 15, 25, 187
Jewish identity, 192
Jewish law, 25
Jewish legion, 43
Jewish nation, 31, 46, 48, 56, 61
Jewish people, 22, 26, 28, 34, 45–46, 61, 105, 120, 186–87
Jews, 6–7, 9–10, 15, 22, 25–26, 28, 31, 42–46, 51, 66, 79, 108, 119–20, 124, 128, 131, 134–35, 168, 175
Josephus, 21
Joyce, James, 200
Judaism, 7, 24–25, 116, 173, 195, 242, 258; and women, 176, 178, 179, 188, 240n21
Judges, 21, 40–41, 44, 46, 86, 138, 186

Kartun-Blum, Ruth, 187, 195
Katzir, Yehudit, 11, 150–54, 169, 180, 185, 202
Katznelson, Berl, 163
Keats, John, 190
Kenan, Amos, 3–4, 32–35
Kenaz, Yehoshua, 11, 32, 66–67, 76–77, 80, 82–88, 90–94, 180–81; *The Way to the Cats*, 181
Keret, Etgar, 153–54, 169–71. *See also Ha-Kaitanah shel Kneller*
kibbutz, 4, 6, 8, 10, 35, 51, 59–60, 62, 71, 81–83, 104–8, 114, 126–28, 141, 164
kibbutz movement, 104–6, 118
kiddush hashem, 22, 25–26. *See also* martyrdom; Middle Ages
Kishniev pogrom (1903), 43

Labor Party, 9, 59; decline of, 148
Labor Zionism, 3, 10–11, 59, 79, 104–5, 140, 144, 148, 156, 167, 170. *See also* Zionism
Lady Macbeth, 190
Lady of Shallot, 189, 191
Lahav, Pnina, 175, 239n21
lamentation, 186–87
land, 5–6, 10, 15, 33, 39, 42, 44, 46, 59, 63, 98, 100, 102, 104–5, 107, 111, 114, 118, 120, 124

landscape, 6, 8, 141, 150, 158–60, 162, 169
Lang, Fritz, 150
language, 8, 13–14, 16–17, 21, 23–24, 34, 36, 50, 73–74, 98, 116, 145
Lebanon War (1982), 9, 68, 73, 122
legacy, 57, 110–11, 121, 123
legend, 13, 45, 55–56, 60, 81, 103
LEHI, 65
Lester, David, 210, 213–14, 218, 243n4, 244n5, 244n13, 245n22
Levin, Hanoch, 68–69
Likkud Party, 9
literacy, 7–8
literary suicides, 37, 64, 192, 209, 211–12, 214, 217, 223, 225–26
literature, rabbinic, 186–87
London, 26, 29, 101, 171, 190, 222
longing, 147–48, 170
love, unrequited, 28–30, 170, 189, 191, 198
loyalty, 32, 67, 87–89, 158, 175, 209

madness. *See* insanity; mental illness
Maid of Ludmir, 188
Mandate Palestine, 6, 31, 39, 43–44, 48, 65, 123. *See also* pre-state Palestine
Mann, Barbara, 145–46, 162
Mapu, Avraham, 30
marriage, 41, 173, 183, 188, 193–96, 201, 207, 240
martyrdom, 21, 23–26, 31–32, 35, 41–42, 45, 86, 228, 250; commemoration of, 22; and Samson, 22. *See also* Samson
martyrological literature, 20, 22–23. *See also Beautiful Death*
martyrs, 22–24
Marx, Karl, 105–7
Meir, Golda, 137
memory, 13–14, 49, 56, 103, 140, 199, 202, 226; collective, 13–14, 95–96; national, 9, 13–14
mental illness, 69, 76
Middle Ages, 22, 24, 26, 32, 41, 45, 141; and second crusade (1144–47), 23
militarism in Israeli society, 45, 47; militarization, 39, 42, 50, 53, 119
military, 7, 9, 34, 58, 62–63, 65–66, 68–70, 75, 77–78, 85, 88, 94, 99, 206
military police, 83, 91
military service, 4, 6–7
Mintz, Alan, 77, 123

Zionism (*continued*)
agricultural, 6; cultural, 5; critique of, 8, 18, 20, 43, 50, 62, 80, 94, 96, 139, 140, 145, 164, 184, 205, 225 (*see also* national narratives); and literature, 8, 18–20, 29, 36; urban, 141, 143–72 (*see also* Tel Aviv, creation of); and women, 7, 174, 179, 195; Zionist history, 12, 34, 59, 104, 106, 122, 124, 133, 140 (and First Zionist Congress, 1897), 98; Zionist ideology, 8, 20, 76, 80, 99, 118, 156, 179, 188, 205–6; Zionist project, 100–101, 147, 157